Civil War Generals in Defeat

MODERN WAR STUDIES

Theodore A. Wilson
General Editor

Raymond A. Callahan
J. Garry Clifford
Jacob W. Kipp
Jay Luvaas
Allan R. Millett
Dennis Showalter
Series Editors

Civil War Generals
in Defeat

Edited by Steven E. Woodworth

University Press of Kansas

Published by the University Press of Kansas (Lawrence, Kansas 66049),
which was organized by the Kansas Board of Regents and is operated and
funded by Emporia State University, Fort Hays State University, Kansas
State University, Pittsburg State University, the University of Kansas, and
Wichita State University.

Library of Congress Cataloging-in-Publication Data

Civil War generals in defeat / edited by Steven E. Woodworth.
    p. cm. — (Modern war studies)
   Includes bibliographical references and index.
   ISBN 0-7006-0943-1 (alk. paper)
   1. United States—History—Civil War, 1861–1865—Campaigns.
2. Generals—United States—History—19th century. 3. Generals—
Confederate States of America. 4. Command of troops—History—19th
century—Case studies. 5. Military art and science—United States—
History—19th century—Case studies. 6. United States. Army—
History—Civil War, 1861–1865. 7. Confederate States of America.
Army—History. I. Woodworth, Steven E. II. Series.
E470.C59 1999
973.7'3—dc21   98-44859

British Library Cataloguing in Publication Data is available.

To Ira D. Gruber

Contents

Introduction

"The test of merit in my profession," wrote Gen. Albert Sidney Johnston, "with the people is success." For him the test was not merely an academic problem but a matter of current pressing need. The Confederate defeats at Forts Henry and Donelson in February 1862, with the resulting loss of a quarter of his army and more than half the state of Tennessee, had happened on his watch. Across the South, newspaper editors and their readers knew little and appeared to care less about the convoluted details of the almost freakish debacle at Fort Donelson or the events that had led up to it. For them it seemed enough to know that Albert Sidney Johnston had been in chief command in that theater, and far from achieving success, his efforts had met with failure on an appalling scale. So they denounced him, asserted that he was incompetent or had been drunk at key moments, and demanded his immediate removal from command, "because," as one complainant put it to President Jefferson Davis, "he is no general." Johnston had not achieved success. In the public's simple test of merit, he had been weighed in the balances and found wanting.[1]

And as modern students of war—and readers of this book—will no doubt be quick to point out, that test has a certain stark validity. Johnston thought so too. "It is a hard rule," he wrote, "but I think it right."[2] Few today would disagree with Johnston's admission as a sort of final-analysis conclusion. War is a hard business, and well may its rule, its test of merit, be hard. Mistakes in war are costly not only in treasure but in blood. For the man who would command an army, lives are the fee paid for lessons of practical instruction. He had better be a quick study.

Most of all, he had better produce results. The general is not employed to make a good attempt, fight nobly, and lose impressively. His society has staked all on his achieving the results it needs. Either he fulfills those expectations or he does not—and is rated a failure. With very few exceptions, the men who held major independent commands during the Civil War were selected on the basis of reasoned analysis of their abilities. They owed their high positions solely—or almost solely—to the conviction of their governments that they could deliver success, that they could pass the people's test of merit.

Having failed signally to fulfill such expectations during the winter of 1861–62, Albert Sidney Johnston admitted the fairness of the hard rule by which the public was then condemning him, but he went on to write that he hoped soon to change the people's verdict by achieving success. His attempt culminated at the battle of Shiloh, where he died leading his troops. Victory had seemed possible during the closing hours of his life, but ultimately it eluded both him and his successor. In the starkest and most summary analysis, then, Albert Sidney Johnston may be counted a failure. He did not achieve that for which his society had invested him with the rank of general.

Yet such a verdict has limited value in enhancing our understanding of the man, the conflict, or the nature of command. To say that Johnston, or any general, ultimately failed in his task is far from explaining why a campaign turned out the way it did. All too often, history sorts out generals and their reputations with a logic that amounts to the assumption that if a campaign failed, the commanding general must have been incompetent, and therefore the campaign failed *because* he was incompetent. Put in those bald terms, such reasoning can clearly be recognized as an impediment to our understanding of the past. In practice, however, it often takes the form of progressively more extreme vilification of a losing commander, until every mishap that befell his army is held to be the result of some egregiously, almost incomprehensibly wrongheaded decision on his part. Braxton Bragg and John Bell Hood have been particular victims of this type of history writing. Some recent accounts of these two hapless generals lead the reader to wonder not why they held command of an army but rather why they were not in an insane asylum. Does this offer a satisfying explanation for the events of the past? The fact is, it creates the necessity of an even more difficult explanation, namely, why governments engaged in a desperate war for their existence frequently opted to entrust the command of their armies to dangerous lunatics. While Hood and Bragg may be the most striking examples of such treatment, other generals, including several of the subjects of this study, have come in for a greater or lesser share of the same sort of oversimplified summary judgment. Clearly it is time to step back and take another look at the war's losing (or sometimes losing) generals, as well as the entire process of seeking complete and sufficient explanation for failure in the inadequacies of the commander.

There is far more to be learned in trying to understand how and why a general fell short—why a particular course of action seemed desirable to a highly intelligent and motivated man—than there is in multiplying denunciations of his alleged stupidity. This book seeks to ask those more productive questions. It examines a number of the war's most capable "failures"—officers of high prewar reputation among their peers, some of whom had distinguished Civil War records before military mishap marred their careers and some who went on to creditable exploits later in the war. The selection of this type of officer focuses even more sharply the need to explain failure. Clearly these were not poltroons or half-wits whom demagoguery or cronyism had tragically propelled into a position to slaughter their troops and ruin their countries. They all had displayed considerable talent. They were all selected by high authority for extremely responsible commands, and somehow, despite all this, they were not able to shape events and achieve success in at least one important epoch of their careers.

The fact that these men were all intelligent, trained, experienced, and capable of making good tactical and strategic decisions on a number of occasions forces us to delve deeper into their characters and capacities, as well as into the circumstances of the campaigns they waged, to find explanations for what happened. Doing so initiates a process of exploration that will tell us a great deal more about not only why commanders fail in war but also what makes them succeed.

Of course, this is not the first book to deal with losing generals. A number of books have appeared from time to time, each examining the career of one or another defeated general and usually asserting that the fault lay with his subordinates, his superiors, or other circumstances beyond his control. Since this formula is familiar to readers of Civil War history, some readers may hope to see none of it here. They will be disappointed. The fact is that *sometimes* a general's failure *was* primarily the fault of subordinates, superiors, or other uncontrollable factors, and in those cases, we ought to recognize as much if we want to understand what really happened. But we can also ask in such cases whether there was anything the commander could have done to overcome such difficulties and, perhaps more to the point, what else can be learned about the situation once it has been established that the commanding general's alleged incompetence is not a full and sufficient explanation for all that took place. The various authors whose work is presented in this book do not always agree on the rights and wrongs of any given general's case, but they do agree that something is to be learned by taking a closer look at the cases of generals who at least seemed meritorious yet nevertheless failed. That is the unifying principle of the book.

The first chapter deals with Albert Sidney Johnston himself, seeking the explanation for the early 1862 Confederate strategic debacle that befell his command. Johnston faced extreme challenges but not an impossible assignment. As a fifty-nine-year-old general with long service and a towering reputation in the old army, Johnston faced a situation unprecedented in his experience or in that of any other living American. Much depended on his ability to adapt and adjust to the new situation as it pertained to not only the size of the conflict and the resources at his disposal but also a hodgepodge of inexpert and uncooperative subordinates.

Almost no Confederate general has attracted more controversy than the quiet, dapper, and very ambitious Joseph E. Johnston. Highly ranked and rated in the old prewar U.S. Army, and with a reputation respected by both friends and enemies throughout the course of the war, Johnston somehow failed to achieve a major battlefield victory or to wage a successful campaign. In the second chapter, Alan Downs explores Johnston's pivotal first major command in the Virginia theater and examines the factors that denied an otherwise meritorious officer the success he ardently desired.

Ethan S. Rafuse looks at George B. McClellan's peninsula campaign, the strategic centerpiece of the popular Army of the Potomac commander's Civil War career. In the spring of 1862, McClellan faced a complex problem of military engineering set in the midst of a ticklish strategic situation, complicated by persistent problems of military intelligence, and immersed in a daunting thicket of political pressures and expectations. He attempted to solve the military problem while maintaining the political requirements that he personally believed were necessary to a successful conclusion of the conflict. But at the same time, he was compelled to respond to the political stipulations of those whose agendas differed from his own. The result reveals much about the subtle and not so subtle ways that politics can influence military operations and even shape the perceptions of success and failure.

Stephen D. Engle next examines Don Carlos Buell's summer 1862 advance toward Chattanooga. Buell's experience, even more clearly than McClellan's, points out that military operations within a republic are never conducted in a political vacuum. Nor, as Buell learned to his sorrow, is the political environment of a war bound to remain stable even during the course of one campaign. Buell's experience illustrates the sort of political skills and sensitivities that were every bit as necessary to the Civil War commander as his sense of strategy or tactics.

Maj. Gen. Joseph Hooker is the subject of Stephen W. Sears's chapter. Sears aggressively challenges previously held views of Hooker. As commander of the Army of the Potomac in the spring of 1863, Hooker faced the Confederacy's first team in the persons of Robert E. Lee and Thomas J. "Stonewall" Jackson. Hooker's effort against these fell opponents—a product of the interaction of terrain, politics, the contributions of his subordinates, and, finally, a well-placed Confederate artillery round—came up short. The result was Lee's and Jackson's most renowned victory and an indelible blot on Hooker's otherwise impressive record. Not all will agree with Sears's verdict on "Fighting Joe," but his careful research and analysis will challenge students of Civil War command to rethink their assessment of this general, the nature of his performance, and the factors that denied him success.

Michael B. Ballard looks at John C. Pemberton, the unsuccessful defender of Vicksburg, and demonstrates that military merit is not all of one sort. An officer with great skills in some areas might be badly lacking in others. When employed in the areas of his weakness, an officer of considerable merit might nevertheless prove a dismal failure. Like Hooker, Pemberton faced the opposing side's best commanders in the spring of 1863—in this case, Ulysses S. Grant and William T. Sherman. It was a situation that called for aggressive, audacious action and sharp strategic and operational insight. Yet Pemberton's strengths were in administration and staff work. In the crisis created by Grant's stunningly rapid and powerful turning movement, Pemberton needed to perform immediately at world-class level in areas outside those that had gotten him promoted to the rank he held.

In the final chapter, Brooks D. Simpson takes a collective look at issues of success and failure—and the perception thereof—at the battle of Gettysburg. The Army of Northern Virginia marched into Pennsylvania in the summer of 1863 with a reputation of all but invincibility. Its commander, the already almost legendary Lee, claimed that it could go anywhere and do anything "if properly led," and the army's leaders—Lee, Longstreet, Stuart, Ewell, and Hill—had all won great and deserved renown. At Gettysburg, however, they failed to achieve their accustomed success. What went wrong? Simpson demonstrates that much more is involved in assessing an officer's merit than the simple outcome of a battle. A changing set of circumstances, including the performance of the opposing army, can mean that a level of achievement that once produced success now results in failure. His study points up once again the bankruptcy of an approach to military history that makes the analysis of success and failure little more than an exercise in finger-pointing. While success may be the standard of merit ultimately demanded of commanders, that end result may not necessarily show a direct correlation with the skill, intelligence, and dedication that a general displays.

Some of the conclusions advanced in the following pages are controversial, in that they challenge long-accepted simple explanations for battlefield failure. Sometimes the contributors suggest that real merit went unrewarded because of difficult circumstances; sometimes that the missing component in an officer's merit was not what it was often thought to be. It should be obvious as well that the contributors do not always agree with one another about the merits of the officers under discussion here. That, however, is beside the point. The purpose of this book is not to rehabilitate the reputation of any one Civil War general or even of the whole group of officers discussed here. Rather, the purpose is to make a case for— and a substantial beginning at—a deeper inquiry into questions of Civil War command, not just to ask whether this or that general should have succeeded but also to assess the circumstances and characteristics that made the difference between success and failure.

Chapter One

When Merit Was Not Enough: Albert Sidney Johnston and Confederate Defeat in the West, 1862

Steven E. Woodworth

He was a soldier's soldier. Albert Sidney Johnston was a tall, powerfully built Kentuckian who had graduated eighth in his West Point class of 1826. Resolute, steady, dependable, and forceful, he was a born leader. A veteran of the Black Hawk War and a former commanding general of the army of the Republic of Texas, he had also compiled an excellent combat record in the Mexican War and had held with credit one of the most coveted commands in the pre–Civil War U.S. Army, as colonel of the crack Second Cavalry regiment. When the army had needed someone to lead the difficult 1859 expedition against rebellious Mormons, it had given the job to Johnston, along with a brevet brigadier generalcy. Zachary Taylor called him "the best soldier he had ever commanded," and for Winfield Scott, Johnston was, perhaps second only to Robert E. Lee, the best man to command all the nation's armies. Johnston had achieved more than any other officer of the old army and all that any 1826 West Point graduate could have hoped in the three decades prior to the Civil War. No one familiar with the prewar army could have chosen a more promising officer to hold a large and difficult command of vital importance.[1]

Yet Albert Sidney Johnston failed, and nothing could have been more of a surprise to knowledgeable observers, to his commander in chief, or to himself. His defeat during the late winter and early spring of 1862 constitutes one of those strange and all but inexplicable events that continually beg for reexamination. Within a period of two months in early 1862, the army he commanded was driven from the entire states of Kentucky and Tennessee. The whole navigable lengths of the Tennessee and Cumberland Rivers were in enemy hands, and the strategic situation had shifted to such an extent that no point on the Mississippi could be held north of Vicksburg. Little hope remained of saving the vital Memphis and Charleston Railroad, some 150 miles south of what had been, only a few weeks before, the Confederacy's front lines. Over 24,000 Confederate soldiers had become casualties or gone into captivity, and among the 2,000 or so who were killed outright was Johnston himself. How could a man of such obvious intelligence, experience, and character be so completely defeated?

In part, at least, it was a matter of factors beyond his control, and the foremost of these was the quality of his opposition. Few if any members of the old army's officer corps would have predicted that the unprepossessing Ulysses S. Grant was, beneath that shabby exterior, something like a practical military genius. Most of them were reluctant to concede that much even after the dramatic series of victories of which Albert Sidney Johnston was the victim. Clearly, however, Johnston could not possibly have faced a more formidable Federal opponent. If he is to be numbered among those defeated by Grant, he at least has plenty of company.

Another factor that was beyond Johnston's control was the inadequacy of the manpower and equipment at his disposal. In all the length and breadth of the huge department that was his to defend, Johnston had less than 40,000 troops at the time of his appointment in September 1861, and though he endeavored to raise more from the various states of his department, he was hindered by a lack of firearms to place in the hands of any volunteers that might come forward. In the same month that he took command, he reported to Richmond that he needed an additional 30,000 rifles, but at that time the Confederate authorities could send him only 1,000. The situation gradually improved over the months that followed. Weapons trickled in, and so did recruits. A few reinforcements even arrived from the East, but Johnston's situation could never have been called adequate. Partly that was the result of the failure of the Confederate high command in Richmond to pay enough attention to the threat west of the Appalachians, and partly it was simply the handicap that the outnumbered agrarian South had to accept in taking on the populous and industrialized North. If Southern generals needed equal or near-equal manpower or equipment to blunt Federal incursions into their territory, their cause was doomed from the outset.[2]

The fact is, however, that the defender did not need anything near equal numbers to make the invader's task nightmarish if not downright impossible. The attacker in war always has the more difficult role, and the state of military technology in the mid-1800s made the defender's tactical advantage even more pronounced. Northern forces would also carry the burden of the strategic offensive: they would fight in the enemy's country, on unfamiliar terrain, and among a hostile populace. Nearly every feature of the landscape could be made to work against them by a resourceful defender, and they would have to depend on a long and tenuous supply line that would require more men to guard it with every mile that the invading army advanced. Feeding the army as it moved into enemy territory and keeping its cartridge boxes full as it fought its way southward would require the presence of a substantial wagon train that would make maneuvers slow and clumsy. All of that added up to the fact that the 90,000 men in the ranks of Johnston's opponent in late 1861 were none too many—indeed, were not really enough—for the offensive operations that the North would have to carry on if it was to have any chance at all of winning the war.

Thus while Johnston's circumstances were certainly not favorable, they were not exactly hopeless either. If the factors working against him meant that success would be difficult and failure disastrous, they did not put victory beyond reach—at least not if victory meant stalling, disrupting, and punishing Northern offensives. The circumstances can explain some of what occurred, but not all. As the spring of 1862 approached, the rest would depend on the decisions that Johnston and his subordinates made in the coming campaign.

The fall and early winter of 1861 and 1862 were a prelude to the opening of active operations in the western theater. During that period Johnston had chosen and carried out a successful policy of bluffing his Northern opponents. Distributing his forces along the frontier and pushing them as far forward as possible, he tried to create the impression that his troops were far more numerous than they were. So admirably did this stratagem work that William

Tecumseh Sherman suffered something like a nervous breakdown at the thought of Johnston's imaginary hordes. Sherman's replacement, Don Carlos Buell, was perhaps more stable but far less dangerous. Of special value to Johnston was the fact that Buell was not at all given to haste. Some would say that he was dead slow. At any rate, he offered more of what Johnston needed: time to raise, train, and equip a respectable army and prepare defensive positions. Sooner or later, however, the Federals were bound to advance resolutely, whether under one commander or another, and Johnston's defensive line was so long that it faced the sectors of several Federal commanders. In midwinter 1862, those on both his flanks began to move. Neither Union advance was coordinated with the other, but both were disastrous for Johnston.[3]

On Johnston's right flank, along the upper Cumberland River, Union Brig. Gen. George H. Thomas marched his small army southward toward east Tennessee and the vital rail link that connected Johnston's sector with Virginia. Thomas was under Buell's overall command, and though he was by nature about as slow as his commander, he was more capable, more resolute, and, most important, under considerable pressure from Abraham Lincoln to make a move in the direction of east Tennessee, where pro-Confederate Tennesseeans were severely persecuting the Union-loyal mountaineers. On January 19, 1862, at Mill Springs, Kentucky, Thomas's army met and decisively defeated the Confederate force under Maj. Gen. George B. Crittenden that was to have defended that sector. So complete was Thomas's victory that the way was open to Lincoln's cherished goal of occupying east Tennessee. Only the poor quality and bad condition of the roads that led there prevented Union troops from penetrating that region at once. The shattered fragments of Crittenden's force joined Johnston's main body at Bowling Green, Kentucky. Crittenden, an officer of questionable merit who may well have been drunk during the battle that brought disaster to his army, faced court-martial.[4]

Before Johnston could react to the virtual annihilation of his right flank, his left-center came under attack. Here, in west Tennessee, the crucial terrain features were the Mississippi and Tennessee Rivers—the latter of which bisected the state along north-south lines—and the lower reaches of the Cumberland, which slanted northwestward out of middle Tennessee past Nashville and then

Albert Sidney Johnston

joined the Ohio near the mouth of the Tennessee River. All three streams were fully navigable. Johnston knew about these rivers, of course, and he knew that they were strategically important. One of his chief goals during the preceding months had been to make them secure, but in this he had failed.

Partially the failure had been due to the chronic lack of resources that hampered everything else Johnston tried to do in defense of the Confederate heartland. Partially, however, it was the result of a command problem. The problem was not of Johnston's making originally, but the failure to correct it well enough and soon enough was a major ingredient in his downfall. Prior to Johnston's assumption of command in the region, Kentucky had been at least theoretically neutral, closed to the military forces of both sides. That effectively gave protection to most of Tennessee. Only along the Mississippi River, on the state's western boundary, could Union forces pose a threat. Accordingly, Confederate efforts had been concentrated there, under the command of Confederate president Jefferson Davis's old West Point crony Leonidas Polk. Polk had never held a commission in the old army, having resigned upon graduation to enter the Episcopal ministry. By the time the Civil War came, Polk was a bishop. Smooth, ingratiating, and persuasive, Polk was also headstrong, self-willed, and largely ignorant of military matters. The Confederate president, however, never forgot a friend, and when Polk had come browsing around the War Department the previous summer, Davis had rewarded him with the most important command in the West—defense of the Mississippi River. Polk repaid Davis's favoritism by violating Kentucky neutrality—and Confederate policy—in occupying the Mississippi River town of Columbus, Kentucky. Columbus was indeed a key terrain feature and an excellent point from which to defend the middle stretch of the Father of Waters. Unfortunately, however, Polk's occupation placed the South in the apparent role of aggressor, alienated many Kentuckians, and led to the state's formally declaring itself on the side of the Union. State loyalty being what it was in the America of the 1860s, Polk's political blunder undoubtedly led to large numbers of Kentuckians shouldering rifles for Uncle Sam who might otherwise have fought for the South or remained neutral.[5]

This was the situation when Johnston took command in September 1861. Polk remained in command on the Mississippi, but now he would answer to Johnston in Bowling Green rather than directly to Davis in Richmond. Johnston, however, was for months unaware of a crucial fact: Davis's original orders to Polk had given the bishop-general command of both banks of the Mississippi but had extended his district only as far as the banks of the Tennessee on the east. That was of prime importance, because it placed the defense of the Tennessee and Cumberland Rivers outside Polk's bailiwick. The Mississippi could not be held without the other two rivers, and Johnston seems to have assumed that Davis had logically given Polk responsibility for all three. Such would indeed have been the logical course had Kentucky neutrality not shaped Confederate decisions prior to September 1861. In the confusion of Polk's seizure of Columbus, the end of Kentucky neutrality, and Johnston's assumption of supreme command, no one had seen to it that the new situation was accounted for in Confederate preparations.[6]

The Tennessee River flows northward into Kentucky at a place where the two states' generally straight boundary makes a slight jog. As a result, at the point where the river leaves Tennessee, the east bank is Tennessee and the west bank is Kentucky. Back in the spring of 1861, when the state of Tennessee had just seceded and had not yet officially joined the Confederacy and was handling its own defense, officers with little background in military engineering had decided to place the river's main defenses precisely there, at Tennessee's northernmost spot of riverbank, and on that site they built Fort Henry. That was all very well politically, but militarily it made little sense. The location was low and swampy and offered no commanding position for artillery. Worse still, it was dominated by the high hills on the Kentucky side of the river. Finally, since it was on the Tennessee shore, the east bank, it was out of Polk's district, so the work on it idled forward without any great sense of urgency throughout the remainder of 1861. The Cumberland River defensive position, called Fort Donelson, was better sited but suffered from the same bureaucratic problems. Nothing much of importance was done about either fort.[7]

All this might have changed when Johnston took command, except that Johnston placed too much confidence in Polk. He considered moving Fort Henry from its unfortunate site but finally decided that with time so short before a probable Federal attack and with so much work already having been invested at the current location, it would be best to press on, inferior position and all. He thus gave immediate orders to Polk to see to the improvements of the two forts, and particularly to make sure that the hills on the Kentucky side across from Fort Henry were occupied and fortified, since Kentucky neutrality was a thing of the past. Polk simply ignored the order. It was not his district, he apparently reasoned, so he need not concern himself with it. Yet inexplicably, he neglected to inform Johnston. Johnston, for his part, failed to see to it that his orders were being carried out. And so four more months went by with little sense of urgency on the part of anyone in authority about the construction of the forts on the Tennessee and Cumberland Rivers—Johnston because he did not know their condition, and Polk because he did not care.

Rather than expediting the work on the forts, Polk actually hindered their construction. For a time the works languished without any trained engineer officer because Polk had corralled the whole stock of engineering talent in the department to direct the elaboration of his vast defensive works at Columbus, apparently oblivious to the fact that Columbus would be utterly indefensible if the Cumberland and Tennessee Rivers should fall into enemy hands. Johnston was unaware of this problem but did sense the need to strengthen the garrisons of the half-finished forts. Once again Polk stood in the way of the necessary steps. With Confederate manpower desperately short throughout Johnston's department, Polk's Columbus garrison constituted the only available surplus of troops, so Johnston directed Polk to send 5,000 men to strengthen the works on the Tennessee and Cumberland. Polk refused. The orders were reiterated. Again Polk refused, yet he had troops enough to allow him to contemplate various far-fetched schemes for adventures against the Federal forces in Missouri. The fact was that Polk simply did not want his personal importance diminished by having the size of his force reduced, but he wrangled on week after week, steadfastly refusing to obey orders and going through the motions of resigning his commission to enlist the sympathy of his friend President Davis. Ultimately his tactics were successful. He kept his troops, and Johnston gave up on the most practical means of bolstering the forts.[8]

Johnston's instincts had been correct about the Tennessee and Cumberland Rivers, but in the confusion of his first few months in an enormous and difficult command, he had not shown the ruthless drive necessary to make his wise plans become reality. Polk, after all, had been his West Point roommate and was the choice of their mutual friend Davis. Johnston's reluctance to crush Polk's insubordination lay behind many of the problems that followed. Johnston probably ought to have gone personally to Forts Henry and Donelson to push the work there and demand obedience. Indeed, his best course, viewed in the abstract, would have been to ensure that he was personally present at whatever position Polk commanded, thus relegating the contentious and incompetent bishop-general to a secondary role. That, of course, would have been problematic, since Polk was a favorite of the president's, had been assigned by the president to command along the Mississippi, and was second in rank only to Johnston within the department. There was no easy solution to the problem of Leonidas Polk, but finding a solution of some sort was an important missing element of success for Johnston.

If Johnston needed any further indication that the Tennessee and Cumberland Rivers were dangerous weak points in his defenses, that warning came on January 14, five days before the battle of Mill Springs destroyed the opposite end of his defensive line. On that day a small squadron of Union gunboats moved up the Tennessee River and briefly shelled Fort Henry. While Polk insisted that the incident was nothing more than a feint intended to draw attention away from his beloved heap of fortifications at Columbus, Johnston correctly recognized it as a scouting expedition that presaged a much larger and more dangerous Union advance. He began to issue orders for the final preparation of the river forts to receive the expected attack, and only then did he learn the full extent of their unpreparedness. At Fort Henry the situation was particularly grim. The heights that frowned down upon the fort from the Kentucky shore remained unoccupied, despite Johnston's orders of the previous autumn. For the Confederate western commander, the news came as a considerable shock. "It is most extraordinary," he almost gasped, "I ordered General Polk four months ago to at once construct those works. And now, with the enemy upon us, nothing of importance has been done. It is most extraordinary."[9]

It *was* extraordinary, at least by the regular-army standards that Johnston had known, but the question was what to do about it now. There was no time to fortify an alternative position, although Johnston quickly had inquiries made whether a stand could be made at

Clarksville, Tennessee, upstream on the Cumberland from Fort Donelson, but found it was no use. To abandon the forts without a fight would be to give up two-thirds of the state of Tennessee, along with access to the Southern heartland. It would have been so devastating to morale as to be unthinkable. The only option, then, was to try to hold the forts as they were. To the commander at Fort Henry, Johnston wired, "Occupy and intrench the heights opposite Fort Henry. Do not lose a moment. Work all night." But once again the urgency that Johnston expressed in his orders did not carry over into action on the part of his subordinates. It was another three weeks before the real test of that fort's strength came, but by that time the officer in charge of the fort had made no serious attempt either to strengthen his works or to build the all-important twin fort on the heights across the river. Again, Johnston's shortcoming had been that he did not go personally to the most intensely threatened site and press the work forward.[10]

And so the result when Johnston's left-center was tested was very similar to that when his right flank had been struck a fortnight earlier. On February 6, Ulysses S. Grant brought 15,000 men and a gunboat flotilla up the Tennessee to rattle the lock on Fort Henry. The struggle was over within a matter of hours. The fort was gone and the Tennessee River open to Union gunboats and transports all the way into northern Alabama. The affair could have been an even greater disaster for the Confederacy, save that the Union naval commander was in such a hurry to test his boats against the fort that he did not wait for Grant to get his troops into position to cut off a Confederate retreat. The Confederate commander wisely availed himself of this opportunity and got most of his garrison safely to Fort Donelson.[11]

Thus within eighteen days Johnston's entire strategic situation had been drastically altered. It was no longer any use to keep up his bluff of strength all along the front, since by now it was obvious that his defenses were fatally weak at any number of points. The course of action for any commander endeavoring to defend Tennessee in these circumstances was fairly obvious. He must concentrate his forces and strike a counterblow. The place for this concentration of forces was equally obvious. Corinth, Mississippi, at the junction of the important Mobile and Ohio Railroad and the even more important Memphis and Charleston Railroad, lay just a score or so miles from the Tennessee River, at the point where that stream completed its broad turn from a westward to a northward course and started its long descent parallel to the Mississippi. A Union army advancing southward to turn Confederate defenses on the Mississippi River would be likely to leave the Tennessee near here, and Federal possession of such a key rail junction would paralyze Confederate transportation in the northwestern part of the South's heartland and give the Union all but insurmountable strategic leverage there. With Johnston's forces deployed on either side of the Tennessee, as they had been all winter, and with Union gunboats now plying that stream, no concentration of Confederate troops could take place anywhere north of Corinth, since the long north-south stretch of the lower Tennessee would prove an unbridgeable chasm to maneuvering Southern armies. In short, any student of strategy who studied a map of the South's rivers and railroads could hardly fail to recognize Corinth as the key point of the campaign.

On the Union side, Maj. Gen. Henry W. "Old Brains" Halleck recognized it. He was the overall Union commander on the western end of Johnston's front, as Buell was on the eastern. Grant took orders from Halleck, and it was Halleck whom Grant had persuaded to let him try Fort Henry. The area's importance was equally obvious to Confederates all the way from Johnston himself down to Brig. Gen. Daniel Ruggles, who suggested a concentration of forces at Corinth. It was obvious as well to Louisiana general Pierre Gustave Toutant Beauregard, the hero, at least in the popular mind, of both Fort Sumter and First Manassas (Bull Run). Beauregard had just arrived from Virginia, having been transferred by Davis in the hopes that he might do Johnston some good or at least cease making such a political nuisance of himself by interacting with Confederate congressmen at Richmond. Having been in the theater of operations for less than a week, Beauregard too had no trouble recognizing the importance of Corinth. Discussions of who first conceived the idea of a Confederate concentration at Corinth are thus pointless. That sort of strategic insight belongs to the class of things German philosopher of war Carl von Clausewitz referred to when he stated, "In war, everything is very simple, but the simplest thing is very difficult." Seeing the need to concentrate Confederate strength at Corinth was simple. Actually bringing the troops together there in a timely manner was another thing entirely.[12]

That was the task that faced Johnston. His own main body would have to move southward, around the head of navigation of the Tennessee River in northern Alabama. Polk's wing of the army, now supervised by Beauregard, would have to abandon the possibly impregnable but now thoroughly useless bastion at Columbus. Reinforcements, which the Confederate government was only now beginning to see as necessary, would be the first to arrive at Corinth, but the place could be held only if the two widely separated Confederate wings could converge there before the Federals arrived in force. Accomplishing that maneuver would be made even more difficult by the presence of the Cumberland River in the rear of Johnston's main force at Bowling Green. Curving through middle Tennessee, the Cumberland swept directly across Johnston's line of retreat at Nashville, and it was navigable all the way there. Worse, the only thing keeping the Federal gunboats off that river was Fort Donelson, the other of the two neglected forts.

Johnston consulted with Beauregard as the latter passed through on his way to take over supervision of Polk's force. Together they decided on their strategy for the coming campaign. Fort Donelson, they agreed, could not possibly hold out for long, yet it was vital that they hold the fort as long as possible in order to secure Johnston's retreat from Bowling Green. So Johnston determined to send substantial infantry reinforcements to the garrison at Fort Donelson. At first glance, it was a strange decision. Johnston and Beauregard had agreed in their discussion that the major threat to the forts came from the Federal gunboats, not the Union land forces, and that had certainly been the case at Fort Henry. Johnston obviously would have entertained no thought of combating enemy gunboats with his own infantry. In fact, only one sensible explanation exists for Johnston's thinking behind this order. If Fort Donelson was to resist up to the last possible moment against the seemingly invincible Union gunboats, then its garrison would not have the luxury of making a timely withdrawal like that at Fort Henry and escaping before Union infantry could get into position. If the Donelson garrison was to hold the Union gunboats back as long as possible and still make good its escape, it would require an infantry force of its own sufficient to keep the Federal ground troops at bay. This alone can explain Johnston's thinking in ordering major infantry support for the fort, and indeed, Johnston gave orders that the garrison should withdraw whenever it appeared that the fort could no longer be held.[13]

That this was the Confederate purpose is borne out by the behavior of the fort's officers when the expected Union attack came. Grant marched his Union troops across the neck of land separating the two rivers. Bad roads and other hindrances prevented him from drawing his lines around the fort until February 12, and the dreaded gunboat squadron was not ready to make its attack for another two days. When it did, everyone, including Confederate general John B. Floyd, commanding the fort, seems to have believed that it would make short work of the Confederate batteries. In fact, quite the opposite was the case, as Fort Donelson proved to be a far sturdier and better sited work than its counterpart on the Tennessee River. Within the space of about half an hour, all the gunboats were forced to drop back down the river, badly shot up. Damage to the fort was slight and Confederate casualties virtually nil.[14]

If the Confederate purpose had been to have the Fort Donelson garrison fight to the finish within its entrenchments, the gray-clad troops would simply have hunkered down and waited for the gunboats—or Grant's infantry—to try again. Instead, Floyd, in consultation with his two next ranking officers, Brig. Gen. Gideon Pillow and Brig. Gen. Simon B. Buckner, decided that the time had come to pull out. They probably underestimated both the amount of time the fort could hold out and the amount of time that Johnston would need to make good his retreat and reconcentration. Yet their decision was a reasonable one, for they could not know how much longer the balance of forces locally would allow their escape, and in the event, the time gained was indeed sufficient for Johnston to get his forces across the Cumberland at Nashville.

Accordingly, Floyd, Pillow, and Buckner made plans for a massive breakout assault on the morning of February 15, to be followed by the retirement of the entire garrison southward. Well before dawn, Confederate troops scrambled out of their trenches and across the hard, frozen ground toward Union lines. Surprise was all but complete, and after a fierce battle that lasted through the morning and into the afternoon, success was achieved. The Southerners shoved the Federals out of the way and opened the road to Nashville and a rendezvous with Johnston's withdrawing main body.

So far, Johnston's plan for recovering the desperate situation in his department had functioned pretty much as he had hoped, but at this point it suffered a major malfunction in the persons of the three ranking Confederate officers in Fort Donelson. With almost inconceivable stupidity, Pillow, at the very moment of victory, decided that the thing to do was to pull the Confederate garrison back into the fort so that they could rest, eat, and gather up their effects before leaving. He was able to prevail on Floyd to order such a movement, despite the vehement protests of Buckner, who was the only one of the Confederate generals present who had any military training or any acquaintance with Grant. What happened next would have been predictable to someone like Buckner. Grant seized the initiative and recovered his army's former position and then some. That night the Confederate commanders held another conference, and this time it was Buckner's turn to contribute to Confederate disaster. Morosely he asserted that the fort was doomed and the only possible course was to surrender at once. This time he prevailed with the commander, and the next morning nearly the entire force went into captivity. Col. Bedford Forrest led his unit and a few others out of the trap, and Floyd and Pillow fled to avoid sharing the fate of their men.[15]

The debacle at Fort Donelson cost the Confederacy perhaps 13,000 men. The other factors were, by this time, secondary. Johnston had known that the fort was bound to fall, and the three days that it had already held out, coupled with some confusion within the Federal high command regarding departmental boundaries between Halleck and Buell, sufficed to give Johnston the time he needed to get south of Nashville. The loss of manpower, however, was devastating. Even after reinforcements arrived from other parts of the Confederacy, the troops that had surrendered at Donelson still would have constituted approximately one-fourth of the army Johnston finally led into battle at Shiloh seven weeks later. What the result might have been lies in the realm of speculation, but it could have made a considerable difference.

Johnston's failure once again involved controlling his subordinates. Floyd and Pillow were hopeless incompetents and miserable poltroons. Their presence in such key positions seems in retrospect to have been a horrible mistake. Yet Floyd's date of rank made him senior to every other Confederate officer in the department save

Beauregard, Polk, and Johnston himself. Johnston had just learned his lesson about Polk's capacity and had sent Beauregard to oversee the bishop-general. As strange as it may seem, the only viable option by which Johnston might have avoided disaster was to go to Fort Donelson and take command himself. Under his resolute and skillful leadership, it is hard to imagine how the Confederates could have failed to make good the escape of the entire garrison. In Johnston's absence from the main body, Brig. Gen. William J. Hardee would have been more than adequate to lead that force to safety on the south bank of the Cumberland at Nashville, and there Johnston and the Fort Donelson garrison could have rendezvoused with them for the continued march southward to Corinth. In all fairness, Johnston can hardly be faulted for choosing to stay with the largest portion of the troops in his department. Nevertheless, the fact stands out that in a desperately threatened region with a critical shortage of qualified generals, there is no substitute for the active, personal presence of the commanding general at the key point of contact with the enemy. Choosing to entrust this job to subordinates while trying to function in the more traditional role of department commander had now twice cost Johnston severely.

By late March, Johnston had succeeded in bringing his scattered forces together at Corinth and was trying to shape them and the new reinforcements into some semblance of an army. By April 2 the time had come to take the initiative. Grant's Union army, roughly comparable in size to Johnston's now united force, was encamped on the banks of the Tennessee River at Pittsburg Landing, about thirty miles from Corinth. While Grant's 40,000 men rested there, Buell's 35,000 additional Federals were marching overland from Nashville to join them. Once again the proper military solution to the problem Johnston faced was obvious enough to be grasped by any strategist who studied the rival armies' positions. All Johnston had to do was take his army up to Pittsburg Landing and destroy Grant before Buell arrived, and then destroy Buell in turn. And once again the task of actually carrying out such a purpose would prove infinitely more difficult and complicated than simply conceiving it.

Johnston gave orders for the army to march on Pittsburg Landing on April 2, but at once things started to go wrong again. Partly this was because the weather turned rainy and the roads turned boggy, and no one's army could have made good time across the northern Mississippi and southern Tennessee countryside. Partly it was because this was an army of neophytes led by largely inexperienced officers. All armies have to learn the art of swift and orderly marching sometime. Unfortunately for Johnston, his was learning it now. Finally, part of the reason for the slow and confused march up the road toward Pittsburg Landing was that Johnston had once again made the mistake of placing too much confidence in a subordinate.

P. G. T. Beauregard had come highly recommended, the ostensible hero of Fort Sumter and First Manassas. The fact was that Fort Sumter had been an exercise in the emplacing of artillery batteries, and Beauregard's victory at Manassas had been more in spite of his planning than because of it. Johnston, of course, could not know this. Beauregard had been sent west to help defend the region at a time when his reputation was very high and Johnston's, because of the fall of Fort Henry, was very low. Johnston may have believed that only his personal friendship with Jefferson Davis had kept him from being relieved outright and replaced with Beauregard, and that may well have been the case. At any rate, Johnston seems to have felt compelled to give Beauregard a large amount of responsibility, and so it was that he directed Beauregard, his second in command, to prepare the order for the movement to Pittsburg Landing.[16]

With characteristic admiration for Napoleon but remarkable disregard for historical context, Beauregard chose to pattern the march order after Napoleon's order for the march to Waterloo. That in itself might have been no problem, but the real difficulties arose from the fact that Beauregard's orders called for elaborate maneuvering by green troops and did not make the best use of the available roads.

All these factors led to a considerable traffic snarl. When his subordinates managed to lose track of an entire division of infantry, Johnston at last decided that it was time to intervene personally. "This is perfectly puerile!" he exploded. "This is not war! Let us have our horses." With that, he and his staff mounted and rode off in search of the missing troops. It seems that Polk had messed up the march order and had his wagons in the wrong place, thus blocking the march of the missing division. Johnston was able to get matters sorted out, and the army was on the march again fairly quickly.

Nevertheless, the roads, the weather, the army's inexperience, and Beauregard's poor planning delayed the operation. Johnston had hoped to be in place to launch his attack no later than the morning of April 5, but the troops were not up and deployed until late that afternoon. The assault was rescheduled for the morning of Sunday, April 6.

Even worse from Johnston's point of view was the way in which the Confederate army was deployed. Johnston's battle plan called for hitting hardest at the Federal left, tearing it loose from Lick Creek and the Tennessee River at Pittsburg Landing, and crowding it into the pocket formed where Owl Creek angled northeastward through swampy ground to join the Tennessee below the landing. For this purpose, he planned to have Braxton Bragg, the most aggressive of his four corps commanders, lead an oversized unit amounting to about one-third of the army's total manpower against the crucial Federal left. Hardee's corps would go in on the Confederate center, and Polk's on the left. John C. Breckinridge's would be in reserve. It was a good arrangement, and Johnston described it in a letter to Jefferson Davis. Unfortunately for the Confederacy, it was never carried out.[17]

Besides letting Beauregard draw up the plans for the march, Johnston also allowed the Creole general to direct the deployment of the troops. Either because he did not understand Johnston's plan or because he thought he knew better, Beauregard spread Hardee's and part of Bragg's corps across the entire front line. The rest of Bragg's corps formed a second line behind it, and Polk's behind that. It was a disastrous arrangement that guaranteed confusion on the battlefield. Once the fight started, the three lines would compact together, forming a jumble of units that no one could maneuver and in which few soldiers would be familiar with the officers they would be expected to obey in the heat of combat. Worst, perhaps, it completely negated Johnston's plan to hit hardest at the Federal left.

Once again, Johnston had been burned by giving too much discretion to his subordinates and not exercising enough personal direction. Admittedly, it would have been an extremely tall order for Johnston to have anticipated the key times and places in his vast department and been there in person at each of them. Yet without doing that, no general could have succeeded in the Confederate West in the winter and spring of 1862.

By the evening of April 5 it was too late to change the army's deployment.[18] The attack would have to proceed with the present arrangement or not at all. Beauregard, until then Johnston's most trusted subordinate, was vehemently in favor of not attacking at all. He moaned that the element of surprise would now be lost and that the army should retreat to Corinth at once. Bragg and several other officers took up the theme and continued to press their case the following morning. This was the same sort of council of war that had surrendered Fort Donelson, and it was headed in the same direction. At this point, however, the value of Johnston's personal presence became apparent. "I would fight them if they were a million," he declared. The attack would go on, and that was that. "Tomorrow," he added, "we will water our horses in the Tennessee River."[19]

It appears that Johnston did eventually learn his lesson about placing too much responsibility in the hands of subordinates. That mistake had cost him dearly over the last few weeks—at Mill Springs, Fort Henry, Fort Donelson, and now on the road to Pittsburg Landing. But when the Confederate attack commenced on the morning of April 6, Johnston himself was on the spot and leading the assault in the key sector on the Confederate right, and in that capacity he met his death around 2:30 that afternoon.

A final analysis of his generalship in the Confederate West in the winter and spring of 1862 reveals a capable and resolute officer with excellent strategic and tactical abilities and exceptional leadership qualities. If he had an Achilles' heel, it may have been that his learning curve was not quite steep enough. Despite all his experience with volunteer soldiers in Texas and in the Mexican War and his obviously superb ability to inspire such troops, he was simply too slow to anticipate the blundering and willfulness of the war's first batch of volunteer officers and even some professionals carrying unwonted responsibilities. Things that had been matters of course in the old army—such as simple obedience to orders by senior officers—just did not happen much of the time in this new service, and up until the evening of his next to last day on earth, Johnston seemed to be one step behind in heading off his subordinates' miscues.

Johnston had the misfortune to exercise his first major Civil War assignment in a massive command of crucial importance under the eyes of the whole nation. Like Robert E. Lee in West Virginia the preceding fall, he learned that one dare not leave vital matters in the hands of weak subordinates. Given time, he would no doubt have learned which subordinates were weak and which strong. He was not given that time. Instead, circumstances required of him an extreme quickness in learning and exacted a high price for mistakes already made.

Chapter Two

"The Responsibility Is Great": Joseph E. Johnston and the War in Virginia

Alan Downs

On November 12, 1862, Joseph E. Johnston reported for duty at the War Department in Richmond. It had been almost six months since he had been severely wounded in the shoulder and chest at the battle of Seven Pines. Although recovered enough in early November to resume riding horseback, the general still suffered from an "obstinate adhesion of the lungs to the side, and a constant tendency to pleurisy."[1] Ideally, Johnston would have liked to regain his old command, the Army of Virginia (now the Army of Northern Virginia). The chances of this occurring were minimal, since his replacement, Robert E. Lee, was now established as a favorite among Virginians and Jefferson Davis, in spite of his recent failure in Maryland. Johnston instead learned that the president intended to place the departments of Tennessee and Mississippi under his direction—an assignment that would ultimately dash any hopes he entertained for personal fame and military distinction.

Accompanied by his wife, Lydia, and his personal staff, Johnston boarded a train in Richmond, Virginia, to begin what would become an arduous trip to his new headquarters in Chattanooga, Tennessee. He took with him more than just his personal baggage. He took along a year's worth of experience in fighting this war and a relationship with the president that was anything but convivial. In fact, the events of the previous year had all but transfixed the general's concepts for waging the war and his attitude toward the administration in Richmond. Much of what Johnston did or did not do (his strategic and tactical decisions) for the remainder of the war could find precedents during his tenure in command in Virginia. These precedents and their legacies became for many the criteria for the overall assessment of Johnston's generalship.

Historians, in general, have been quick to point out Johnston's failures, ultimately relegating him to the second tier in the pantheon of Confederate heroes. As Frank Vandiver noted in his introduction to the 1959 edition of Johnston's memoirs, the general is considered by many to be a "first-rate second-rater, if not worse."[2] One explanation for this prevailing point of view can be linked to Johnston's apparent lack of climactic battlefield engagements and, consequently, victories. He won no Cannae or Austerlitz during the American Civil War. More akin to Roman consul Quintus Fabius Maximus, the Confederate general conducted campaigns that were frequently characterized by maneuver, delay, and withdrawal. Historians of the Civil War have argued that Johnston's preference for trading space for time was inappropriate for the Confederacy and merely a reflection of the flaws in his character. T. Harry Williams argued that "Johnston undoubtedly had real ability, but he never did much with it. It is reasonable to expect that a general who has sustained opportunities will sometime, once, achieve something decisive. Certainly Johnston had the opportunities, but there is no decisive success on his record."[3] In *Battle Cry of Freedom*, James McPherson includes the general in his list of "bumblers," noting that he "fought too little and too late."[4] Clement Eaton states in his biography of Jefferson Davis that Johnston was an "egotist, afraid to launch what might be an unsuccessful adventure in battle."[5] Richard McMurry wrote a similar critique: "A lifetime in the army's bureaucracy had taught him that one could win promotion if one avoided mistakes and that the way to avoid mistakes was to avoid risks. For an army commander, this meant avoiding battle—if he did not fight, he could not lose."[6]

These historians and others have contributed collectively to an image of Johnston that has become the standard interpretation. He was a reserved, stubborn man with the pompous air of an intellectual. His animosity toward Davis and jealousy of Lee led him to be secretive, self-serving, and overly cautious on the battlefield. His unwillingness to take risks led to campaigns characterized by retreats or withdrawals. The general's subsequent feuding with the War Department and the Davis administration was detrimental to Confederate morale and military cohesiveness. The ultimate manifestation of this last sin was Johnston's link to the anti-Davis faction in the Confederate government led by, among others, Johnston's friend Senator Louis T. Wigfall of Texas. In short, Johnston was indeed a "second-rate" general.

Juxtaposed to these highly negative interpretations of the general are contemporary accounts that offer overwhelming praise. Former Confederate general James Longstreet stated publicly that he believed that Johnston was the Confederacy's best general.[7] "Stonewall" Jackson's staff member and devotee Henry Kyd Douglas wrote, "For clear military judgment and capacity to comprehend and take advantage of what is loosely termed 'the situation,' General Johnston was not surpassed by any general in either army."[8] Even former foes such as Ulysses Simpson Grant and William Tecumseh Sherman argued in their memoirs that Johnston's responses to their respective operations in Mississippi and Georgia were usually correct, even the best choices for the Confederacy.

How, then, can one man foster such diametrically opposed impressions? One answer is that whereas many contemporaries found much to admire in the general, some of Johnston's detractors were influenced by often bitter postwar retrospectives that frequently examined events out of context. They committed what one historian has labeled the "fallacy of responsibility as cause." Critics merged two different questions and demanded a single answer: "How did it happen?" and "Who is to blame?"[9] Adherents to this approach have isolated events during the Civil War that either were lost opportunities for the Confederacy or contributed to its eventual defeat. In the majority of these "turning points," Johnston played a prominent role: the Confederate failure to follow up on its victory at Manassas in 1861 with a march on Washington, the failure to retain Vicksburg in 1863, and the failure to stop Sherman from taking Atlanta in 1864. Robert E. Lee, in contrast, "saved" Richmond from capture after Johnston retreated up the peninsula in front of McClellan in 1862.

Another, more common error is to equate failure with lack of merit. To be sure, Joseph Johnston was, and remains, a difficult person to know and understand. But it is hard to dismiss his record of military achievement prior to Virginia's secession. If Johnston was a failure during the Civil War, there is little in his record prior to Confederate service indicative of things to come. What, then, accounts for his apparently unstellar, "all-but-mutinous" performance during the war?[10] At the beginning of the American Civil War, Johnston was fifty-four years old with over thirty years in the military behind him. He experienced highs and lows in both military and civilian life before the Civil War that played an integral part in forming the context in which the general's actions and decisions as a Confederate officer must be examined.

Joseph Johnston was the son of Peter Johnston, a Revolutionary War veteran, state politician, and judge of the Virginia General Court. His mother, the former Mary Wood, was the niece of Patrick Henry.[11] Joseph spent the first four years of his life in Farmville, Virginia, at Cherry Grove, the home of his birth. In 1811, Peter moved his family to Abingdon, located in southwest Virginia and better suited for his judicial circuit. Living in an area populated with veterans of the battle of King's Mountain (Johnston's great-aunt married Gen. William Campbell) and having a father who had fought for American independence, young Joseph grew up listening to numerous military reminiscences.[12] Evidence of the impact these war stories had on Joseph and of the deep respect he had for his father's military accomplishments can be found in Joseph's desire to make the military a profession and, ultimately, to wear his father's sword during his own early campaigns in the American Civil War.[13] In fact, the course of Johnston's Civil War career was almost predetermined, because he had inherited from his family and environment a burden of responsibility (almost an obligation) to assume a leadership role in the South's own war for independence and to see to its success.

Entering the U.S. Military Academy at West Point in 1825, Johnston was one of 105 new cadets that year. Among his entering class was Robert Edward Lee. The Johnston and Lee families were no strangers to each other. Joseph's father had enlisted in the patriot cause at the age of sixteen and served under Lee's father, "Light-Horse Harry" Lee, during the American Revolution. At West Point the sons of these two Revolutionary warriors became intimate friends as well as competitors—especially as the ranks of their entering class

Joseph E. Johnston

dwindled and the two became the sole representatives of their native state. Graduating thirteenth (behind Lee and ahead of another future Confederate general, Theophilus Hunter Holmes) in a class that had eroded to forty-six in 1829, Johnston experienced a variety of military assignments prior to the Civil War.

The newly commissioned second lieutenant of the artillery saw his first duty in garrison at Fort Columbus, New York, and at Fort Monroe, Virginia.[14] At the latter post, Johnston was reunited with Robert E. Lee. He participated but saw no action in the Black Hawk Expedition of 1832. With the exception of an excursion to Fort Dearborn with Maj. Gen. Winfield Scott on board the *Sheldon Thompson,* Johnston sat out most of the Black Hawk War in garrison at Charleston Harbor, South Carolina.[15] He was on hand, however, when that state threatened to nullify Federal authority in 1832. This was a difficult assignment for Johnston, because three of his brothers were drilling with the state militia in Columbia, and a fourth brother in the U.S. Congress was actively supporting states' rights.[16]

After three more years of garrison and topographical duty, the twenty-nine-year-old Virginian received his first taste of warfare in 1836 while serving as aide-de-camp for Gen. Winfield Scott fighting the Seminole Indians. Very little was accomplished during this campaign, which ultimately resulted in the recall of Scott (along with his staff) and an appearance before a board of inquiry. Scott defended himself and his command by stating that he would have gladly fought the Seminoles but was never able to find them. He surmised that it was the intention of the Indians to remain deep in the wilderness of southern Florida, allowing the American army to defeat itself in the hot, swampy, and disease-ridden terrain. To make matters worse, Scott continued, the sinkholes and ponds that were to supply water for his troops had dried up, and the men had overheated because they were still wearing cold-weather uniforms.[17] This experience could do nothing but impress Johnston with the difficulty of conducting a campaign in a hostile climate and under the watchful eyes of civilian superiors.

On May 31, 1837, now holding the rank of first lieutenant, he resigned from the army and went into civilian service as a civil engineer. Despite this rather abrupt change, Johnston clearly had not lost his love for the military life. When hostilities in Florida flared up again in September 1837, Johnston offered his services to the army. The secretary of war appointed him adjutant and topographical engineer (without military rank) and assigned him to Lt. L. M. Powell of the navy, along with a hodgepodge of other soldiers, sailors, and civilians.[18] Johnston's assignment was to select and mark sites along the Indian River for possible outposts and depots. As the expedition left the interior on January 15, 1838, it was attacked by Seminoles near the mouth of the Jupiter Inlet. Lieutenant Powell was wounded, along with several other officers and men. Johnston himself was wounded in the forehead after effectively directing the rearguard action of the army regulars.[19] According to one account, "Mr. Johnson [sic] took command . . . ; and the coolness, courage, and judgment he displayed at the most critical and trying emergency was the theme of praise with every one who beheld him."[20] This experience inspired Johnston to reenter the regular army on July 7, 1838, as a first lieutenant in the Corps of Topographical Engineers. His engineering duties sent him to the border between the United States and the Republic of Texas in 1841, to Lake Erie that same year for harbor improvements, to the Topographical Bureau in Washington, D.C., in 1842, and on various boundary and coastal surveys from 1843 to 1846.[21]

Within a year the nation was at war with Mexico. Now a captain of topographical engineers, Johnston was reunited with Gen. Winfield Scott in his campaign into central Mexico. Also along on the campaign was Capt. Robert E. Lee, with whom Johnston shared a cabin on board Scott's ship, the USS *Massachusetts*.[22] With Scott and Lee, Johnston participated in the landing at and capture of Vera Cruz in March 1847. In early April he was promoted to lieutenant colonel of the "Voltigeurs," a new regiment of regulars raised for the war. Following the occupation of Vera Cruz, Johnston was wounded in the arm and groin while conducting a reconnaissance near Cerro Gordo on April 12.[23] The action brought him a brevet promotion to colonel for "gallant and meritorious conduct." The American victory in the ensuing battle opened the road to the Mexican capital.

The Voltigeurs participated in all the major engagements against the defenses of Mexico City. Their standard flew at Contreras, Churubusco, and Molino del Rey and was the first to be planted on the wall at Chapultepec.[24] Johnston, wounded again at this latter battle, drew from General Scott the comment that "Johnston is a great soldier, but he has the unfortunate knack of getting himself shot in nearly every engagement."[25] Lee remarked, "Joe Johnston is fat & ruddy. I think a little lead, properly taken, is good for a man."[26]

The fall of the Mexican capital meant the end of the campaign for Johnston. In August 1848, the Voltigeurs were mustered out of the service, but Johnston was reinstated in the regular army with his prewar rank of captain of topographical engineers. From 1853 to 1855 he was on assignment west of the Mississippi in charge of river improvements. With the addition of two new cavalry regiments to the army in 1855, the captain was commissioned a lieutenant colonel and assigned to the First Cavalry under Col. E. V. Sumner. The Second Cavalry was under the command of Albert Sidney Johnston, with Robert E. Lee serving as lieutenant colonel. Johnston served with his regiment out of Fort Leavenworth, Kansas, in quelling disturbances in that state in 1856 and, after a brief stay at Jefferson Barracks, Missouri, in patrolling the southern border of the territory in 1857. He served in a variety of posts in 1858, including Fort Riley, Kansas, and Washington, D.C., and participated in the Utah Expedition as inspector general.

In these postwar years, the relationship between Lee and Johnston grew more formal as the two lost touch with each other.[27] Relationships grew, however, between Johnston and some of the other young officers in the army. Particularly close to Johnston was George Brinton McClellan. The two corresponded frequently, and when McClellan traveled to Europe to observe military developments, Johnston asked his friend to bring him back a "good sword for fighting" and books on cavalry tactics.[28]

On June 10, 1860, the quartermaster general of the army, Thomas S. Jessup, died. The quartermaster general was next in rank to the aging General Scott. Whoever replaced Jessup should be capable of assuming command of the army if something were to happen to "Old Fuss and Feathers," now seventy-four years old. The War Department requested that Scott name the officer that he thought would be best suited for the job. Declining to limit himself to a single choice, Scott submitted four names: Joseph E. Johnston, Robert E. Lee, Albert Sidney Johnston, and Charles Ferguson Smith. Secretary of War John B. Floyd favored Joseph Johnston, and the Senate confirmed his selection with a vote of thirty-one to three in the lieutenant colonel's favor.

The office of quartermaster general carried with it a promotion to brigadier general. Robert E. Lee, whom Johnston now outranked, wrote, "My dear General: I am delighted at accosting you by your present title, and feel my heart exult within me at your high position."[29] Privately, however, Lee expressed the belief that Johnston was the object of favoritism from his cousin by marriage, the secretary of war.[30]

With the secession of South Carolina from the Union on December 20, 1860, followed by six more Deep South states in January and February 1861, attention in Washington focused on, among other things, the resignation of military and civilian employees of the United States government. Personally and privately, Johnston, the grandnephew of Patrick Henry, was opposed to secession, but he believed that it was the duty of an officer of the army to take no part in political debates.[31] On March 15, 1861, Confederate Secretary of War LeRoy Pope Walker wrote to Johnston to notify him of his appointment to the Confederate army with the rank of brigadier general. No extant record indicates whether Johnston received Walker's letter or replied to it. What we do know (or can at least surmise) is that with the news of the firing on Fort Sumter on April 12, 1861, and Abraham Lincoln's call for state troops three days later, Johnston began to reevaluate his situation. The Virginia convention went back into session on April 16 and recommended that the state secede from the Union. The convention also suggested that Governor John Letcher organize volunteers for the defense of the state and seek to lure away militarily experienced Virginians from the ranks of the U.S. Army and Navy. General Scott anticipated that Johnston might leave Federal service and attempted to persuade him to remain, as he did with Robert E. Lee.[32]

On Friday, April 19, Johnston received official notification of the Virginia convention's decision to secede from the Union. Feeling bound by his state's decision, Johnston determined to resign. Johnston's wife, Lydia, was not at all convinced that this was the wisest course of action for her husband. She did not want to leave her home, family, and friends. Furthermore, ever since the debate over Johnston's appointment to the office of quartermaster general, Mrs. Johnston had doubted Jefferson Davis's loyalty to Joseph. She told her husband, "he hates you, he has power & he will ruin you."[33] Johnston replied, "He can't, I don't care, my country."[34]

Leaving behind most of their personal possessions in their home on H Street in Washington, Joseph and Lydia boarded a train for Richmond on Tuesday, April 23. The Johnstons carried with them only their clothing and Joseph's personal arms—including his father's Revolutionary War sword. The weather had been bad, and floods had swept away or damaged many of the bridges on the road to Richmond, causing delays. Consequently, the Johnstons did not reach the Virginia capital until the morning of April 25. As he and Lydia settled into their temporary lodging, Johnston unpacked expectations unseen by others that would serve as internal burdens for the remainder of the war.

Robert E. Lee was already in town. Having resigned his commission as colonel of the Second Regiment of Cavalry on April 20, Lee arrived at the Richmond depot on April 22 and checked into the Spotswood Hotel.[35] The state secession convention had mandated that someone be appointed to command the military forces of Virginia. That person would be given the rank of major general. Governor Letcher's advisory council recommended Lee for the job, and the governor promptly offered it to him. Lee accepted, and his appointment was quickly confirmed by the convention. Johnston called on Lee in the latter's office near the state capitol. Lee recommended to Governor Letcher that Johnston be commissioned (as was Lee) in the Virginia military with the rank of major general. The governor agreed, and Lee assigned his friend the task of organizing and instructing the volunteers arriving daily in Richmond.

Johnston remained busy at his task in Richmond for almost two weeks, during which time he discovered, to his surprise, that the Virginia government had decided to commission him only at the rank of brigadier general. The rationale for this move was that public policy dictated that only one man should hold the higher rank of major general, and Lee, possibly owing to his arrival in Richmond before Johnston, had secured that position. Johnston's private feelings about what essentially amounted to a demotion are unrecorded. Lee was a close friend—a fact that helped ease what must have been feelings of bitterness and frustration. Now Johnston would be in a subordinate role to a man whom he had outranked in the U.S. Army just a few weeks earlier, supposedly because of the sequence of their arrival in Richmond. One wonders what thoughts flashed through Johnston's mind. It was not the first time he had lost out to Lee. The memories of West Point reminded him of that. Were he and his long-time friend going to resume where their fathers had left off?

Endeavoring to psychoanalyze an individual is risky at best, even with what appears to be strong evidence. The task becomes all the more perilous when the individual has been dead for over 100 years. But it is perhaps worthwhile in an effort to comprehend Johnston's state of mind (his motives) to examine what was probable through evidence that, short of written testimony, is necessarily circumstantial.

As the Confederacy strove to evolve into legitimacy, it made deliberate and tangible ties to the American War for Independence almost a century earlier. The great seal of the Confederacy highlighted George Washington on horseback while the new nation's statesmen and soldiers worked to establish and maintain "home rule."[36] Relatively few of the more prominent civilian and military leaders of the Confederacy had direct and immediate links to the Revolution. As sons of Revolutionary War officers, Johnston and Lee were the exception rather than the rule—and Johnston had the added distinction of being the grandnephew of Patrick Henry.

From his early days at West Point through the Civil War, Johnston parlayed his heritage into what can be best described as an insatiable desire for prominence, manifested by his keen sensitivity regarding rank and reputation. This obsession frequently translated into arrogance and at West Point won him the epithet "The Colonel"—a response to his often haughty demeanor. Throughout his antebellum career, Johnston's impressive military record was paralleled by his own crusade for professional advancement and distinction. This pursuit was at times successful, but it was not without its share of disappointments.

Beginning at West Point, Johnston experienced the first of what amounted to a series of perceived demotions in rank (and all the things that rank symbolized, such as status and authority), just when he felt that he should have been the recipient of accolades. During his senior, or first class, year, Johnston was the only cadet out of sixteen to hold rank the previous year and not receive a reappointment. While his friend Lee served as cadet adjutant, Johnston turned in his chevrons and joined the unacknowledged majority of his classmates.[37] Eight years later, after being promoted to the rank of first lieutenant and serving with Scott in Florida, Johnston went so far as to resign from the army over his dissatisfaction at being bypassed for promotion in favor of junior officers simply because (as he saw it) they belonged to regiments that received favorable treatment.[38] Low pay and firsthand experience with governmental interference in the Seminole campaigns also contributed to his disenchantment. After returning to the army the following year, Johnston continued to climb the rocky road of promotion, battling with then Secretary of War Jefferson Davis over his correct rank following the war with Mexico. He reached his peak in the U.S. Army as quartermaster general with the staff rank of brigadier general in 1860. That promotion was paramount in Johnston's list of professional objectives is obvious by a declaration he made in a letter written to his brother, Edward, in 1851 in which he stated, "promotion, [is] a thing I desire more than any man in the army."[39]

Of course, it would be inaccurate to imply that Johnston was atypical in his hunger for promotion, but it is reasonable to conclude that Johnston's desire for professional laurels was never far from his thoughts. There is no evidence that Johnston's noteworthy performance on antebellum battlefields—his military merit—was undertaken simply in the pursuit of rank. It is accurate to conclude, however, that for Johnston, promotion fairly won ought not be surrendered or denied. As war appeared inevitable in 1861, Johnston found himself assuming a prominent commanding role in a state military establishment that professed ties, both real and imagined, to a similar scenario in 1775. He was to continue the legacy of his father and kinfolk by helping chart the course for the revolution of 1860. For a man whose first instinct was to support neither slavery nor secession, the burden of responsibility must have been great. His actions would not be justifiable unless the "revolution" worked. Success must be guaranteed.

After word arrived of Johnston's new subordinate role to Robert E. Lee, he grew increasingly depressed at what he saw as a demotion from his leadership role in this Southern war for independence. His despondent mood was soon lifted, however, when he was invited to meet with Confederate president Jefferson Davis at the capital in Montgomery, Alabama. Davis offered Johnston a commission in the provisional Confederate army with the rank of brigadier general—the highest rank attainable at the time. Johnston accepted. This appointment ameliorated his previous vexation over his commission in the service of Virginia, thus restoring his parity with Lee. He later wrote, "as it was certain that the war would be conducted by the Confederate Government, and its officers had precedence over those having like state grades, I preferred the Confederate commission."[40]

Almost immediately after accepting his commission and while still in Montgomery, Johnston received orders from Confederate Adjutant and Inspector General Samuel Cooper assigning him command of the troops in Harpers Ferry, Virginia. Harpers Ferry, the northernmost garrison of the Confederacy, was already a target of the Union army. Six days prior to the general's arrival, Johnston's old friend George B. McClellan (now a major general in the U.S. Army and commander of the department of the Ohio) reported to Winfield Scott's assistant adjutant general that he had developed a plan for "driving the rebels from Harper's Ferry."[41]

Johnston arrived in Harpers Ferry on May 23. The task of turning the town into a viable military garrison was difficult for many reasons, one being that the troops assembling in the town were undisciplined and poorly equipped.[42] Many of those men who were assigned to duty at Harpers Ferry were unable to train or perform their duties because of illness. Johnston reported that nearly 40 percent of his troops were either sick in the hospital or debilitated with measles or mumps.[43]

The topographical features at Harpers Ferry also posed potentially serious problems for Johnston. The town was situated at the point of land formed by the confluence of the Potomac and Shenandoah Rivers. It was surrounded on three sides by high ground, making the terrain unfavorable to a defensive force. The Potomac River could be easily crossed both above and below Harpers Ferry, making the retention of the town for defensive purposes rather pointless. Finally, Harpers Ferry was twenty miles away from the main transportation route into the Shenandoah Valley from Maryland and Pennsylvania. Thus the garrison was out of position to defend the valley.[44]

Johnston faced varying degrees of loyalty among his troops and among the inhabitants of the surrounding countryside. On the same day that he arrived at Harpers Ferry, the state of Virginia officially approved the referendum on secession. The mountainous western part of the state, on which Harpers Ferry bordered, was strongly

Unionist and opposed to secession. Consequently, many of the troops from that part of the state were no longer interested in serving, especially now that Virginia troops would clearly be incorporated into the Confederate army. The result was an increase in desertion among these troops and a general deterioration of discipline.

William Henry Chase Whiting, major of engineers and member of Johnston's staff at Harpers Ferry, confirmed the general's difficulties when he wrote:

> To hold this post . . . either as a fortress or as a condition of the defense of the Virginia Valley, we [would] require a force of from twelve to fifteen thousand men, of which two regiments should be cavalry. The strengthening and re-enforcement of this force, as now constituted, seems to have ceased when most necessary. [W]e are so deficient in ammunition that this force must, on the advance of the enemy, move out from the Ferry and maneuver, to prevent being shut up in a cul-de-sac.[45]

In retrospect, Whiting did not possess the qualities one would hope to have in a staff officer. He would later reveal a tendency toward moodiness and depression—emotions that often translated into pessimistic advice.[46] But in the late spring of 1861, there was good reason to have great faith in Whiting's ability, for he had graduated at the top of his class at West Point with the highest grades ever recorded at the academy up to that point. Alternatives to withdrawal were not forthcoming from Johnston's staff. To even consider other options, Johnston would have had to ignore this apparently brilliant engineer's advice, be influenced by someone claiming to be more knowledgeable than Whiting, or be given a specific order from Richmond to remain at Harpers Ferry.

Given these circumstances, it is not surprising that Johnston was concerned as he received intelligence of Federal troop buildups to his north and northwest. In addition to Maj. Gen. Irvin McDowell's army in the District of Columbia, Federal forces threatening Virginia were located in Chambersburg, Pennsylvania, under the command of Maj. Gen. Robert Patterson and in northwestern Virginia under the command of McClellan. Johnston communicated his concerns to the authorities in Richmond, now undergoing the transition from the capital of Virginia to the capital of the Confederate States of America. The ensuing correspondence inaugurated the rocky relationship between Johnston and the administration in Richmond—a relationship that would steadily erode and be at its worst during Ulysses S. Grant's campaign against Vicksburg.

Johnston stated his position early during his command at Harpers Ferry. In a memorandum dated May 26 he wrote, "The only way in which this force can be made useful, I think, is by rendering it movable, and employing it to prevent or retard the enemy's passage of the Potomac, and, should he effect the crossing, in opposing his advance into the country. This I shall endeavor to do, unless instructed to the contrary."[47] On May 28 Johnston, in an effort to determine quickly whether his plan was approved by the Richmond authorities and to discover the latter's strategic concept for Harpers Ferry, wrote to Col. Richard Garnett, the adjutant general of Virginia forces, requesting clarification and adding, "If the Commander-in-Chief has precise instructions to give, I beg to receive them early."[48]

Information from scouts, friends in Maryland, and the Northern press indicated to Johnston that the armies of Patterson and McClellan had as their objective a unification of their forces at Winchester, Virginia.[49] He wrote to Lee that "This place cannot be held against an enemy who would venture to attack it. Would it not be better for the troops to join one of our armies, which is too weak for its object, than be lost here?"[50] The reply that Johnston received from Lee, coming in two letters dated June 1 and June 3, provided no meaningful answer to the question of the former's mission and to Johnston belied a seeming lack of comprehension of the situation. The first letter from Lee reflected confidence in Johnston's judgment but implied that the troops in Harpers Ferry should be prepared both to defend Harpers Ferry, as a garrison, and to contest any Federal advance across the Potomac into the interior of Virginia (an offensive defensive). Lee added that if Johnston was unable to resist an attacking force or defend the frontier, he should move out of Harpers Ferry and "destroy all facilities for the approach or shelter of an enemy."[51] Two days later, Lee apparently decided against leaving the decision making to Johnston when he wrote, "As regards Harper's Ferry, its abandonment would be depressing to the cause of the South."[52] He further suggested that Johnston deploy more troops to guard the major route into Virginia at Martinsburg.

Johnston, probably frustrated with Lee's implied warning—and wanting to know if political considerations outweighed those of the military—fired back a lengthy letter to Richmond clarifying his position. He argued that the Confederate government had not made it clear how Johnston's command was to be used. Was it to be a garrison or a corps of observation? He explained that either of these roles would be difficult for his troops, given their present condition. In closing, Johnston declared:

> A retreat from the presence of an enemy is the most difficult of military operations to the best troops. To very new ones it is impossible. It would soon become a flight. You say that "the abandonment of Harper's Ferry would be depressing to the cause of the South." Would not the loss of five or six thousand men be more so? And, if they remain here, they must be captured or destroyed soon after General McClellan's arrival in the valley.[53]

In the midst of his communications with Lee, Johnston continued preparing his troops for a possible confrontation with the ever-increasing body of Federal troops to the north and northwest. Cartridge boxes and belts were manufactured in neighboring towns. Cartridges were assembled, using powder provided by Governor Letcher and lead found at the armory or in town. Percussion caps were smuggled in from Baltimore in small quantities. Caissons were put together using the chassis of farm wagons. Most important, defensive positions on the heights around the town were improved.[54]

Lee decided to bring Johnston's most recent letter to Jefferson Davis. On June 7 Lee wrote to Johnston that the Confederate president placed great value on the retention of the Shenandoah Valley and the position at Harpers Ferry. Specifically, Davis worried that the loss of Harpers Ferry would damage the Confederate cause in Maryland. Lee, however, added that Johnston should exercise his good judgment—even if that meant retiring from the town if enemy forces could not be successfully opposed.[55]

What Lee and Davis appeared to be suggesting was that Johnston prepare to engage the enemy if necessary to hold Harpers Ferry, and if things did not go well, he should break off contact and withdraw. At this point the North and South had yet to become involved in a major military engagement on land. Thus Johnston would have the chance to participate in the first real battle of the war. He could easily predict the outcome. His men were outnumbered, poorly trained, poorly equipped, depleted by illness, and bottled up in an indefensible location. Moreover, Johnston was out of position to defend the natural invasion routes into Virginia that would likely be used by an army under the leadership of someone whose abilities he knew and respected. The psychological importance of emerging victorious from the initial encounter of the war was also clear.

P. G. T. Beauregard had assumed command of the Confederate and state troops at Manassas Junction. Clearly, military principles called for the troops at Harpers Ferry to become mobile, giving them the option to strike the Federal force when Johnston had the advantage or to unite with Beauregard to repel activity on his front. Because of his indefensible position at Harpers Ferry, Johnston resolved "not to continue to occupy the place."[56]

On June 13 information reached Harpers Ferry that advance units of McClellan's force were at Romney, Virginia, fifty miles to the west. The Federals were now in a position to turn Johnston's flank or participate with Patterson in a pincers movement against the Confederate garrison. Johnston dispatched the Thirteenth Virginia Infantry under A. P. Hill, along with the Tenth Virginia, by railroad to Winchester, whereupon they were to move toward Romney to check McClellan's advance. Hill would be reinforced by the Third Tennessee Infantry, which had just arrived at Winchester. The remainder of the troops at Harpers Ferry spent the thirteenth and fourteenth loading baggage and public property onto railroad cars for transportation to Winchester and burning the bridges across the Potomac. On the fifteenth, Johnston's army evacuated the town.

Johnston's decision to withdraw from Harpers Ferry was his own. In retrospect, his movement was premature. Federal forces were themselves unorganized and of insufficient strength to pose an immediate threat to Harpers Ferry. The advantages of retaining the position had tangible military and political rewards. To Johnston, however, the picture looked quite different. He knew McClellan to be a capable soldier. Spies in Grafton, a key railroad junction due west of Harpers Ferry on the Baltimore and Ohio (B&O) Railroad, obtained information that as of June 2, Federal troops were indeed advancing by train toward Harpers Ferry.[57] To remain in the "cul-de-sac" would be a gamble, and gambles by their very nature do not guarantee success. Johnston's self-imposed burden of responsibility prevented him from throwing caution to the wind. Nevertheless, this brief episode in his early career in the Confederate military planted the seeds of discord with the government, in the areas of both communication and strategic thinking.

Following the evacuation of Harpers Ferry, Johnston assisted Capt. Thomas R. Sharp of the Confederate Quartermaster's Department in his orders to remove from Martinsburg as much of the captured B&O rolling stock (including locomotives) as possible. Those that could not be removed were burned—ultimately, 42 locomotives and 386 cars.[58] In retrospect, Johnston erred in destroying so much B&O property. The necessity for demolition was not nearly as great as Johnston imagined, nor did he ever seem to contemplate choosing dismantling over destruction. Stockholders and Unionist politicians in neutral Maryland were outraged and expressed their indignation in local papers. Yet it is an exaggeration to argue, as some historians have, that Johnston made an "egregious blunder" and "vastly exceeded" his orders.[59] It was already clear to him that Union forces were using the railroad as part of their offensive operations in western Virginia. His own troops were retiring up the rail line toward Winchester. His orders from the War Department specifically stated, "Everything should be destroyed which would facilitate [the enemy's] movements through the valley."[60] Lee even specifically instructed Johnston to "deprive them of the use of the railroad."[61] This he did. Even Johnston's most severe critic of his handling of the railroads admits that the destruction "appreciably delayed the combined movement of Union Armies against Harpers Ferry late in June 1861."[62]

It was now clear to both Johnston and Beauregard that their armies faced an ever-increasing enemy to the north. Therefore, the best means of defense for northern Virginia would be to ascertain where the major Federal attack would occur, rely on interior lines of transportation to concentrate the two armies, and defeat the enemy before it could move in counteraction. The success or failure of this defensive strategy necessarily depended on timing and execution. Moving too early or too late would result in failure.

On July 9, after hearing from Confederate cavalry leader J. E. B. Stuart that Federal troops were arriving in Martinsburg, Johnston wrote to Davis, "The object of reinforcing General Patterson must be an advance upon this place. Fighting here against great odds seems to me to be more prudent than retreat."[63] He requested that troops from Beauregard's command be sent to him as soon as possible. Beauregard, however, was receiving information through an elaborate spy ring, which included Mrs. Rose O'Neil Greenhow and other Southern sympathizers in Washington, that a Federal army of 40,000 men commanded by Gen. Irvin McDowell was preparing to move on his position at Manassas.

The time for ascertaining Federal intentions was upon the Confederate command. Both generals were threatened. Which was the main attack, or were both attacks of equal weight? The question was answered the following day when a message arrived at Johnston's headquarters from Adjutant General Cooper calling for "a juncture of all your effective force."[64] Unconvinced that Beauregard was indeed the more seriously threatened, Johnston reluctantly prepared to move eastward.

Unifying two armies in the field is a difficult and dangerous maneuver, with plenty of room for confusion, especially during combat. With the issue of rank (both his own and that of others) never far from his mind, Johnston recognized the potential for problems and requested clarification from Richmond "to prevent the possibility of doubt of the relative rank of General Beauregard and myself in the mind of the former."[65] The reply was clear— Johnston was a full general, Beauregard was a brigadier. Consequently, Johnston would be in command of both the Army of the Shenandoah and the Confederate Army of the Potomac. This point was apparently understood by Beauregard when the two met on the afternoon of July 20 at the latter's headquarters in the home of Wilmer McLean.

Johnston expressed his desire that Confederate forces attack McDowell on the following day. Beauregard agreed and proceeded to outline his plan for battle. Johnston approved the plan, requested that the order of battle be drawn up quickly for his signing so that copies could be distributed that evening, and then went to bed. Not until 4:30 in the morning on July 21 were the orders ready for distribution. Johnston hesitated briefly, noting that they were not in the usual form for the U.S. Army; moreover, Beauregard had affixed his signature to the documents, making it appear as if troop movements were under his direction, not the commanding general's. Johnston signed nevertheless, noting that it was essentially immaterial and too late to make corrections—the troops needed to be moving.[66]

The Confederate attack never had the chance to get under way —General McDowell stole the initiative. The Federals launched their assault shortly after dawn on July 21. The plan was a good one. It included a feint against the Confederate right, followed by an envelopment of the latter's left. Johnston's forces would be required to fight on the defensive in the rear of, and at a right angle to, his original front line. Johnston placed Beauregard in command of the troops "immediately engaged," while he himself remained free to supervise the whole field.[67] The Confederate armies won a decisive victory over the Federals that day, but the defeat of the enemy in the field led to immediate bickering over who should get the credit. The Confederate victory resulted in part from Johnston's accurate assessment of the situation on his left flank and his timely dispatch of troops in that direction. Beauregard, in contrast, was slow to recognize the Federal envelopment as the main assault. Capt. (later Gen.) Edward Porter Alexander, observing much of the battle from his position atop a signal tower behind Confederate lines, stated in his private memoir:

> Apparently Gen. Johnston was disposed to go there [the left flank] but Beauregard seemed to hesitate. . . . The roar of firing continued to increase . . . [and] Gen. Johnston said sharply, "I am going there," & jumping on his horse . . . set off at a gallop without another word to anyone.[68]

The commanding general moved regiments into place and steadied frontline troops. It was Johnston who directed the brigades of Jubal Early and Arnold Elzey to move to strengthen the Confederate left. The arrival of these two fresh brigades opposite the Federal right broke any remaining resolve of McDowell's forces. A general rout of the Federal army began at 4:40 in the afternoon as the attackers withdrew in confusion back to Centreville and Washington.[69]

President Davis arrived on the field of combat just as the battle was closing. Unfortunately for the president, he arrived too late to take part in the battle. Nevertheless, Davis left Manassas Junction, rode briefly in the direction of McDowell's fleeing troops, cheered the Southern soldiers on as they continued the pursuit, and went to find Johnston.[70] According to the president, the two rode back to Manassas Junction, where they were joined by Beauregard.

What transpired during the meeting of the three is unclear, since Davis, Johnston, and Beauregard left conflicting accounts. One issue of discussion was the feasibility of following up the Manassas victory with a pursuit of the Federal army. Davis inquired about plans for pursuit. Beauregard responded that none had been ordered, whereupon the president began to dictate orders to Beauregard's chief of staff authorizing such a move immediately. Davis changed his mind, however, after learning from an unreliable source that the Federal army was in a state of chaos as it streamed through Centreville. A night pursuit, therefore, might not be advisable.

After the war, Davis argued that his intentions were for the Confederate forces to conduct a full-scale pursuit. Beauregard refuted Davis and stated that the agreement was for a reconnaissance in force. Johnston stated that he was not even present at this discussion. Regardless of who said what, a pursuit of the Federal army, followed by an attack against Washington, was impractical for several reasons. For one thing, inadequate and often inaccurate intelligence, combined with poor staff work, kept the commanding general from ascertaining the magnitude of the Federal defeat. For another, the Confederate force was disorganized, disintegrating (some volunteers assumed that the war was over and they could go home), poorly trained for an offensive operation, and ill equipped. Federal troops, although in full retreat, were nevertheless consolidating in and around the capital. Johnston would be required to take his army across the Potomac and advance against what were believed to be heavily defended fortifications. It was a logical assumption that low morale and panic would be counteracted by the need to defend the Northern capital. The likely result would be defeat for Johnston's command and the negation of all that had been accomplished at Manassas.

This assessment of the situation finds support from Jubal Early, whose brigade had been in a good position to evaluate the state of both armies during the late afternoon of July 21. Early wrote in his memoir:

> Without having been in General Johnston's confidence, or professing to know more about the motives actuating him at the time than he has thought proper to make public, . . . [I will state that] it was utterly impossible for any army to have captured Washington by immediate pursuit, even if it had been in condition to make such pursuit, and that it would have been very difficult to cross the Potomac at all.[71]

While this argument may have been clear to Johnston and Early, other people both inside and outside the army remained unconvinced. For months after the battle, newspaper editorials and reports from the Federal capital revealed a high level of panic and unpreparedness on the part of the Union army as it retreated back into Washington. The optimists believed that the South could have defeated the North once and for all.

The initial target for the accusations of failure was the Confederate president. Worried about the possibility of an increasing lack of confidence in the administration (especially during an election year), Davis asked Johnston to issue a statement on whether the president had "obstructed the pursuit of the enemy." Johnston voluntarily accepted full responsibility for the decision not to attack Washington. After the war he wrote:

> If the tone of the press indicated public opinion and feeling in the South, my failure to capture Washington received strong and general condemnation. Many erroneously attributed it to the President's prohibition; but he gave no orders, and expressed neither wish nor opinion on the subject, that ever came to my knowledge.[72]

Thus Johnston placed the blame at his own doorstep. In so doing, the general ultimately contributed to the erosion of his own reputation. The lost opportunity at Manassas, combined with the earlier evacuation of Harpers Ferry, emerged in the minds of a few as examples of failure on the part of the commanding general.

Ironically, the individual who received the most public acclaim (as well as credit) for the Confederate victory on July 21 was Beauregard. Still basking in the glory from his role at Fort Sumter, the Louisiana Creole gladly accepted his status as hero of the Confederacy. Songs were written in his honor, and babies were named after the conquering hero.[73] Women often wrote to him with romantic intentions. Most significant of all, Davis promoted him to full general.

Unable to promote Johnston above the rank he already held, Davis offered the general command of Confederate forces in western Virginia. Johnston viewed the situation in western Virginia as less important and therefore less attractive than his current location. More than likely, he also saw western Virginia as a minor theater of operations compared with his position as the defender of the Confederate capital. There would be few opportunities for climactic victory in that part of the state. He anticipated a buildup of a large Federal force in Washington ready to begin offensive operations by the end of the fall. In his mind, he needed to stay where he was in order to operate against it.[74] His suspicions appeared to be confirmed by early September. Writing to Davis, Johnston warned, "if any active operations against us are intended, they must be directed against this army—from Washington—My opinion of M'cClellan [sic] confirms this idea."[75]

Overall, the Confederacy's first summer appeared to be a success in Virginia, in spite of the loss of Harpers Ferry. Yet the question of what to do next remained unresolved. Most important, the South had yet to decide who would answer that question. During the late summer and early fall of 1861, the ambiguities of the civil-military relationship inherent in the infant nation created fissures that grew wider as the war progressed. The relationship between the Confederate president and his senior commander in the field soured, largely as a result of the latter's unwillingness to relinquish anything that resembled power, combined with his self-imposed burden of responsibility for this revolution's success or failure.

As generals and politicians discussed strategy, Johnston consistently erred on the side of caution. This is not to say that he was a consistent advocate of the defensive. By the end of August, Confederate forces had advanced to a point near Washington where they could see the unfinished dome of the Capitol. Beauregard favored an immediate offensive into Maryland, and Johnston eventually concurred. The morale of the Southern troops was high, winter would soon be at hand—thus the end of campaigning season—and a delay until spring would give McClellan too much time to build up and train his army. The two generals proposed to concentrate the forces of the Confederacy by shifting troops from North Carolina, South Carolina, and Georgia (unthreatened areas in the South) to northern Virginia, whereupon the combined armies of Johnston and Beauregard would move across the Potomac toward the rear of Washington. They hoped that this flanking movement would place McClellan at a disadvantage by forcing him to leave the defenses of the district. If all went well, Southern victory would bring Maryland into the Confederacy, and a new defensive line would be established in northern Maryland. The operation required reinforcements to the army, increased supplies, and additional wagons.

President Davis visited his army near Fairfax on September 30. The following day Davis met with Johnston, Beauregard, and Maj. Gen. G. W. Smith. While agreeing that activity was needed to keep up troop morale, the Confederate president declared that the manpower and supplies requested could not be supplied "without a total disregard for other threatened positions."[76] Davis suggested that Confederate forces along the Potomac conduct raids into Maryland against detached Federal units. Davis believed that these small-scale operations would bolster morale in the army and encourage civilians (and potential recruits) in northern Virginia and Maryland. Johnston disagreed with the president's proposal, contending that adequate water transport was presently not available and Federal gunboats controlled the river, making such operations a high risk.[77] The conference ended with the president victorious. Through the remainder of the year, Johnston was charged with holding his line in the face of what he saw as an ever-increasing threat to his north and east.

Despite the rejection of what was, in essence, Beauregard's plan of invasion, in many ways, Johnston and Davis thought alike in their overall strategic concepts for winning this war. Both men preferred limited risks, especially considering the Confederacy's disadvantages in manpower and material.[78] Time could be on the side of the Confederacy if its military avoided mistakes. The precedent established by Washington in his war of attrition against the British during the Revolution must have been obvious to both. However, similar to Washington and unlike Davis, Johnston was willing to surrender space to buy time. This fundamental difference of opinion over how to fight a protracted war with limited risks was at the core of the conflict between the two men. Compounding the issue was the general's lifelong cognizance of anything that smacked of intrusion on his authority—itself engendered by experience and promotion. Unfortunately for both men and for the Confederacy, the differences between the two came to the forefront during the remainder of Johnston's command in Virginia and carried into the campaigns of 1863 and 1864.

It was during the months immediately following the battle at Manassas that the well-documented "debate" over Johnston's seniority in relation to the other full generals in the Confederate military materialized. Johnston was operating under the assumption that he was the ranking general in the Confederate army. In his mind, Davis had confirmed this on July 20 by stating that Johnston was a full general and in overall command at Manassas. However, in early September, Johnston learned that on August 31 Davis had sent to the Confederate Congress nominations for five individuals to receive officially the rank of full general, as well as a listing of their relative seniority. Davis's ranking of generals placed Samuel Cooper first, followed by Albert Sidney Johnston, Robert E. Lee, Joseph E. Johnston, and P. G. T. Beauregard. Congress assented and endorsed the commissions.

Johnston was simultaneously informed of the nominations and their confirmation. The news came as a complete shock, and he made his position clear, claiming, "notwithstanding these nominations made by the President, and their confirmation by Congress, I still rightfully hold the rank of first general in the Armies of the Southern Confederacy."[79] Davis's action, in Johnston's words,

transfers me from the position of first rank to that of fourth. The relative rank of the others among themselves, is unaltered. It is plain, then, that this is a blow aimed at me only. It *reduces my rank* in the grade I hold. This has never been done heretofore in the regular service in America but by the sentence of a court-martial, as a punishment and a disgrace for some military offense. It seems to *tarnish my fair fame* as a soldier and as a man, earned by more than thirty years of laborious and perilous service. I had but this—the scars of many wounds, all honestly taken in my front and in the front of battle, and *my father's Revolutionary sword.* . . . If the action against which I have protested be legal, it is not for me to question the expediency of degrading one who has served laboriously from the commencement of the war on this frontier and borne a prominent part in the one great event of that war, for the benefit of persons [A. S. Johnston and Lee] neither of whom has yet struck a blow for the Confederacy.[80]

If Johnston was ever in a panic, this was the time. In his mind, all that he had striven to establish—his position of leadership in this Southern war for independence—was being taken from him. It was another demotion, but this time of the most serious kind.

The question of who was right and who was wrong in their interpretation of the law has been exhaustively debated over the years and is of little consequence here. What is important in our effort to evaluate Johnston's ability is to examine what the general thought was the motivation for this act and the consequences that his conclusions had on the war effort. Johnston saw this as an action aimed at him alone and for the betterment of Robert E. Lee and Albert Sidney Johnston. Although the general's position is usually dismissed as oversensitivity and pettiness on his part, there is some merit to his point of view.

The competitive relationship between Johnston and Lee (at least from Johnston's point of view) was of long standing, with Johnston "losing" out to his friend more often than not. But what about Albert Sidney Johnston? The only time that there was any real competition between the two Johnstons was when they were both candidates for the position of quartermaster general. That competition was too recent to have been forgotten by Joseph Johnston, and his victory gave him the brigadier general's rank he was using to claim his position as "first general in the Armies of the Southern Confederacy." There is a persuasive argument that Davis indeed held up submitting his nominations to Congress until A. S. Johnston had committed to Confederate service, in an effort to ensure that his old friend received the highest position possible.[81] For Joe Johnston, however, there was tangible evidence that the president favored the Kentuckian.

Having vented his feelings on paper, Johnston put his letter to Davis aside for two days so that he could review it dispassionately. Making no alterations, the general dispatched his protest to Richmond on September 12. The president's response was quick, to the point, and uninformative. He made no effort to explain his reasoning, nor did he attempt to counter Johnston's accusation that his action had been aimed at Johnston alone. If one looks at the extant original letters written by Davis to Johnston during these critical first two weeks of September, a small but not insignificant detail is characteristic of them all. In every one, Davis misspells Johnston's name—referring to the recipient of each letter as "Gen. J. E. Johnson."[82] Given their contact over the past ten years (longer, if one assumes that they knew each other at West Point), this mistake seems hard to explain. What makes this all the more peculiar is the fact that in two of the letters (September 5 and September 8), Davis makes reference to Albert Sidney Johnston and spells his name correctly. Johnston could not have missed this error, and the timing could not have been worse. The president, signing his letters "your friend" and "ever, truly, your friend," appeared less than sincere and clearly focused on the whereabouts of Sidney Johnston.

These personal matters remained unresolved but would arise again and again to bedevil Johnston in his relationship with Davis. In their correspondence with each other, neither Johnston nor Davis referred to this exchange again for the remainder of the war. For the rest of Johnston's tenure in Virginia, the general's name was spelled correctly, because much of the correspondence from Richmond to the field commander was handled by Davis's new secretary of war, Judah P. Benjamin. A Louisiana lawyer with no military experience, Benjamin had attained his current position through his perceived loyalty to the Confederate president and the latter's belief in Benjamin's organizational abilities.[83] Benjamin did not have a very high opinion of Johnston's (or Beauregard's) abilities, arguing that the general would not fight and consequently needed few reinforcements.[84] The secretary's concern for the affairs in Johnston's department led the latter to remark, "The Secretary of War will probably establish his headquarters within this department soon."[85]

The immediate problem facing Johnston was the buildup of Federal forces in Washington. In all likelihood, these troops would move again toward the Confederate positions in northern Virginia and eventually to Richmond. Information coming out of the Federal capital indicated that there had been a change in command. McClellan had come from western Virginia to replace McDowell. This was troubling news for Johnston. The latter was fully aware of the capabilities of his old friend. McClellan had yet to reveal the leadership flaws that later kept him from winning the decisive victories his army was capable of achieving.

In the ten months between the battle at Manassas and his next major engagement in southeastern Virginia, Joseph Johnston faced numerous challenges in his dealings with the president and the War Department while preparing to counter Federal operations to the north and east. They, along with his actions at Harpers Ferry and Manassas, served as the basis (both during the war and after) on which the public, the executive, and the War Department evaluated the general's capabilities in the field.

Determined not to surrender any authority to politicos, Johnston remained true to his own ideas and decisions while sometimes giving the appearance of a willingness to cooperate. Although he no longer encouraged the president to leave civil affairs behind and take to the field, he did urge Davis from time to time to visit the army and bolster the morale of the troops.[86] He also became less communicative with those in Richmond, in the probable hope that the less they knew, the less they could interfere with his handling of the army. This latter policy had the opposite effect, because the president, who took the role of commander in chief literally, wanted more, not less information. It also encouraged the president's tendency to communicate with other general officers directly, bypassing Johnston and subverting the chain of command.

Beginning in October, Johnston fought a series of what amounted to managerial battles with the administration over army reorganization, furloughs, and staff appointments. Johnston held stubbornly and vociferously to his position on all these issues, only to find himself up against a foe of equal caliber in Secretary of War Benjamin. Unfortunately for the sake of harmony, Benjamin knew how to win the sympathy of the president, and Johnston did the same with Beauregard and Smith. Thus the lines were drawn as the campaign season of 1862 drew nigh.[87]

During the latter part of February and early March, Johnston began the process, agreed on at a February 20 meeting in Richmond with Davis, of shifting his supply base from Manassas fifty-four miles southwest to a more secure location at Gordonsville, with a portion of the supplies deposited at Culpeper Court House and Orange Court House in anticipation of a withdrawal of the army. Concern for the safety of his troops and the need for speed led the general to remark, "We may indeed have to start [withdrawing our men] before we are ready."[88] The president wrote to Johnston that he relied on his "special knowledge and high ability to effect whatever is practicable in this our hour of need."[89] Johnston notified Davis that some materials might have to be destroyed, and the latter asked the Confederate quartermaster for more rolling stock to help with the withdrawal.[90]

The reason for Johnston's anxiety was information coming from Brigadier General Whiting informing him that a division of Federal troops on the opposite bank of the Potomac from Dumfries appeared to be preparing to take the offensive. Johnston had taken care during the winter months to analyze McClellan's options for the spring. He narrowed down the possibilities to four: a direct overland route from Washington to Richmond—similar to what McDowell had attempted in July; a maneuver southeast of Washington, crossing the Potomac to the mouth of Potomac Creek, then to Richmond via Fredericksburg; or moving the army by water to either the lower Rappahannock (Urbanna) or Fort Monroe and then to Richmond by way of direct roads. Johnston determined that the most difficult option to defend against (given the current placement of troops) was the second. Federal forces could potentially move to a position opposite Potomac Creek without being detected until the river crossing began. This meant that McClellan would have a two-day jump in marching time on Johnston's forces moving from Centreville to defend the capital.[91] Whiting's report implied that the Federals had indeed chosen this route.

Ascertaining that the Federals were preparing to cross the Potomac, or at the very least turn the Confederates out of their position at Centreville, Johnston decided on a complete withdrawal.

His decision was aided by independent information collected over the months by operators in three Confederate spy rings that monitored Federal troop deployment, obtained accounts of Lincoln's cabinet meetings, and recorded descriptions of private discussions with McClellan. The intelligence collected by Southern agents revealed Lincoln's desire for McClellan to advance directly against Johnston at Centreville and McClellan's preference for the Urbanna route. This information, combined with Whiting's, indicated that it was McClellan's plan that was in operation.[92] Consequently, on March 7 Johnston issued orders for troops positioned on the two flanks of the Confederate line to fall back to a temporary position on the south bank of the Rappahannock River. Units located at Centreville and Manassas were to remain until March 9 in order to facilitate the continued evacuation of food, property, and military supplies. The provisions and equipment that could not be evacuated were to be destroyed—including the meat-packing plant at Thoroughfare Gap. In the latter case, civilians living in the environs of the plant were allowed to divide the surplus meat among themselves before the buildings were burned or demolished.

On March 10 General Stuart's cavalry set fire to the storehouses and supplies remaining at Manassas, including four days' rations for men and horses deposited there.[93] One of Stuart's cavalrymen, Lt. Col. William Willis Blackford, observed that the troopers burned "huge piles of bacon . . . as high as a house . . . and the smell of fried bacon was wafted for twenty miles."[94] Also destroyed in the withdrawal were the railroad bridges of the Orange and Alexandria between Manassas and the Rappahannock River.

Davis, however, was of another opinion. On March 10 (while Stuart was applying the torch at Manassas) Davis telegraphed Johnston to notify him of the "assurances" he had received that the general would "be promptly and adequately reinforced, so as to enable you to maintain your position, and resume first policy when the roads will permit."[95] Johnston could not reverse his movements three days into the withdrawal of the army (not to mention the problem of provisions—both those removed and those burned) and occupy his old position on the "assurance" of reinforcements. It was a moot point anyway, considering the apparent maneuvering of the Federal army toward the east. Like his evacuation of Harpers Ferry the previous year, Johnston's movement from Centreville to the

Rappahannock was to Davis an example of the general's proclivity for premature retreats. In 1865 Davis remarked that he had been "surprised" by Johnston's "hasty retreat without giving notice to do so."[96] Later, in 1878, the ex-Confederate president wrote that Johnston "fled, though no man pursued."[97]

Debate over the wisdom of the movement notwithstanding, the withdrawal was completed by March 11, and Johnston's infantry and artillery were, for the time being, on the south bank of the Rappahannock River. Confederate troops from the department of northern Virginia were deployed from Fredericksburg to Culpeper Court House, with Stuart's cavalry advanced as far as Warrenton. Jackson, commanding the valley district within Johnston's department, was also forced to fall back from Winchester to Mount Jackson in the face of a large Federal force in the lower Shenandoah Valley under Maj. Gen. Nathaniel Banks. Johnston's instructions to his district commander were to remain close enough to Banks to keep his attention, thereby discouraging any attempt to reinforce McClellan from the west.

On March 18 Johnston shifted his troops once again, this time to the south bank of the Rapidan River, placing him in a more advantageous position to move to Richmond in a single day's time if necessary. Maj. Gen. Richard Stoddert Ewell's division and Stuart's brigade were left in advanced positions near the Rappahannock for observation. Theophilus Holmes remained near Fredericksburg, where he had been since the previous June.

During the following week, Johnston received reports from scouts that transports in large numbers were moving down the Potomac but not entering the Rappahannock. That left two possibilities—either the Federals were bound for North Carolina to reinforce Ambrose Burnside's operations in the eastern part of that state, or they were planning to disembark at Fort Monroe, seventy miles from the Confederate capital. The answer arrived in Richmond on March 24 when messages from Maj. Gen. John B. Magruder, in command of the 11,000 Confederate soldiers at Yorktown, announced the arrival of the enemy. Magruder's reports were corroborated by Maj. Gen. Benjamin Huger, in command of 13,000 Confederates at Norfolk.

While McClellan's objective was still unknown, Robert E. Lee questioned Johnston on the feasibility of sending troops to support

Magruder and Huger while maintaining an adequate defense of the major rail center at Gordonsville to the northwest of Richmond.[98] Johnston's response was to reiterate his belief in concentration, suggesting that a force of 25,000 be sent to the peninsula, leaving behind only the bare minimum to man the Rapidan line. On March 27 the War Department ordered only 10,000 men to meet the possible threat. Johnston replied, "We cannot win without concentrating."[99]

McClellan's intentions became clear in early April as Federal troops began a general advance toward Yorktown. After inspecting Magruder's positions around Yorktown, Johnston reported to Davis in person on April 14 and suggested that an effective means of thwarting the Federal drive would be to concentrate all available troops in North Carolina, South Carolina, and Georgia with those around Richmond (including Magruder's and Huger's commands) and to strike a surprise blow against McClellan while the latter focused on siege operations outside the Confederate capital, expecting only defensive measures from his opponent. With the Federal army so far removed from its base at Fort Monroe, victory would be virtually assured. Johnston believed that the magnitude of the Confederate triumph could be enough to win the war.[100]

President Davis decided to discuss Johnston's proposal and the alternatives with Lee and Secretary of War Randolph before a making a decision. Johnston requested that both Gen. Gustavus W. Smith and Gen. James Longstreet be present at the meeting (Smith was in complete agreement with Johnston's concept for defeating McClellan, and Longstreet had developed into one of the general's favorite subordinates).[101] The daylong discussion began with the Virginia commander outlining his conclusions from his trip to the Yorktown defenses. He then proceeded to review his plan as presented earlier to Davis. Johnston emphasized his belief that a major attempt to defend the peninsula could be successful only temporarily because of the vulnerability of any defensive line to flank attack from the rivers. Therefore, if the Confederates could keep McClellan at bay for only a few weeks at most, it was not worth the detrimental effect the tidal swamps and bad water would have on the men. Furthermore, any victory on the peninsula (if indeed possible) would necessarily be incomplete due to the proximity of Fort Monroe. The latter would provide a haven for McClellan's retreating army and prevent its complete annihilation. If his plan was approved, Johnston argued, Federal forces would be removed from the security of Fort Monroe, exposed to the unhealthy conditions of the Chickahominy and tidewater swamps, and unprepared for a surprise attack by consolidated Confederate forces. In making this latter point, Johnston emphasized that his plan was offensive in nature, not merely a defense of the capital. As was the case earlier at Harpers Ferry, the general maintained that once the enemy was defeated, positions that had to be evacuated could be retaken—in this instance, the Norfolk navy yard.[102]

After outlining these reasons why a withdrawal was necessary and relating his plans for concentration and attack, Johnston listened as General Smith endorsed his recommendation. Longstreet, a bit overwhelmed at being invited to "such august presence," said very little, and only when called upon.[103] Secretary Randolph, a former naval officer, was opposed to the plan because it meant the abandonment of the navy yard at Norfolk, the forfeiture of valuable machinery located therein, and the loss of the base for the CSS *Virginia*. Lee, siding with Randolph, was also against Johnston's proposal because it necessitated the removal of Confederate troops from South Carolina and Georgia—troops that he believed were sorely needed to defend the seaports of Charleston and Savannah from Federal capture.[104] The president's de facto military adviser extolled the natural defensive lines available on the peninsula behind which Johnston's troops would be able to thwart, or at least significantly delay, the Federal offensive. Lee argued that he needed time to finish the reorganization of the army, a job that could immediately become more complex if a pending conscription bill was passed by Congress.

After listening to both arguments, Davis chose to heed the advice of his secretary of war and de facto military adviser. Randolph and Lee essentially echoed the strategic views of the president. Their desire was to see Confederate forces hold the peninsula in a defensive designed to prevent the loss of geographic points. For the time being, mobility and threatened flanks appeared to be of slight concern. Johnston, along with the divisions of Smith and Longstreet, received orders to depart for the peninsula, where the former assumed command of over 53,000 troops on April 17.

McClellan, meanwhile, was surprised to find what he interpreted as an elaborate and well-manned defensive position stretching across his projected route to the Confederate capital. The Federal general had expected to outflank Yorktown and press on. However, without making a major effort to test the enemy's defenses, he decided to commence siege operations.[105] His engineers constructed impressive fieldworks and prepared for the arrival of heavy artillery from Fort Monroe.

Johnston was confronted with a different set of problems from those he had faced at Manassas. The men of Magruder's command were tired from the continuous effort to construct and improve their lines. Food was of poor quality and insufficient in quantity. Both health and morale were in a state of decline due to the frequently heavy rains, lack of adequate shelter, and harassing small-arms fire from the enemy. One Confederate private complained of the enemy sharpshooters: "For the most part they were concealed in the tops of tall pine trees and had down shots upon us, against which it was almost impossible to protect ourselves. When we attempted to do so by digging holes back of and beneath our works, the water rose in them and drove us out."[106]

The Confederate commander remained under pressure from Richmond to reorganize his army to reflect state origins and to allow for the election of officers. His main concern, however, focused on indications that McClellan was preparing to bombard the Yorktown position and the York River water batteries with 30 mortars and 100 rifled cannon from a distance too great for the Confederates to adequately respond with their antiquated smoothbore artillery.[107] This information, combined with word on April 22 that Federal Maj. Gen. William Buel Franklin had arrived with his division (approximately 11,000 men) and was still on board ship, indicated an impending turning movement up the York River—just as Johnston had predicted.[108] Lee informed Johnston, "You can best judge of the difficulties before you and know the interests involved in the question."[109] Johnston responded by telling Lee that a withdrawal might be necessary and requesting that bridges to his rear be repaired in the event such a move were required.

On April 27 the general sent word to the War Department that he intended to evacuate the Yorktown–Warwick River line before the Federals began their bombardment. A retrograde movement prior to McClellan's assault was preferable to one attempted during an attack in which soldiers could succumb to artillery fire and confusion. Major General Huger was directed to prepare to evacuate Norfolk, removing as much property from the navy yard as possible. Flag Officer Josiah Tattnall, of the James River Squadron, was queried on the possibility of taking the CSS *Virginia* to the York River to destroy the Federal transports. Tattnall responded that the operation could not be safely done.[110] Lastly, Johnston reiterated his suggestion that a large army be concentrated in Richmond for a strike against McClellan.

Johnston's position was supported by his subordinates. Jubal Early wrote that it would have been "easy" for the Federals to shell the Confederates out of their positions and advance into their rear, blocking off all avenues of retreat and "thus rendering the capture or dispersion of our entire army certain."[111] E. P. Alexander acknowledged Johnston's willingness to risk being assaulted by McClellan's main body but added, "we could not afford to become entangled in siege operations with McClellan before Yorktown, for the river flank was too weak."[112] On April 29 word reached Yorktown from forward observers that the Federal batteries were almost all in place and the cannonading would surely begin soon. The general wrote to Lee: "The fight for Yorktown, as I said in Richmond, must be one of artillery, in which we cannot win. The result is certain; the time only doubtful. Should the attack upon Yorktown be made earnestly, we cannot prevent its fall; nor can it hold out more than a few hours. We must abandon the Peninsula soon."[113] At midnight on May 4–5, concealed by heavy artillery fire, Confederate forces withdrew from their position astride the peninsula and fell back toward the old colonial capital of Williamsburg. The opportunity for a decisive battle on the peninsula would have to be postponed.

McClellan immediately organized a pursuit. Advance units of Federal cavalry caught up with the Confederate rear guard under Longstreet on May 5 two miles outside of Williamsburg. A heated contest ensued as infantry on both sides joined in the fray. The battle of Williamsburg cost the Confederates 1,560 casualties; the Federals suffered 2,239.[114] Johnston had protected his supply train, obstructed the enemy's advance, and demonstrated to McClellan that he was not unwilling to turn and fight. As a consequence of this latter lesson, the Federal general thereafter avoided a vigorous pursuit, never again initiating combat on a large scale with his Southern counterpart, and returned to his efforts to outflank Johnston.

The presence of the enemy on both the York and the James Rivers caused Johnston to fall back across the Chickahominy on May 15 to be in a better position to counter a movement from either direction. The unhealthy conditions in the Chickahominy lowlands, combined with a scarcity of water, forced an even further withdrawal on May 17 to higher ground within three miles of Richmond.[115] In leaving the Chickahominy to the Federals, Johnston (who had seen the effects of swamps on an army during his service in the Second Seminole War) deliberately forced McClellan to occupy unhealthy terrain, thereby weakening his army with the adverse effects of sickness and disease—something the Confederates, already outnumbered, could ill afford. That Johnston was aware of the medical hazards of McClellan's position is clear in a statement the general made in answer to criticism of his apparent inactivity. Johnston remarked, "Is it nothing that I compel the enemy to inhabit the swamps, like frogs, and lessen their strength every hour, without firing a shot?"[116]

Although tempered by the defeat of Federal gunboats below Drewry's Bluff, the movement up the peninsula to the outskirts of the city created fear and consternation in Richmond. Many wondered whether the city and even the war would be lost. Visible efforts were being made to safeguard valuables from the enemy, and plans for the destruction of tobacco and cotton supplies were discussed. The possibility of evacuation was apparent as a railroad bridge was planked for wagons, limbers, and caissons. The president's wife and children were even put on a train and sent to Raleigh, North Carolina, for reasons of safety.[117]

The situation appeared to be going from bad to worse as word reached Richmond that McDowell's First Corps, now essentially an army numbering over 30,000, was preparing to move toward Fredericksburg fifty miles north of the Confederate capital. With Jackson moving southwestward in the Shenandoah Valley away from Washington, President Lincoln and Secretary of War Stanton were less hesitant to release the First Corps to join the Army of the Potomac. The unified commands of McDowell and McClellan would number approximately 135,000—double Johnston's strength.[118] Responding to orders, the commander of the Army of the Potomac positioned his troops in such a way as to maintain pressure on the Confederate capital from the east while at the same time facilitating a juncture with the First Corps as it moved southward from Fredericksburg. This meant that the Federal army would be forced to straddle the Chickahominy River—a waterway originating north of Richmond and flowing southeastward to the James.[119]

The proximity of the Army of the Potomac to Richmond led Davis and Lee to meet with Johnston to discuss the general's plans for defeating McClellan. Although there is no official record of their discussion, the participants left their own accounts. Davis claimed that he and Lee agreed that Johnston had no plan other than improving fieldworks and waiting "for the enemy to leave his gunboats, so that the opportunity might be offered to meet him on land."[120] Johnston wrote that he explained to the president and his military adviser that the withdrawal to the outskirts of Richmond was necessary to protect his flanks from a turning movement by water from either the York or James River. He stated further that the position he had chosen was excellent, and he planned to defend it against an anticipated Federal attack. Beyond this Johnston said very little.

To many, Johnston's reticence implied the absence of a plan to defend the capital. While remaining secure behind Richmond's defenses, the general sought flexibility to react quickly to any mistake or opportunity presented by his Federal counterpart. In an effort to keep his options open and to limit risks, Johnston avoided making a commitment to a fixed plan. Davis must have been content at the time with what he heard. Three days after their meeting, the president wrote to Johnston: "If the enemy proceeds as heretofore indicated, your position and policy, as you stated in our last interview, seems to me to require no modification; . . . it is my wish to leave you with the fullest powers to exercise your judgment."[121]

The opportunity Johnston was waiting for materialized at the end of the month. After rebuilding Bottom's Bridge (one of the bridges across the Chickahominy destroyed by retreating Confederates), two Federal corps commanded by Erasmus D. Keyes and Samuel P. Heintzelman moved south across the river. Remaining to the north were three corps commanded by Edwin Sumner, William Franklin, and Fitz-John Porter. Efforts were under way to construct or rebuild eleven bridges between Bottom's Bridge and Mechanicsville to facilitate a speedy reunion of the army when necessary. Thus, by May 25, the Chickahominy physically divided the Army of the Potomac into two "wings."

Johnston, recognizing the opportunity to strike McClellan while his army was divided, determined to attack one or both of the wings. Johnston began to develop his plan after further consolidating his forces by moving Huger from Petersburg to Drewry's Bluff and advising Brig. Gen. Lawrence O'Bryan Branch at Gordonsville and Brig. Gen. Joseph Reid Anderson near Fredericksburg to shift their troops closer to Richmond. He now had 75,000 men available, the largest army ever assembled in the Confederacy to that date.[122] His initial concept was for an assault against the extreme right of the Federal army north of the Chickahominy, in conjunction with a strike against the right flank of the two corps south of the river. His decision to move against the Federal right was based on the urgency created by the belief that McDowell was on his way to link up with McClellan. This presumption was enhanced on May 27 by an engagement fifteen miles north of Richmond at Hanover Court House in which Fitz-John Porter's Fifth Corps defeated 4,000 Confederates under Branch. This action appeared to be in preparation for the arrival of McDowell. A Federal defeat along the Chickahominy would prevent such a union by driving McClellan back, away from Richmond, and freeing Johnston to turn on McDowell.

Johnston planned to attack on May 29, but information coming from Stuart the previous evening indicated a change in Federal plans. McDowell was no longer heading south—the First Corps was being withdrawn to support Banks. Now, with an entirely different situation confronting him, the Confederate commander no longer needed to attack to forestall the unification of Federal forces. Yet circumstances were still favorable for a tactical offensive. Johnston saw an opportunity to eliminate the weaker of McClellan's two wings and then turn on the three corps north of the river.

The 31,500 men south of the river under Keyes and Heintzelman had advanced west of their river crossing and were dispersed in four lines. One division of Keyes's corps was in line one mile west of Seven Pines, a road junction six miles east of Richmond on the Williamsburg Road. Keyes's other division stretched from Seven Pines north to Fair Oaks Station on the Richmond and York River Railroad. Heintzelman's two divisions were located to the rear of Keyes—one at Savage Station, two miles east of Fair Oaks Station, and one near Bottom's Bridge. McClellan did not anticipate a Confederate offensive. In a letter to Stanton, the Federal general dismissed reports surfacing in the newspapers that Johnston would mount an attack against the Army of the Potomac by writing, "I think he is too able for that."[123]

Johnston's battle plan for May 31 directed the divisions of Longstreet and Daniel Harvey Hill to assault Keyes's right and center while Huger's division, moving from the southwest, turned the enemy's left flank. G. W. Smith was ordered first to engage troops that might attempt to cross the Chickahominy to aid Keyes and Heintzelman and then (if no Federal reinforcement arrived) to support Longstreet's attack on the Federal right. All troops were to advance toward the enemy using the existing road network, which conveniently converged at Keyes's position. In the early-morning attack, the latter division would be smashed first; then Heintzelman, moving up to support Keyes, would meet the same fate. These instructions were given orally to Longstreet, who was given tactical command of the operation based on his performance at Williamsburg and his seniority in rank to Hill and Huger.

Although Johnston's plan was tactically sound, he erred by issuing his orders orally and by not informing all his division commanders that Longstreet was in tactical command.[124] The result was confusion and delay. In addition, the weather added its own impedance. The day before the battle, rain turned the roads into quagmires. Both sides, however, were hampered by the weather.

The May 31 battle at Seven Pines did not go well at all for Johnston. Longstreet did not take his assigned route to the attack. Instead, he moved his 14,000-man division farther south to the Williamsburg Road currently occupied by D. H. Hill's division. This shift ultimately weakened the Confederate assault against the Federal right and created a nightmare in coordination when Huger's men prepared to enter this same road to reach their assigned point of attack. Huger, initially unaware that Longstreet was in tactical command, lost the argument that he should have priority over the road.

Johnston became increasingly concerned when the expected sounds of battle did not reach his headquarters during the early morning. His anxiety grew when Brigadier General Whiting, in command of Smith's division, could not locate Longstreet's, which he was to follow into position. Johnston sent one of his own staff officers down Longstreet's appointed route of march to find the missing general. Unaware that he was riding down an empty road, the officer continued until he encountered troops. Unfortunately, they belonged to Keyes, not to Longstreet. After a delay of over six hours, the assault finally commenced at a little after 2 P.M. Only six of the intended thirteen brigades were in position when the battle began. Huger's three brigades and three brigades from Longstreet's division were mired in White Oak Swamp south of Seven Pines. One brigade was held back to protect the Confederate left. The assault, although bearing little resemblance to Johnston's original plan, was nevertheless gallant and determined. Longstreet sent a message to Johnston notifying his commander that the battle had been under way for several hours and requesting support for his left flank in the form of an attack on the Federal right and rear. Longstreet anticipated that such a blow could terminate the battle before nightfall.[125]

Johnston ordered General Smith's division to advance toward Seven Pines to aid Longstreet. The commanding general, reprising his actions at Manassas, left his headquarters and rode to the front to oversee the assault. However, instead of striking a blow against a weakened Keyes near Seven Pines, Johnston found himself facing fresh troops at Fair Oaks. Fire coming from this newly arrived Federal force struck the left flank of Smith's division as it moved past Fair Oaks. Caught by surprise, the Confederates were brought into a general engagement north of Seven Pines and were unable to aid Longstreet in his efforts against Keyes.

By 6:30, Johnston was convinced that the contest would have to be renewed the following day. He rode forward toward his front-line positions, issued orders for a cease-fire, and instructed his men to sleep on their arms. The commanding general was exposed to sporadic enemy fire during this process, and around 7:00 he was shot in the right shoulder. Immediately following this wound, Johnston was hit in the breast by a shell fragment that knocked him, unconscious, off his horse. The general was carried to a less exposed position to await an ambulance that would remove him from the field. He regained consciousness in time to discover that his belt containing his pistols and his father's Revolutionary War sword were still out on the field where he had been wounded. The general insisted that someone go back and retrieve them, rewarding the obliging courier with one of the pistols.

President Davis and General Lee, who had been at Johnston's headquarters earlier in the day, rode up on what must have been a shocking scene. Davis expressed his deep regret that Johnston had been wounded. The general smiled in response and informed the president that he was not sure of the seriousness of the wound.[126] Johnston was then placed in an ambulance and taken to Richmond. The command responsibility fell briefly to Smith. On June 1, however, President Davis ordered Robert E. Lee to assume command of the Confederate army outside Richmond. Nevertheless, Johnston believed that whoever was in charge at the present would be there only temporarily. The general fully expected to return to his army as soon as he recovered from his wounds. This, however, was not to be. In what essentially amounted (at least in Johnston's mind) to another demotion, the prosecution of the war in his native state would remain in the hands of Lee.

Joseph Johnston's record during his twelve-month tenure as commander of Confederate forces in Virginia is one of mixed success. On the surface he withdrew prematurely from Harpers Ferry, destroyed valuable (possibly irreplaceable) rolling stock and supplies in northern Virginia, alienated B&O stockholders in Maryland, repeatedly shied away from a fight on the peninsula, refused to cooperate with Secretary of War Benjamin, and moved steadily away from cordial relations with the president. Yet in almost every case, if one avoids retrospection, a convincing argument can be made that Johnston made the correct military decision—but often at the sacrifice of political considerations. It is true that Johnston's willingness to trade space for time belied an unwillingness to fight under current conditions—conditions that he determined were not worth the risk.

In contrast, Johnston was in favor of the tactical offensive at Manassas and Seven Pines and the strategic offensive following the Confederate advance to Centreville. When Johnston saw the opportunity to attack, he did so with no hint of timidity. Outside Richmond in May 1862, Johnston had the chance he had been looking for, and he committed twenty-three of his twenty-seven brigades to the attack.[127] His plan of battle was mishandled by Longstreet, thereby depriving Johnston of a victory and possibly even continued command in Virginia.

Johnston's failure was in his inability to divorce himself from the past and look to the present and future. Clearly he had military merit and was deserving of his high place within the Confederate military hierarchy. However, the expectations he placed on himself—largely as a result of his heritage—did not allow him to play second fiddle in the revolution of 1861. His burden of responsibility would not allow him to gamble when all could be lost during his watch. Joseph Johnston's father had literally passed along the torch when he gave his son his Revolutionary War sword. To some, this may seem to be misplaced psychoanalysis. But why did Johnston choose to wear this rather plain sword, the least attractive of the ones in his possession? Evidence abounds that he was always strikingly well dressed in his close-fitting uniform.[128] Why did he wear this particular sword only during the Civil War? Lee, by way of contrast, had an entirely different relationship with his father and, as his most recent biographer maintains, "attempted throughout his life to come to terms with his father's memory."[129] Unfortunately for Johnston, the revolution of 1861 was much different from the revolution eighty-five years earlier.

When Lee assumed command of Johnston's old army, he inherited a responsibility to a nation that was no longer experiencing the uncertainty of infancy. Lee inherited a status quo in which the civil-military relationship as personified by himself and Davis was already established. Lee had waited out the storm and could now steer a course that was favorable to both.

Chapter Three

Fighting for Defeat?
George B. McClellan's
Peninsula Campaign and the
Change of Base to the James River

Ethan S. Rafuse

"Circumstances make your presence here necessary," the telegram from Washington read, "come hither without delay."[1] Four days after receiving this message, thirty-four-year-old Maj. Gen. George Brinton McClellan completed his journey from the mountains of western Virginia. He found the capital badly in need of a ray of sunshine in the aftermath of the stunning defeat of Union arms at Bull Run and was greeted with far more enthusiasm and deference than his modest accomplishments in western Virginia merited. Expectations that a man had arrived who could make things right were further elevated by McClellan's success in restoring order and transforming the armed mobs of volunteers around Washington into a well-disciplined army. He found himself proclaimed a military genius, a young Napoleon who would crush the rebel army and restore the Union. That would change.

McClellan's generalship has long been the target of sharp criticism from students of the Civil War. The general's foremost biogra-

The author would like to thank the following scholars for reading and offering helpful comments on earlier drafts of this essay: Stan Adamiak, Mark Grimsley, Joseph L. Harsh, Herman Hattaway, and Steven E. Woodworth. But unlike the essay's subject, he fully accepts that the shoulders on which responsibility for any faults must rest are his own.

pher, Stephen W. Sears, argues that McClellan "was a man possessed by demons and delusions . . . inarguably the worst" commander the Army of the Potomac ever had. In his Pulitzer Prize–winning book *Battle Cry of Freedom,* James M. McPherson concludes, "[M]ilitary success could be achieved only by taking risks; McClellan seemed to shrink from the prospect. He lacked the mental and moral courage required of great generals—the will to act." In 1978, Michael C. C. Adams advanced the argument that McClellan was a member of a segment of Northern society that questioned whether a democratic North could defeat an aristocratic and therefore more martial South, and infected the Union war effort in the eastern theater with a defeatist mentality. As long as McClellan had influence, Adams argued, the Army of the Potomac would, in spirit and on the battlefield, fight not for victory but for defeat.[2]

Few actions appear to support the arguments put forward by these scholars so well as McClellan's conduct of the peninsula campaign and his decision at the beginning of the Seven Days battles in June 1862 to retire his army from a position only six miles from Richmond on the Chickahominy River to a new base on the James River. To Sears, the outcome of the campaign was attributable to McClellan's deluded mind "imagining overwhelming [enemy] force wherever he looked." To McPherson, McClellan's decision to retreat after Gaines's Mill showed that even minor defeats could render him "a whipped man mentally." In the context of Adams's thesis, the retreat to the James, and McClellan's cautious conduct of the campaign on the peninsula as a whole, reflected a mind-set that viewed success in terms of avoiding defeat rather than actively seeking victory.[3]

Yet in order to fully understand McClellan and his actions on the Virginia peninsula, it is necessary to look beyond whatever flaws may have existed in his character and take into account the actual circumstances he faced in the spring and summer of 1862 and the potential and real effects his move to the James River had on the Union war effort in Virginia. It is also important to consider the cultural outlook that shaped McClellan's perception of the sectional conflict, approach to the problem of restoring the Union, and strategic and tactical decisions through which he managed to accomplish a great deal on the peninsula, but ultimately undermined his larger goals.[4]

Although McClellan was a member of the wing of the Democratic party led by Stephen A. Douglas in 1858 and 1860, his cultural outlook, or the system of beliefs and attitudes that shaped his problem-solving techniques,[5] actually reflected his early socialization in an environment where, as he would write in 1866, "traditions and associations . . . were all on the side of the old Whig Party." His father, the renowned Philadelphia surgeon Dr. George McClellan, was a member of the emerging cosmopolitan, nationalistic, and upwardly mobile Northern bourgeoisie that embraced the Whig vision of a nation in which enlightened statesmen gave paternalistic encouragement and direction to the development of a market economy and worked to preserve social order and institutional stability by conciliating competing interests through compromise. From the time it was organized in the 1830s until his death in 1847, Dr. McClellan was a steadfast supporter of the Whig party and not only deeply admired the party's two great statesmen, Henry Clay and Daniel Webster, but considered them intimate friends as well. And, like his father, the future general was unwavering in his support for the Whigs throughout the 1840s.[6]

Whig culture was distinguished by the tendency of Whigs to view the world as a place where the forces of narrow-minded passion and extremism and the forces of enlightened reason and moderation battled for ascendancy, a perspective that McClellan developed at an early age. Preoccupied with the preservation of social order, Whigs feared that the rowdy, democratic spirit of Jacksonian America would compromise the ability of enlightened statesmen to provide the reasoned, moderate leadership necessary to maintain the stability of established institutions, such as the Union, the Constitution, and the rule of law, that gave rational order and direction to society. To many Whigs, particularly in the industrial and commercial cities of the Northeast, it was Webster who personified the values they held dear: heroic statesmanship that prized the good of the nation above parochial, party, or self-interest; reason and moderation; and the preservation of the Union, social order, and sectional harmony over all other concerns.[7]

Among Webster's admirers was a young George B. McClellan, who in 1852 hailed the Massachusetts statesman as "an intellectual giant" and, when given the honor of naming the largest mountain in the Wichita mountain chain during the Red River Expedition that same year, christened it Mount Webster. By 1852, however, McClellan's attachment to the Whig party, like Webster's, had been shattered by the rise to power of a new generation of leaders within the party whose support for the Wilmot Proviso and the opposition to the Compromise of 1850 imperiled the institution that old-line Whigs prized above all others, the Union. In response to the danger to the Union posed first by an increasingly free-soil Whig party and then by the militantly antislavery and sectional Republican party, Dr. McClellan's son, like Clay's and Webster's, became a Democrat.[8]

To McClellan, the sectional crisis was the product of the ultimate Whig fear coming to fruition: the forces of passion and extremism—fire-eaters in the South and antislavery fanatics in the North—stirring up irrational fears in the minds of the people. If sectional harmony was to be restored, it was essential that reason and moderation regain ascendancy. This was possible only if the North pursued a carefully crafted and implemented war policy that would accomplish the task of coercing the South back into the Union without further inflaming passions on both sides. To this end, McClellan became one of the most committed adherents to, and the leading symbol of, what historian Mark Grimsley labeled the "rational, even enlightened policy: of conciliation that guided Union war policy toward Southerners and their property through the summer of 1862.[9]

Conciliation was based on a belief that secession was the work of a small group of extremists in the South that had been able to seize power only by stirring up irrational fears that the election of a Republican president would be fatal to Southern republicanism. Their continued success in this endeavor depended on their ability to preserve and nurture a false perception in the minds of the Southern masses that a small faction of antislavery fanatics in the Republican party had gained control of the federal government and spoke for the North as a whole. By ignoring the calls of antislavery extremists for a hard war against the slave power that fueled Southern resistance, adopting an attitude of paternalistic forbearance toward the people of the South, and rigidly respecting their constitutional rights, advocates of conciliation believed that Northern policy makers would expose the fraudulence of the secessionist argument. Once this happened, Southern nationalism, which was not particularly

George B. McClellan

strong to begin with, would rapidly dissipate, and the atmosphere of sectional harmony, with the authority of the Union firmly established, that Webster and Clay had worked so hard to foster could finally be established.[10]

McClellan's rationalism and desire to restrain passion also shaped his formation of strategy and conduct of operations. Although he recognized that the war could not be won without hard fighting, by taking advantage of the North's overwhelming advantage in manpower and industrial resources, he looked to limit the actual number of battles and carefully control the conditions under which they would be fought to ensure that they would produce decisive Union victories. Fighting battles obviously meant accepting casualties; an unnecessarily large number of either would exacerbate sectional enmity and jeopardize the effort to restrain passions on both sides. In addition, McClellan was aware that any battle, no matter how well managed, could result in defeat. Further setbacks on the battlefield could not be afforded. First, they would encourage rebel resistance by strengthening Southern confidence in the viability of the Confederacy as a nation. Second, they would foster frustration and exasperation in the North, giving irresponsible politicians the opportunity to stir up passions against the South and adopt measures, such as emancipation, that would stimulate Southern resistance by increasing the consequences of secession.[11]

McClellan laid out the strategic vision that was to guide his operations on the peninsula in a letter to Secretary of War Edwin M. Stanton on February 3, 1862. In response to criticisms raised by President Abraham Lincoln, who favored an advance against the Confederate army at Manassas commanded by Joseph E. Johnston via the Occoquan River, McClellan argued that sending a massive force to the lower Chesapeake offered the best means for compelling the enemy to fight a major, decisive battle it could not win. For the point of landing, McClellan selected Urbanna on the lower Rappahannock River. A rapid movement from Urbanna, he reasoned, would enable the Army of the Potomac to isolate the small Confederate army on the peninsula and either occupy Richmond before Johnston could arrive from the north or force him to fight an offensive battle "in a position selected by ourselves . . . in which all is in our favor," or both. In the unlikely event that neither occurred between Urbanna and Richmond, the Federal army would have the option of using the navy to cross the James and approach the Confederate capital from the south bank, "forcing the enemy to come out and attack us, for his position would be untenable with us on the southern bank of the river." Another option, although one that did not offer the "celerity and brilliancy of results" of a move from Urbanna, would involve making an overland march up the peninsula, using Fort Monroe as a base. "It is by no means certain," he concluded, "that we can beat them at Manassas. On the other line I regard success as certain by all the chances of war . . . success [that] must produce immense results."[12]

When one looks at Virginia on a map, the logic of basing operations on the lower Chesapeake is undeniable.[13] In the Virginia tidewater, the North would be able to exploit its overwhelming naval superiority. Three major rivers—the Rappahannock, the York, and the James—reached from the Chesapeake Bay straight into the Virginia heartland, providing perfect routes for an invading army working in cooperation with a strong navy. The navy could be used to transport troops rapidly and securely upstream to cut off any enemy forces that might resist an army advancing toward Richmond, a tactic the Confederates would find difficult, if not impossible, to counter. Using the lower Chesapeake as a base also ensured lines of supply and communication that would be secure from the threat of raids or turning movements that accompanied an overland line. In addition, the navy could be used to protect the flanks of any army advancing on Richmond, and should siege operations be necessary, gunboats would be in close enough proximity to augment the Union's already overwhelming advantage in firepower. The river best suited for combined operations was the James, the widest and deepest of the three major rivers. During the Revolutionary War, British forces had conducted a number of successful operations in Virginia using the James as a line of operations. Only when the French navy was able to wrest control of the Chesapeake and its tributaries were the allied forces able to stop these invasions. The Confederacy, except for the few weeks that the CSS *Virginia* (the former USS *Merrimack*) operated, never had any hope of challenging Northern naval supremacy.[14]

Upon receiving McClellan's letter and assurances that enough troops would be left behind to protect Washington, Lincoln reluctantly gave his consent to the Urbanna plan. But when Johnston pulled his army back from Manassas to a position behind the Rapidan River in March 1862, he nullified the advantages of a movement to the lower Rappahannock. McClellan reacted to this by changing the point of landing and initial base of operations from Urbanna to Fort Monroe at the tip of the peninsula between the York and James Rivers. McClellan was denied use of the James, however, by the ironclad CSS *Virginia*. Although the *Virginia*'s threat to the Union navy was neutralized by the USS *Monitor*, its presence at the Norfolk navy yard was enough for the navy to consider the James closed as a line of operations. McClellan therefore decided to base his initial operations on the York River. In a letter to Stanton on March 19, he proposed "a combined naval and land attack upon Yorktown," with the navy first reducing the Confederate batteries at Yorktown and then ferrying "a strong corps" up that stream to take West Point. Besides cutting off Confederate defenders on the lower peninsula and securing the York River and Richmond Rail Road as a possible supply line for operations against Richmond, this would also provide "every facility for developing and bringing into play the whole of our available force on either or both banks of the James."[15]

McClellan's plans, however, had already started to unravel by the time he reached the peninsula. On March 12 he was demoted from general in chief to commander of only the Army of the Potomac, thus losing his ability to coordinate his army's movements with those of other Union forces. On March 31 a division was transferred from the Army of the Potomac to John C. Frémont's army in western Virginia. Then, in a meeting with Flag Officer Louis Goldsborough shortly after his arrival at Fort Monroe, McClellan learned that the navy would "furnish no vessels to take an active part in the reduction of the batteries at York and Gloucester or to run by and gain their rear." Finally, on April 4, as the Army of the Potomac began probing the rebel line at Yorktown, McClellan was informed that the entire First Corps, 30,000 men under Irvin McDowell, was being withheld from the Army of the Potomac in order to protect Washington.[16]

With the navy unwilling to participate in a bombardment of Yorktown or even test Confederate batteries along the York, the campaign of amphibious maneuver that McClellan desired was reduced to an overland march up the peninsula. After making a tough march to Yorktown through heavy rains that turned the roads to mud, the Federals learned that the Warwick River, instead of flowing from east to west as indicated on their maps, actually flowed across the peninsula from Yorktown to the James. The problem of getting across the Warwick was made particularly difficult by strategic damming of the river by the Confederates, which turned it into a formidable obstacle. This rendered impracticable McClellan's plan of quickly pushing forward to the halfway house on the Yorktown-Williamsburg Road, the occupation of which would have forced the Confederate commander at Yorktown, John Magruder, to either hastily abandon the lower peninsula and Gloucester, thus opening the York and James to navigation by Union warships, or be trapped in the Yorktown defenses. When the withholding of the First Corps precluded an effort to open the York by attacking Gloucester via the Severn River, McClellan decided to undertake siege operations against Yorktown and commenced petitioning the administration for restoration of some or all of the First Corps for an operation against Gloucester.[17]

Few actions on the peninsula so well illustrate McClellan's political-strategic approach as his decision to besiege Yorktown rather than break Magruder's lines by assault. Clearly, the decision for a siege cost McClellan valuable time. Had he carried the Confederate position by assault in early April, he would have denied the South time to implement conscription, conduct a successful campaign in the Shenandoah Valley, construct effective obstructions to navigation on the James, or make an orderly evacuation of the lower peninsula. More importantly, he could have avoided feeding a growing disenchantment in the North with his approach to the war. As historian Eric T. Dean, Jr., has pointed out, in 1862 the Northern public had an unrealistic expectation—reinforced by the reporting of journalists, who had determined by the 1860s that sensationalism sold more newspapers than sober, careful explanations of events—that a quick, decisive, and climactic victory that would end the rebellion could easily be achieved if only Northern generals had the nerve to pursue it with vigor. McClellan recognized (and Lincoln was sure to remind him) that in deciding to sacrifice time in order to preserve lives, ensure victory, and thus restrain Northern passions, he risked feeding sentiments in the North that a dispassionate approach to the war and a controlled, rational conduct of operations reflected lack of a "proper" martial spirit.[18]

It is difficult, however, to challenge the rationalism of McClellan's decision to besiege rather than launch frontal assaults on the enemy's entrenchments at Yorktown. When one keeps in mind the general's desire to avoid unnecessary loss of life, maintain control over the battlefield, and ensure certainty of results, there was no contest between the merits of a "slow but sure" siege versus those of a frontal assault. By choosing siege operations, he placed the Confederate military authorities in an impossible position. Impotent to disrupt McClellan's siege preparations or resist the power of his heavy guns once they opened fire, they faced the dilemma of either abandoning the lower peninsula, and thus freeing the waters of the York and the James to Union warships, or maintaining the position on the Warwick at the risk of losing their army.

Ironically, McClellan's decision to take the time to carefully prepare for a siege gave the Confederate high command an opportunity to push more trophies into the bag he was planning to close once preparations were complete. Against the advice of Johnston, who recognized a trap when he saw one, President Jefferson Davis and his military adviser Gen. Robert E. Lee ordered his army into the Yorktown trenches, hoping that together with Magruder's force they could gain time to raise troops and prepare defenses near Richmond or beat back an assault. And there was hope that McClellan would at least attempt an assault. Davis and Lee recognized as well as Johnston did that the Confederate position on the peninsula could not withstand a siege. Yet if McClellan were to attempt an assault with Johnston's as well as Magruder's men behind the trenches, there was a chance that a defensive victory could be achieved that would inflict significant casualties on the Union army and might even open up an opportunity for a counteroffensive to drive the Army of the Potomac back to its ships. They recognized that this was a long shot, but it was their only hope for saving the lower peninsula. McClellan, however, refused to oblige them.[19]

Prospects for avoiding a drawn-out operation brightened considerably when William B. Franklin's division of the First Corps was restored to the Army of the Potomac on April 11. This enabled McClellan to revive his scheme of seizing Gloucester to open up the York to combined operations. While waiting for Franklin's division to arrive (Franklin himself would not reach the peninsula until April 19), McClellan continued perfecting his siege preparations. Once Franklin's force was ready, McClellan intended to use his heavy artillery to pin the Confederate army in Yorktown while Franklin, after reducing Gloucester, cut off its line of retreat. To ensure that a trusted hand would be in charge of operations against Yorktown, McClellan appointed Fitz-John Porter director of the siege.[20]

On May 3, just as McClellan was prepared to pound the Confederate defenses with his heavy artillery, Johnston evacuated Yorktown. Two days later, McClellan sent Franklin's division up the York River in an unsuccessful attempt to cut off the Confederate retreat. (The delay getting the expedition off to West Point was a consequence of McClellan's decision to disembark Franklin's troops upon receiving false reports that the enemy was contemplating a sortie against the Federal right.) On May 10, after a sharp fight with Johnston's rear guard at Williamsburg, the Army of the Potomac fully established connection with Franklin's command near West Point. On May 15 and 16 three divisions were sent forward to establish a depot at White House on the Pamunkey River.[21]

The rebel occupation of Norfolk became untenable with the fall of Yorktown. On May 10 Norfolk was abandoned and quickly occupied by the federal army. On May 11 Stanton informed McClellan that "the *Merrimac* was set-fire to and blown up by the Rebels this morning at five o'clock." A flotilla of Union gunboats, under the command of Commodore John Rodgers, was then pushed up the James. It came within eight miles of Richmond before being stopped by batteries at Drewry's Bluff on May 15.[22]

It is significant, and points up another reason for McClellan's cautious approach to operations on the peninsula, that he did not entrust the main components of his plan to take Yorktown to any of his three corps commanders but rather to two division commanders, Franklin and Porter. As Albert Castel noted, a prerequisite for success in carrying out tactical flank attacks—and, by extension, the more complicated and risky strategic turning movements that McClellan hoped to execute—is confidence on the part of the army commander in the ability of subordinates to exercise semi-independent command responsibilities.[23] This McClellan lacked. One of the actions Lincoln took prior to the commencement of the peninsula campaign was to mandate the organization of the Army of the Potomac into corps and appoint the four senior division commanders—McDowell, Edwin V. Sumner, Samuel P. Heintzelman, and Erasmus D. Keyes—to lead them. The organization of corps was a necessary step, and the selection of these four men on the basis of seniority was certainly appropriate. McClellan, however, would have undoubtedly preferred Porter, Franklin, and perhaps William F. Smith, as he had serious reservations about whether the four senior officers possessed sufficient professional competence, respect for his authority, and confidence in his strategy. Of the four, only Keyes endorsed the plan to operate from the lower Chesapeake when it was first presented to them.[24]

The inauspicious performance of the corps commanders during the battle of Williamsburg confirmed McClellan's concerns about his command structure. In letters to his wife and to Stanton after the battle, McClellan fumed over the "utter stupidity & worthlessness of the Corps Comdrs" and requested "permission to reorganize the army corps . . . either to return to the organization by division or else be authorized to relieve incompetent commanders."[25] Stanton granted McClellan authority to suspend the corps organization. However, accompanying the communication in which Stanton granted this authority was a letter from the president expressing uneasiness with such a move. He warned the general that to overturn the corps organization would be poorly "received in quarters which we cannot entirely disregard." Lincoln then expressed concern over reports that McClellan had "no consultation with [Sumner, Heintzelman, and Keyes]; that you consult and communicate with nobody but General Fitz John Porter and perhaps General Franklin," and he urged McClellan to consider the "practical and very serious question" of whether he was "strong enough, even with my help— to set your foot upon the necks of Sumner, Heintzelman, and Keyes all at once?"[26]

McClellan took Lincoln's advice and backed away from any notion of removing Sumner, Heintzelman, or Keyes. He did, however, take advantage of Stanton's permission to adopt "any [reorganization] you see fit." When McClellan issued orders laying out the army's order of march to Cumberland Landing on May 12 and to White House Landing two days later, Franklin's and Porter's divisions were treated as independent commands. (Of course, Franklin's corps commander, McDowell, was not with the army anyway.) Then, on May 18, he formally announced the reorganization of the Army of the Potomac. He kept Sumner, Heintzelman, and Keyes in command of corps but created the Fifth and Sixth Provisional Corps and gave them to Porter and Franklin, respectively.[27]

In mid-May 1862, with the James open to Drewry's Bluff and the prospect of a more comfortable—although by no means ideal—corps organization before him, McClellan faced the decision of which line of operations to take in his advance on the Confederate capital: "that of the James on the one hand, and, on the other, the line from White House as a base, crossing the upper Chickahominy." McClellan let his preference be known to Washington in a telegram on the tenth. "West Point Railway is not very injured," he noted. "Materials for repairs . . . may be sent to me. Should Norfolk be taken and the *Merrimac* destroyed, I can change my line to the James River and dispense with the railroad."[28]

That McClellan would make a move to the James greatly concerned the Confederate high command. "I suspect," wrote Johnston, "that McClellan is waiting for iron-clad war vessels for James River. They would enable him to reach Richmond three days before these troops . . . [and] should such a move be made, the fall of Richmond would be inevitable." "To be prepared for the enemy's advance up the river or on the south side, as well as from the direction of West Point," Johnston, who had been urging a concentration of force in front of Richmond rather than on the peninsula from the moment it became clear that McClellan intended to operate from the lower Chesapeake, pulled his army back to a position behind the Chickahominy River less than ten miles from Richmond, with his right flank anchored by the defenses at Drewry's Bluff.[29]

Davis and Lee shared Johnston's concern that McClellan would make a move to the James. On May 17 both wrote letters urging Johnston to strike a blow at the Union army to prevent McClellan from reaching that stream. Moving to the James, in Lee's opinion, was clearly "[McClellan's] best policy. . . . [I]t is fair for us to conclude that his operations in front of Yorktown will be re-enacted in front of the obstructions on the James River, unless you can prevent it."[30] Little did Davis, Lee, or Johnston know that relief from their anxiety was to come the very next day.

Any thoughts McClellan may have had of changing his line of operations to the James were rendered superfluous by orders that arrived from the War Department on May 18. Stanton informed him that the rest of the First Corps was finally being sent to the peninsula, but not by water, as McClellan had urged four days earlier. Instead, McDowell would march south from Fredericksburg, keeping himself "in position to save the capital from all possible attack." McClellan was ordered to extend his right wing north of Richmond to link up with McDowell's left wing and was informed that "when General McDowell is in position on your right his supplies must be drawn from West Point."[31]

McClellan would later claim that he had decided to use the James River at his line of operations by the eighteenth, and that the order to cooperate with McDowell denied him this option and forced him to establish his depots on the Pamunkey and operate from the Chickahominy.[32] On this point there has been scholarly debate. Rowena Reed accepts McClellan's assertion that he intended to change his base to the James from the moment he reached West Point, pointing to the May 10 letter to Stanton and a June 24 communication to naval officer John Rodgers in which McClellan stated that "circumstances force me to begin my attack at some distance from the James. . . . [I]n a few days I hope to gain such a position as to enable me to place a force above Ball's and Drewery's Bluffs." Stephen W. Sears, however, argues that at no point did McClellan seriously consider a change of base before the Seven Days battles.[33]

The evidence as to McClellan's thinking in mid-May 1862 supports Sears's argument. There is no record of McClellan making any specific plans to change his line of operations from the time he learned that the James was open to Drewry's Bluff on May 15 to the moment he received orders to cooperate with McDowell three days later. Yet the May 10 and June 24 telegrams—and the fact that the reason McClellan had brought the Army of the Potomac to the lower Chesapeake in the first place had been to take advantage of the Union navy—make it difficult to accept Sears's argument that he had abandoned any notion of using the James.

Sears is correct, however, to point out that McClellan was by no means as disappointed with the overland approach as he would make out in his later writings. Although less preferable to operating from the James, it would still be possible to conduct a campaign that would achieve his larger political-strategic objectives from the Chickahominy through a deliberate, controlled operation in which unnecessary bloodshed would be avoided and chance would be neutralized by the force of science and reason. This would be accomplished through siegecraft, where heavy guns and well-engineered entrenchments would give the Confederates little or no realistic possibility of preventing the fall of Richmond.

If operations along the Chickahominy were to be completely secure, however, it was essential that Washington fulfill its promise to send reinforcements from the north. Yet only a few hours after assuring McClellan on Saturday, May 24, that "McDowell and [James] Shields say they can, and positively will, move Monday morning," Lincoln, in response to the defeat of Federal forces in the Shenandoah Valley, suspended McDowell's march to the Chickahominy. McDowell, who warned the administration that it was playing into the hands of the rebels, was then ordered to send Shields to the valley with 20,000 men to deal with the Confederate army under Thomas J. "Stonewall" Jackson. After failing to accomplish anything worthwhile in the valley, Shields returned to McDowell three weeks later. The game resumed. "For the third time," McDowell advised McClellan on June 8, "I am ordered to join you. . . . I will be with you in ten days with the remainder by land from Fredericksburg."[34]

By May 24, the Army of the Potomac had reached Mechanicsville, north of the Chickahominy River, and began crossing that stream to get in position to attack Richmond. The army's efforts were impeded by the heaviest rains the peninsula had seen in years, which in addition to making life extremely unpleasant for McClellan's men, swelled the Chickahominy and made bridging it a difficult and time-consuming task. On May 31 Johnston attempted to destroy the two Union corps that had crossed the Chickahominy before the rest of the army could join it but was bloodily repulsed at the battle of Fair Oaks (Seven Pines).[35]

Despite the obstacles laid before him, McClellan's operations, if not as spectacular as his critics or he might have wished, had brought the Union army within ten miles of the Confederate capital. The Confederates, however, were clearly concentrating their forces for defense of Richmond; it was critical that reinforcements arrive as soon as possible.[36] On June 12 McClellan made another appeal for McDowell to be sent by water, arguing strenuously against the overland approach. "The destruction of the railroad bridges by flood and fire," McClellan noted, "cannot probably be remedied under four weeks . . . the exigencies of my present position will not admit of the delay."[37]

The source of McClellan's concern over his position along the Chickahominy was the vulnerability of the Richmond and York River Railroad, the long line upon which the Army of the Potomac was dependent for supplies. McClellan kept a force under Porter— the Fifth Corps and George McCall's division—north of the Chicka- hominy so that it could link up with McDowell's forces and protect the supply line to the depot at White House Landing. Although in an extremely strong tactical position behind Beaver Dam Creek, Porter's force was simply too small to carry out the mission of pro- tecting the supply line and was intended to perform this function only until McDowell arrived to make the line completely secure. McDowell never did.

Although battling a severe attack of dysentery, McClellan did not spend the month of June sitting idly by waiting for McDowell to arrive or for the Confederates to exploit this weakness. Instead, he investigated and made preparations for a possible move to the James River. During the last week of May and the first week of June, reconnaissance forces were sent to the James to establish communi- cations with the Union fleet, and detailed surveys were made of the terrain between the Federal army and the James. The navy was also ordered to send supplies to that river—just in case.[38]

After Johnston's wounding at Fair Oaks, Davis assigned com- mand of the Confederate army in front of Richmond to General Lee. Lee had already surmised McClellan's intention to repeat his tac- tics before Yorktown and make the battle for Richmond one in which artillery and engineering would determine the outcome. "McClellan," he warned Davis, "will make this a battle of posts. He will take position from position, under cover of heavy guns, & we cannot get at him without storming his works, which with our new troops is extremely hazardous. . . . It will require 100,000 men to resist the regular siege of Richmond, which perhaps would only prolong not save it."[39]

If he hoped to save Richmond, Lee determined that he would have to change the contest from a "battle of posts," in which Northern superiority in artillery and engineering would be irresistible, to a war of maneuver, in which the odds would be more favorable to the Confederacy. The condition of the Union right gave him the opportunity to do this. To exploit it, Lee constructed strong defensive works around Richmond that would allow him to shift the bulk of his army to operate against the Union position north of the Chickahominy. He then ordered Jackson to bring his army from the valley to get into position to "sweep down between the Chickahominy and Pamunkey, cutting up the enemy's communications." Lee believed that this would compel McClellan "to come out of his intrenchments, where he is strongly posted," and fight in the open field.[40]

On June 24 "a very strange case of desertion" informed McClellan of Jackson's planned attack on the Union flank and rear. The next day McClellan advised Washington that "several contrabands just in give information confirming the supposition that Jackson's advance is at or near Hanover Court House." He also confided to Stanton, and later to his wife, his expectation that Jackson would attempt an attack on the Union right and rear.[41]

The Confederates attacked just as McClellan expected. Jackson, however, failed to make the planned move on Porter's rear, and the Confederate offensive degenerated into a serious of frontal assaults on Porter's position behind Beaver Dam Creek that were easily repulsed. Nonetheless, McClellan, "satisfied that Jackson would have force enough next morning to turn Porter's right," decided to extricate himself from his soon to be untenable position on the Chickahominy by retiring to a new base on the James River. He directed Porter to send his wagons and heavy guns to the other side of the Chickahominy and fall back to a position closer to the forces on the south side of the river. A concern that "the abandonment of [Porter's] position at that time would have placed our right flank and rear at the mercy of the enemy" induced McClellan to keep Porter north of the Chickahominy on June 27. This would buy time "to perfect the arrangements for the change of base to the James River." Orders were given to the quartermasters to "throw all our supplies up the James as fast as possible" and prepare for the evacuation and destruction of the White House depot.[42]

Lee renewed his attack the next day at Gaines's Mill, and in the evening a brigade commanded by John Bell Hood achieved a breakthrough, but Union reinforcements managed to contain the damage.

When Jackson's participation in the fighting at Gaines's Mill indicated that he might be abandoning, or at least suspending, his move on the Union rear, McClellan briefly considered a counterattack. At the end of the day, however, he reported a "severe repulse to-day, having been attacked by greatly superior numbers, and I am obliged to fall back between the Chickahominy and the James River." That night, he called together his corps commanders and informed them of his intention to retire to the James River. Then, with his patience and moderation exhausted, he sent an ill-conceived telegram to Stanton, stating: "the Government has not sustained this army. . . . If I save this army now . . . I owe no thanks to you or to any other persons in Washington. You have done your best to sacrifice this army."[43]

McClellan would later claim that he had actually given up hope of McDowell's arrival and decided to abandon the base at White House and take up a new one on the James on June 25, the day before the exact nature of Lee's attack had been established. This is contradicted by the fact that even after being informed the day before of Jackson's coming attack, he persisted in carrying out plans on June 25 for pushing Heintzelman's corps forward to place it in position to support an attack, scheduled for the next day, on the rear of Old Tavern. Had McClellan already made the definite decision to retire his army to the James, it is unlikely that he would have persisted in planning and carrying out this operation.[44]

Clearly, however, a move to the James was on McClellan's mind before Jackson's attack. From the time he reached the Chickahominy, McClellan had pondered the possibility of changing his base to the James River. These, however, appear to have been solely contingency plans due to his orders to cooperate with McDowell. On June 25, when McClellan was convinced of Jackson's coming attack on his right and rear, it began to look like the army would probably, but not necessarily, have to make a move to the James River. Not until late on June 26, when it was clear that Jackson would be able to cut the line to White House and render the position on the Chickahominy untenable, did McClellan make the actual decision to change his base to the James. McClellan, after all, was still under orders from Washington to maintain White House as his base. To have disobeyed these orders by making a move to the James before it was absolutely necessary would surely have exacerbated doubts in Washington as to McClellan's willingness to follow the directions of his civilian superiors and might well have cost him his command.

In assessing McClellan's decision to change his base to the James, it is worthwhile to consider the advantages and disadvantages of this move relative to the other options that were open to McClellan once Lee attacked. The first of these, to stand and fight for his communications from his position on the Chickahominy, if successful, would have kept the army in a position closer to Richmond than the one his move to the James put him in. Yet to maintain this position would have forced McClellan to keep the Pamunkey as his base and the vulnerable York River Railroad as his supply line. He could not have shifted his base to the James and maintained his position on the Chickahominy. From a base on the James he would not have a railroad or any other means of transporting his heaviest siege artillery through White Oak Swamp. Thus, remaining on the Chickahominy would have necessitated keeping the army in the same vulnerable position it was in on June 26 in order to protect the railroad.

A second option would have been to follow the advice of Gen. John Pope, who on June 26 was placed in command of Union forces in the valley and northern Virginia, and retreat in the direction of the York River. This was what Lee hoped McClellan would do, and he kept his force north of the Chickahominy after Gaines's Mill to counter such a move. Lee had anticipated that, in response to the attack on McClellan's rear and the threat to his communications, McClellan "would be compelled to retreat" in the direction of the York "or give battle out of his intrenchments."[45]

The safety of a move to the York is questionable in light of the fact that the Army of the Potomac would have had to make its retreat down the peninsula out of the safety of its trenches and with the Confederates on its left flank. Finally, even had such a move been made safely, it would have placed the army at a greater distance from Richmond than did the move to the James.

The limited options open for future operations had McClellan been able to reach a secure position on the York also support the decision not to pursue this course of action. One option would have been to rest and refit his army in preparation for another advance over the same ground he had already passed and retreated over once. Another would have been to wait until it was determined how he could cooperate with Pope from that position. This would have required time, for until June 25, planning for overland operations in support of the Army of the Potomac had been based on McClellan's being on the Chickahominy. From a position on the York, McClellan might also have transferred the army to the James. Had such a move been made, however, it is unlikely that the army could have placed itself in a more favorable position on the James than the one it had after the Seven Days battles.

It is not unlikely that, had the Army of the Potomac reached a secure base on the York, Lincoln would have ordered it back to Washington so that it could operate with Pope, as he did later. From his self-directed study of military strategy, by January 1862, Lincoln had developed a firm belief in the importance of concentration of force and the need to avoid operating on exterior lines. His appointment of Henry W. Halleck to McClellan's old post of general in chief on July 11 brought to the Union high command a man who fully shared Lincoln's beliefs. Having McClellan on the peninsula and Pope in northern Virginia with a strong Confederate force in between them was a textbook example of the sort of strategic situation that Halleck and Lincoln sought to avoid at all costs.[46]

Another option available to McClellan on June 26 and 27 was to use the left wing of the Army of the Potomac to attack the Confederate position south of the Chickahominy, where the Union forces enjoyed a two-to-one advantage. Although the Union army might have been able to seize the Confederate capital by taking this course of action, the problem of supplying the army, both during the assault and once it had reached Richmond, made the ultimate success of such a move less than certain.[47] Success would have meant not making an all-out defense of the line to White House and operating without a secure base of supplies. Then, in the best-case scenario, before their supplies ran out, McClellan could have assaulted and quickly carried the Confederate defenses, disposed of the other forces protecting the capital, seized Richmond, and, upon clearing the James River of defensive works and obstructions, reestablished communications and a new line of supplies with the navy on the James.

This plan could have worked. But a staff blunder in carrying out orders for the assault on the lightly held but well-prepared rebel works, a breakdown in troop discipline upon occupying Richmond, difficulty in reducing the river defenses, or anything else that may have prevented the rapid occupation of Richmond and reestablishment of a new base could have left the Army of the Potomac destitute of rations and supplies with no base from which to draw new ones. From the time he reached the peninsula, McClellan had seen his best-laid plans upset by factors outside his control. Would it have been reasonable to take this action hoping that luck might finally be in his favor? Had McClellan taken this gamble and lost, in order to resupply his army he might have been forced to make operational decisions that provided Lee the opportunity to force a battle under circumstances disadvantageous to the Union army.[48]

The final course open to McClellan to counter Lee's attack on his communications, and the one he chose to take, was to change his base to the James River and, because he lacked a solid line for bringing forward supplies or moving heavy artillery to the Chickahominy, to retire to the James and make it his line of operations. The drawbacks of this option were the abandonment and destruction of considerable amounts of supplies and a difficult and risky march across White Oak Swamp.

McClellan, however, managed the withdrawal with a skill that even his Confederate counterparts acknowledged. The Army of the Potomac destroyed what supplies it could not carry, leaving little to the enemy. McClellan also covered his movement so well that it was not until the night of June 28 that Lee figured out McClellan's intentions and began his pursuit.[49] In the course of the move across White Oak Swamp, the Union army successfully fought off attacks at Savage's Station and Frayser's Farm and managed to reach Malvern Hill in good enough condition to easily repulse a series of rebel assaults before moving the army downriver to its final stop at Harrison's Landing. In the fighting, the Army of the Potomac also managed to inflict 20,614 casualties on the Confederate forces, while suffering only 15,849 of its own. Victories with such a rate of attrition were not ones that the Confederacy, with its smaller population, could long afford.[50]

Unlike the position on the Chickahominy, the army's new location had a secure line of communications and was too strong for Lee to consider attacking. From its position on the James, the Army of the Potomac could advance Union military efforts in Virginia without even undertaking active operations. Having McClellan within striking distance of the capital made it impracticable for Lee to stray too far from the Richmond defenses. Not until he was certain that the Union army was withdrawing from its position on the James in early August did Lee actively begin offensive operations against Pope.[51]

The James was also a much more advantageous position from which to conduct the sort of irresistible and carefully controlled operations that appealed to McClellan. He could once again utilize the navy, which reopened a number of favorable options for operations. He could undertake an advance on Richmond along the north bank of the James, using the navy to ferry troops up the river to flank any Confederate army offering resistance. Upon reaching Richmond's defenses, the Army of the Potomac would also have the support of navy gunboats for siege operations. Another option would have been to cross the James and campaign along the south bank, which would have placed the army in position to sever Richmond's connections with the rest of the Confederacy. McClellan was working on plans for such a movement when the army was recalled to Washington.[52]

In an effort to analyze the nature of warfare, Prussian military theorist Carl von Clausewitz identified the interplay of "friction" and "genius" as the dynamic that always shapes the outcome of operations in the field. A commander's success or failure is determined not by whether he possesses merit ("genius") per se but by whether he possesses it in sufficient measure to counter the extent and character of the particular problems he faces in planning and executing his strategy. A general who possesses below-average ability may, if confronted with a particularly favorable situation (a preponderance of strength, an incompetent foe, and so forth), achieve great success. Conversely, an officer of outstanding intellect and character might encounter friction of such magnitude that he is unable to attain success.[53]

When viewed from a purely rational perspective—which McClellan maintained throughout the campaign—the merits of his generalship during the peninsula campaign are difficult to dispute. Although he did not capture Richmond, McClellan accomplished a great deal despite the considerable friction he encountered. Throughout the campaign, he found himself unable to exploit the strategic and tactical advantages he had based his plan of operations on, yet he managed to reach the gates of Richmond with a minimum of casualties and the game firmly in his hands. Unfortunately, circumstances that were partially the result of his obstinate rationality (inducing him to disregard the need to indulge the administration's irrational fear of a Confederate attack on Washington) placed him in a position that gave the enemy an opportunity to change the terms of the contest. By changing his line to the James, McClellan regained the strategic initiative and obtained a much more secure and favorable position from which to conduct future operations. Not until Ulysses S. Grant's far bloodier campaign against a far weaker Confederacy would any Union army come so close to Richmond.

Yet in the context of McClellan's larger goal of sustaining a reasoned war policy, what he accomplished through his unyielding rationality from an operational standpoint during the course of the peninsula campaign and Seven Days battles was more than offset by the impact the move to the James had on Northern public opinion. McClellan understood that his carefully calculated, time-consuming, and restrained conduct of operations might strain the ability of a populace that had little understanding of military science and expected a quick victory to restrain their passions and maintain an attitude of conciliation and moderation in dealing with the rebellion. But he believed that a reasoned war policy could succeed only if operations were carefully prepared and executed to neutralize the role of chance, avoid unnecessary casualties, and produce decisive battles that would produce the sort of victories that, in combination with the policy of conciliation, would bring the South to reason as quickly as possible. By late June 1862, however, McClellan had consumed so much time and resources that only a decisive and unambiguous victory followed by the capture of Richmond could have satisfied the North that it had been correct to sustain a cautious general and refrain from conducting a hard war against the rebels. A change of base to the James River, no matter how skillfully conducted or strategically sound, could not. After the Seven Days, toleration for McClellan's "scientific" generalship and the conciliation policy, already badly eroding, collapsed, and calls for "war in earnest" against the rebels increased as the prospect of a quick victory appeared to evaporate.[54]

Although he did not share the popular perception of the Seven Days as a serious military defeat, Lincoln, who had never bought the idea of taking the army to the peninsula in the first place, was personally frustrated with the conciliatory policy and with McClellan. Never slow to react to shifts in public opinion, he decided to take Union war policy in a new direction after the check on the peninsula. Shortly after receiving a letter from McClellan on July 7 urging continuation of the conciliatory policy, Lincoln signed a new confiscation bill and sanctioned a series of orders issued by General Pope that signaled the emergence of a tougher attitude toward Southerners and slavery. Then, on July 22, he advised his cabinet that he intended to issue an Emancipation Proclamation.[55] From that point forward, Northern war policy would be driven by the principle that Southerners were enemies to be vanquished, rather than brothers to be conciliated, and the war for Clay's and Webster's old Union was on the road to becoming Abraham Lincoln's Second American Revolution. Ironically, it was McClellan's own eminently reasoned decisions on the peninsula that dealt the most serious blows to the war policy of reason and moderation that they were intended to sustain.

Chapter Four

Generalship on Trial: Don Carlos Buell's Campaign to Chattanooga

Stephen D. Engle

Scholars and contemporaries of the Civil War have correctly characterized Don Carlos Buell as a commander who suffered from the "slows," from the debilitating effects of failing to reconcile theory with the practicalities of a campaign, and from a flawed notion of civil-military relations. Buell conceived war as a limited exercise, to be conducted by professionals who maneuvered rather than fought for success. Indeed, it might be said that Buell was the George B. McClellan of the West. It was that McClellan-like quality of slowness and unaggressiveness that got him removed from command, illustrating that Union policy makers had learned from his failure.[1]

In November 1862, President Abraham Lincoln relieved Buell from command of the Army of the Ohio, the Union's second largest army. Lincoln's justification for dismissing Buell at the time was that the commander had failed to defeat Braxton Bragg at Perryville and had not pursued him aggressively after the battle. His inability to catch and defeat Bragg confirmed for Lincoln what most senior policy makers had already concluded during the summer: Buell was incapable of success and was uninspired by the political course of the war. This opinion was reinforced by the relentless denunciation of the commander by powerful midwestern politicians, including Governor Oliver P. Morton of Indiana, Governor David Tod of Ohio, and Military Governor Andrew Johnson of Tennessee, who, like

95

most radical Republicans, had long pushed for Buell's ouster. After his dismissal, Buell demanded a trial to exonerate himself from the claims of misconduct and treason stemming from his summer and fall campaigns. Thus, Secretary of War Edwin M. Stanton created the so-called Buell Commission, which provided a venue for judging whether the commander had been negligent, inept, or traitorous in carrying out his duty or simply out of touch with the administration's desires.[2]

The proceedings lasted nearly five months and produced a final report that filled 721 pages summarizing the Army of the Ohio's march to Chattanooga, its pursuit of Bragg, and Buell's conciliatory policy. Although Stanton instructed the commission to examine only the military operations of Buell's army, it was clear that he wanted Buell's attitude toward war condemned and enough evidence produced to bring criminal charges against Buell. Stanton sought not only to placate vengeful midwestern Republicans and a public that wanted to wage a harsh war but also to assert that Buell's brand of "soft war" had led to his failure, not logistical problems, as Buell claimed. Although it was only an investigative body that lacked any legal authority, the commission gave Buell a forum to defend his actions. In essence, it was Stanton's way of making a broad political statement about how much the nature of the war had changed since its inception and how little tolerance the administration had for commanders like Buell who refused to change with it. Not surprisingly, Buell proved as tenacious during the proceedings as he had been during the campaign. Lew Wallace, the president of the commission, recalled in his autobiography forty years later that Buell's status before the commission was peculiar. "There was no charge against him of any kind, not even of failure in command," remarked Wallace. "We were not to investigate him," he added, "but a series of operations conducted by him. We were not a court; he was not a defendant; yet the most extraordinary feature of the whole proceeding [was] the use he made of his privileges of appearance before us."[3] In the end, the commission's verdict was that Buell was slow, unaggressive, inflexible, sympathetic to Southerners and slavery, and not in harmony with the government's aims for waging or winning the war, but not guilty of misconduct warranting a court-martial.

The fact that Stanton restricted the commission to an investigation of Buell's actions and not to Buell himself, yet allowed Buell to defend his case, was important, in that it represented in micro-cosm the doctrines of limited and unlimited war aims. The testimony and cross-examination reflected the shift in the brand of war the administration was waging. The prosecution represented the "war-fare of momentum" and had little regard for the limited-war doc-trine in achieving military objectives. Buell served as his own counsel and defended his operations based on the limited-war doctrine and emphasized the means of achieving his military objectives.

In the proceedings, the commission targeted Buell's Chatta-nooga campaign, commenced in June 1862, as the principal illus-tration of how and why the commander was unsuccessful. The commission attacked the lack of results from this campaign, stress-ing the failure to seize Chattanooga and east Tennessee. They argued that Buell had lost sight of the objectives because he concentrated exclusively on the means of getting to Chattanooga and refused to change either his politics or his tactics. Judge Advocate Donn Piatt emphasized Chattanooga's relatively undefended condition and stressed the short distance Buell's army had to march and the abun-dance of resources awaiting the army in east Tennessee. Wallace, who considered the proceedings an education in the conduct of war, condemned Buell for not adjusting his attitude of war to make his logistical considerations "bend" during the march to Chattanooga. He queried Buell about possible solutions to providing subsistence while keeping his army on the move. In the end, however, Wallace simply concluded that Buell's philosophy of war and temperament made him "either too cautious or too rigidly methodical to be great or successful." The administration learned a valuable lesson from Buell's failure to embrace the kind of war necessary to be successful that summer.[4]

The Chattanooga campaign itself lasted over two months and was an attempt to march quickly into east Tennessee along the Memphis and Charleston Railroad to Chattanooga. In late August, however, Bragg reached the city before Buell and then veered north, launching his famed Kentucky campaign in an attempt to lure Blue-grass residents to the Confederacy. The commission, like Buell's superiors and some of his soldiers, challenged the reasons for Buell's failure to get to Chattanooga. They questioned his apparent fear of Bragg and sympathy with Southerners, his reliance on the railroad for supplies, and his unwillingness to keep pace with the war's political movement and to confiscate property necessary for his army's use. Buell's reasoning that his logistical problems prevented him from reaching the city failed to satisfy the commission. They concluded that Buell had logistical problems because of his failure to move quickly and live off the countryside. This failure, they argued, had less to do with logistics and more to do with his attitude and his contempt for the political direction of the war. Citing Andrew Johnson's appointment as military governor of Tennessee in March, the passage of the congressional mandate the same month prohibiting the return of fugitive slaves, and the adoption of the Confiscation Act of July 1862, the commission concluded that the war had changed. They found that Buell's slowness—caused by his dependence on the railroad, which was caused by his abhorrence of foraging, as well as by his refusal to adjust his practices—ignored this change.[5]

In his defense, Buell argued that from the beginning of the campaign he had had to create the means to overcome the logistical difficulties of moving across the Confederate countryside.[6] Moreover, he claimed that the commission had criticized his Chattanooga campaign as "too slow" based on circumstances that might have been rather than on the actual circumstances at the time. Buell concluded that it was impossible to say "what would have been the consequences of different action." He questioned the value of the commission's opinion, saying that "just and thinking men will hesitate to declare in a judicial verdict . . . that the commander ought to have acted differently."[7] The tenacious commander refused to believe that logistical alternatives and flexibility in attitude might have resulted in success.

On the march to Chattanooga, Buell refused to read the signs that his conduct was not succeeding in getting him to his destination. Buell failed to evolve with the changing circumstances of the Chattanooga campaign because he lacked a complete view of the war itself. A veteran of the Adjutant General's Office and of the War Department, he understood the political side to the war, to the degree that he remained committed to protecting the constitutional guarantees of the Confederate citizens. He never deviated from his desire to prevent his army from trampling the constitutional rights of private citizens of the Confederacy as he marched across northern Mississippi and Alabama.[8]

Don Carlos Buell

This conciliation policy was part of his rationale for keeping the war limited and thus safe. He relied on preparation as an ends as well as a means. When war becomes unpredictable, commanders have to exhibit an intuitive ability and adjust to unforeseen military circumstances. In these situations, Buell was among those who looked backward to the eighteenth century to define his generalship in the Civil War. He envisioned the Civil War as a limited war, fought in the tradition of Antoine Henri de Jomini, and was confident that he understood war and could direct the conflict in that fashion. As one contemporary put it, Buell "had acquired fixed ways of doing things, from which it was difficult to free himself when conditions required new methods and a free hand." He added that Buell "lacked that expansive quality of mind that readily adjusts itself to the broader views that are necessary to success."[9]

If nothing more, Buell's march to Chattanooga was significant in that it highlighted the degree to which Buell's generalship and command were at the mercy of his philosophy of limited war, his flawed concept of civil-military relations, and his conservative temperament. This campaign tested whether he was the kind of commander who could recognize the need for change and adjust. For Buell to be successful in accommodating a warfare of momentum or an unlimited war, he would need to adjust his military thinking. This would require Buell to develop a policy of "bend but not break" when combining theory, doctrine, organization, and operational planning to sustain the tactical and strategic mobility of an army in the field on the offensive. Aside from the problems inherent in military operations, there were problems of politics—problems that Buell refused to consider when they subordinated or threatened his desire to keep war limited.

During Buell's brief career in the West, the one region that Lincoln wanted under Union control was east Tennessee. The fact that the strongest Union area in a crucial border state remained in Confederate hands rankled the president. General in Chief George McClellan had explicitly informed Buell even before he assumed command of the Army of the Ohio that above all else, Lincoln wanted an advance into east Tennessee. Both Lincoln and McClellan had expected Buell to strike for Knoxville in the fall of 1861. The president argued that a Union-occupied Knoxville would cut the northernmost east-west Confederate railroad, thus coming between the secessionists and what Lincoln called their "hog and hominy."[10]

Buell initially shared Lincoln's and McClellan's goal of advancing into east Tennessee through Cumberland Gap. Shortly after his arrival in Louisville in mid-November, however, he changed his mind. He observed correctly that logistical difficulties and the approach of winter precluded an advance at that time. Still, the administration continued to urge Buell to move into east Tennessee and fulfill its political desires, but Buell remained firm in his resistance. The stubborn commander was less concerned with political necessity at the time and offered an alternative route to east Tennessee. Any advance could be realistically achieved, he argued, only by moving through Nashville and establishing links with the Ohio River through the Tennessee Valley, which provided rail, water, and road transportation. Moreover, he was convinced that an advance into west Tennessee along the Cumberland and Tennessee Rivers would prove more militarily advantageous than securing east Tennessee, since it would force the Confederates into making a choice as to where they should concentrate. In the meantime, Buell argued, "constancy will sustain them [east Tennesseeans] until the hour of deliverance." He stated, "I have no fear of their being crushed."[11]

From the outset, the very mention of east Tennessee put Buell at odds with those in the administration and Congress who were eager to see government restored to a loyal region. Succumbing to political desires meant risking his army for a region that he thought had little strategic advantage. Had he been more ambitious or politically astute, he would have recognized that Lincoln would have rewarded the commander of an expedition into that region, even if the commander failed to engage the enemy. Still, the Union had far more to gain militarily, Buell thought, by an advance into west Tennessee or south to Nashville. With Nashville as his base, Buell could not only move into east Tennessee more easily but also rely on the railroad to sustain his occupation of the region. This strategy would keep his army from being forced to live off the countryside and its citizens and thus avoid risk. Although this advance might take longer, in Buell's mind, it was more secure.[12]

Buell's concept of an invasion into Tennessee was based on sound military thinking. The fact that campaigns might be rendered longer due to logistical considerations was crucial only inasmuch as they were made insecure. He was an advocate of securing the means of his military objectives to the point that it reduced the risk that combat would occur, and he closely observed safety in emphasizing preparation over movement. "The object," he wrote to McClellan in December, "is not to fight great battles, and storm impregnable fortifications but by demonstrations and maneuvering to prevent the enemy from concentrating his scattered forces."[13] Moreover, "if precaution and the observance of rule diminish the number of battles, and sometimes miss the accidental success which folly or recklessness might have gained, it is nevertheless true that in the end they usually triumph."[14]

The recklessness in achieving success that troubled Buell could not have been better displayed, in his mind, than by Gen. Ulysses S. Grant's capture of Forts Henry and Donelson in February 1862. Although the amphibious campaign delivered portions of middle and west Tennessee over to Union control, Gen. Henry Wager Halleck had not observed all the rules of campaigning, since he had commenced the movement without "appreciation—preparative or concert." Nonetheless, Grant had accomplished what Buell considered a critical objective in the Union's effort to occupy Tennessee—control of the waterways. These victories allowed Buell to capture Nashville in the same month and thereby accomplish a second objective that he considered essential to permanent Union occupation of Tennessee. Almost two months later at the battle of Shiloh, the Federals completed what Grant had started along the Cumberland and Tennessee Rivers—penetration into the Confederate heartland. The Union drive to Corinth, Mississippi, the following month allowed the Federals to penetrate deeper into Confederate territory, seizing a major railroad terminus and thereby pushing the great barrier between North and South away from the Ohio River, where it had been at the outbreak of the war, and deep into the Confederacy.[15]

By June 1862, the Union's objective in the West remained simply to occupy east Tennessee and restore Union government on Southern soil. Thus, the Union objective in Buell's department had not changed; only the line of advance was new—Buell would march to Chattanooga instead of Knoxville. Halleck's design for the West coincided with this political desire. The Union focus in east Tennessee would divide the Confederates in the West and would facilitate Lincoln's Reconstruction efforts in the South's most loyal region. To achieve these objectives, Halleck dismembered his 120,000-man army and dispersed it east, west, and north. Buell's 40,000 men in the Army of the Ohio were to move toward east Tennessee, connect with Brig. Gen. Ormsby M. Mitchel's division already in northern Alabama, and then head to Chattanooga.[16]

In devising the outline for the Chattanooga campaign, Halleck was certainly more aggressive and ambitious than Buell. He knew that Washington wanted more offensive action in that region but was concerned, like some newspaper reporters, whether Buell had "the *go* in him." Buell's performance at Shiloh did much to buoy up his reputation as a good commander, but it failed to satisfy his critics who had questioned his reasons for not advancing into east Tennessee when prodded by the president, for being too slow to catch the enemy at Bowling Green, and for taking his time to help Grant at Shiloh.[17]

To effect the campaign, Halleck did something that McClellan had refrained from doing the previous winter: rather than merely emphasizing the political importance of the move, as McClellan had done, Halleck *ordered* Buell to Chattanooga and stipulated that he draw on the Memphis and Charleston Railroad to haul his supplies. This meant that Buell would need to repair the severely damaged railroad as he moved. Although Buell suggested his own route to Chattanooga, which would have allowed him "to strike a little farther north, through middle Tennessee and McMinnville" and put him closer to his supply depots, Halleck considered the Memphis and Charleston route to Chattanooga the most favorable. Even for a commander who thrived on using railroads, Buell feared relying on the Memphis and Charleston because for eighty miles the railroad ran south of the Tennessee River, making it susceptible to enemy destruction.

Buell's fear was not enough to force him to live off the countryside or to get to Chattanooga as soon as possible, however. The heat alone that summer would have been an incentive to move quickly. Instead, Buell committed his army to making the supply line a sure thing. Rather than improvising or "bending" his limited-war views, Buell prepared for every contingency that might arise in securing the means of getting to Chattanooga. The sheer logistical problems of moving a 40,000-man army through northern Mississippi and Alabama 300 miles away from its base of supplies would be enough to paralyze operations and frustrate any commander. Placed in the context of Buell's limited-war outlook, the entire campaign proved exceedingly troublesome to the Union war effort, because he refused to forge ahead.[18]

If the president had little to be pleased about in the East in the summer of 1862, given McClellan's problems on the peninsula, he was "greatly delighted" with Halleck's advance on Chattanooga through north Alabama.[19] The strategic importance of Chattanooga was undeniable. It contained the South's chief source of coal for manufacturing and controlled three key railroads vital for Confederate traffic east and west: the Nashville and Chattanooga, the East

Tennessee and Georgia, and the Western and Atlantic.[20] Although Lincoln had been disappointed by Buell's reluctance to advance into east Tennessee the previous winter, he was impressed by the commander's "cautious vigor" in conducting his operations since. Up to that point in the war, Buell's superiors had no reason to doubt his ability to harness enough strength and resources for the drive to Chattanooga. His West Point education and lifetime of military experience, including tours in the Seminole and Mexican Wars, had served him well. Although his soldiers regarded him as distant and austere, he had earned their respect since Shiloh. Indeed, as a commander, perhaps the only thing that Buell lacked up to the summer of 1862 was his enthusiasm for entering east Tennessee.[21]

In mid-June, Buell departed Corinth and advanced eastward with four divisions commanded by Brig. Gens. Thomas L. Crittenden, Alexander McDowell McCook, William Nelson, and Thomas J. Wood. Ormsby Mitchel, who had seized Huntsville, Alabama, in mid-April with 10,000 troops, was holding on to two critical northern junctions of the Memphis and Charleston Railroad in anticipation of Buell's quick arrival: the junction of the Central Alabama Railroad from Athens to the Memphis and Charleston Railroad just north of the Tennessee River, and the junction of the Nashville Railroad at Stevenson. Mitchel had seen the advantage of a swift move into Chattanooga but needed Buell's main army to join him as soon as possible.[22] Halleck based Buell's campaign on three presumptions: first, he anticipated little major Confederate action, especially since the capture of Corinth had severed the only direct rail line between Mississippi and the East, severely handicapping Confederate mobility; second, he thought that Buell's march along the railroad would keep Gen. Kirby Smith's Confederates in east Tennessee from uniting with the Confederates in Mississippi; and third, if Bragg did go after Buell at Chattanooga, it would weaken the Confederate defenses in Mississippi and perhaps give the Union the upper hand in that region. In any event, the Chattanooga campaign appeared to be the decisive campaign for overall success in the West and at the time seemed to be the least troublesome to accomplish. Holding on to the Memphis and Charleston Railroad gave the Union a logistical advantage, because the only way for the Confederates to unite at Chattanooga would be for those at Tupelo, Mississippi, to travel south to Mobile, Alabama, and then proceed northward via

Pollard, Montgomery, and Atlanta back up to Chattanooga. Although this could be accomplished, it would have to be done before Buell, moving straight across northern Alabama, got to Chattanooga. Thus Halleck's plan hinged only on Buell's swiftness in getting to Chattanooga.[23]

What seemed to be a blessing for the Union in this regard turned out to be a curse. In the Buell Commission hearings, Buell argued that Halleck could have done more to enhance his campaign. Halleck had given Washington a false sense of optimism, according to Buell, rather than presenting a realistic picture of the situation. Halleck, he contended, had completely overestimated the condition of the railroads and of the region. By characterizing the region through which Buell would march as "healthy" and by hinting that Buell would not only capture Chattanooga but might also march deeper into the Confederacy and penetrate Georgia, Halleck had set Buell up for failure. Buell argued that Mitchel had already foraged heavily in northern Alabama and that Halleck left the Confederates unattended at other points, thus allowing them to concentrate against his army at Chattanooga. Moreover, he argued that it was not until Lincoln considered transferring 25,000 troops from Halleck's army to McClellan that Halleck released Buell from using the Memphis and Charleston.[24]

From Halleck's point of view, Buell's march was made easier because the Memphis and Charleston Railroad was expected to provide a supply line for the army as it moved east. From the beginning of the campaign, however, Buell attempted to keep open not only the Memphis and Charleston but also the Nashville and Decatur Railroad, which joined the Memphis and Charleston at Decatur, Alabama, and the Nashville and Chattanooga Railroad, which reached the Memphis and Charleston north of the Tennessee River at Stevenson, Alabama. Thus, Buell's complaints stemmed mostly from his inability to keep the railroads open as supply lines.[25]

The fundamental problem of the Chattanooga campaign was one that Buell himself created. In attempting to move across the Confederate countryside unscathed and effect a permanent occupation of Chattanooga, he was convinced that he would need a rail connection to Louisville and that he would need to conciliate Southerners along the way to keep his army safe and at full strength once he got there. Neither Lincoln nor Halleck demanded that his army permanently occupy east Tennessee, nor did they demand that he continue to wage a limited war. By the summer of 1862, political leaders simply wanted him to capture Chattanooga and split the Confederacy, which would have the added benefit of forcing the South to reduce its force in McClellan's front.[26]

As Buell's army marched across the dry, barren countryside of northern Mississippi and Alabama, there was some consolation in discovering that the northern Alabama counties had supported the federal government in 1860 with five Union votes to one for secession. Over 2,000 citizens from this region had enlisted in the Union army, and it encouraged Buell that conciliation was still useful. Unfortunately for Buell, however, Mitchel's division, which had been in northern Alabama since April, had turned the countryside against the Union. Part of this had to do with Col. John Basil Turchin's plunder of Athens in early May in retaliation for being attacked by citizen-assisted cavalry.[27]

The Turchin incident became well known, and when Buell finally ordered Turchin court-martialed in July, he suffered enormously because of his insistence that Turchin's men be punished as well. Buell was making a statement about the kind of war he was conducting by court-martialing Turchin and his men for retaliating against citizens, even though those citizens had assisted Confederate guerrillas. Unfortunately for Buell, the trial hardened soldier animosity toward him, and it began to infect larger segments of the army. Even if there had been no previous reason to think that Buell was fighting a limited war to protect Southerners, the court-martial planted seeds of doubt, insubordination, and demoralization in more than a few soldiers. Although Turchin was ultimately found guilty of failing to restrain his men, and Buell wanted him cashiered from the service, Lincoln retained Turchin and eventually promoted him. As one historian put it, "Short of actually removing Buell, it is hard to imagine what more devastating insult the administration could have offered him."[28]

Mitchel himself was among those who became disenchanted with Buell's soft war even before the summer. After a meeting in late June, in which Mitchel failed to convince Buell to advance to Chattanooga quickly and modify his attitude toward the Southern civilians, he resigned. Mitchel's departure was significant, in that it demonstrated his willingness to make a statement about Buell's lethargic campaign. Buell replaced Mitchel with Lovell Rousseau, a Kentucky native known for his proslavery views. Consequently, Buell increasingly came to be seen by some soldiers and midwestern politicians as a commander who was losing touch with the war.[29]

After almost three weeks of campaigning, Buell's army was spread out from Athens to Huntsville, and he tried to draw supplies from Louisville via the Nashville and Decatur and the Memphis and Charleston Railroads. He used considerable industry in setting up ferries to cross the Tennessee River at Florence and Decatur, but low water prevented the freight boats from navigating beyond Eastport, Mississippi. From there, supplies were hauled by wagon train to Iuka, where they were placed on the railroad and sent to Decatur, where they were again ferried across the Tennessee and then re-loaded on railroad cars, eventually catching up to the army. When Confederate cavalry destroyed the railroad bridge over the Elk River on the Nashville and Decatur line and a long trestle a few miles north of Athens, it did not necessarily stall Buell's operations. Significantly, the army could still move, but with only limited supplies. That exposed another weakness in the expedition: the army lacked adequate cavalry to prevent the constant destruction of supply lines.[30]

Even if the railroads had been open to travel, Buell's sudden demand for supplies placed a considerable burden on them. The lack of adequate quartermaster and commissary officers, coupled with the size of his army, which required 300 tons of food and forage a day, further plagued Buell's operations. McClellan's Army of the Potomac had absorbed almost all available quartermaster and commissary officers in its push to Richmond. Moreover, after getting the railroad repaired, Buell had difficulty bringing forward that volume of supplies, since there was not enough rolling stock to carry it. Consequently, after weeks of campaigning with the summer heat bearing down on the Alabama countryside, Buell was trying to feed his 40,000-man army and hundreds of animals by relying on 300 miles of railroad that just could not carry that much.[31]

Despite knowing how ineffective the railroads were, Buell directed all his energies to preventing their destruction. Consequently, he continued to keep his forces dispersed over some forty miles to protect his overextended front and overextended lines of communication. And because he was guarding the two railroads coming out of Nashville and the Memphis and Charleston, it doubled his work and scattered his troops. Besides the 14,000 officers and soldiers absent from duty without permission, his strength was threatened by the fact that the one-year volunteers who had enlisted in late July 1861 were due to muster out of service. Moreover, Buell's army was suffering from a serious shortage of fresh water as well as unsanitary conditions that led to a mounting sick list. To make matters worse, when Buell tried to compensate for some of these deficiencies by seeking alternatives, it revealed the army's lack of competent and professionally trained staff officers to coordinate the duties of supply. In short, although Buell's army was pursuing the offensive, his attempts to secure logistics transformed his army from a compact, aggressive striking force into a fragmented mass of railroad laborers, watchmen, and ill-trained paper bureaucrats. As one disillusioned Hoosier put it, under Buell, "this war will last 400 years."[32]

By early July, Buell's adversities had snowballed into enormous problems for his army, despite Halleck's relieving him from repairing the Memphis and Charleston Railroad on June 30. His policy of conciliation in a countryside that was barren of food, but infested with slaves and masters procuring their return, added to his army's sense of frustration and disillusionment. From the ranks, his conciliatory policy appeared to favor Southern civilians at a time when the soldiers were suffering from his unwillingness to forage more liberally or to confiscate property. At least under Mitchel's reign, wrote Maj. Joseph Warren Keifer, Southerners "feared the *rope.* . . . Gen. Buell treats these miserable traitors most graciously," he lamented, when they should be "most soundly thrashed."[33]

Part of Buell's problem was that since assuming command of the Army of the Ohio the previous November, he had not cultivated a productive and useful relationship with his men, who, as volunteers, expected more regard from their leader. Had he bonded with his men and been an identifiable leader who deserved their allegiance even when he made unpopular decisions, perhaps there would have been less displeasure over his policy of conciliation. Buell, however, cared nothing for popularity, possessed little charisma or motivational skill, remained distant from his soldiers, and attended more to the smaller details of protocol and management of the army and less to the conceptual aspects of solving his problems by becoming more flexible. In short, the Chattanooga campaign highlighted Buell's worst features. His exploits proved so unproductive that Halleck considered abandoning the expedition. Halleck's exasperation, however, met with stern resistance from the War Department and the president, especially since McClellan had fared no better on the Virginia peninsula. "The Chattanooga expedition must not on any account be given up," wrote Stanton. "The President regards that and the movement against East Tennessee as one of the most important movements of the war."[34]

Halleck and Buell were certainly disheartened by what had become a "pick and shovel" campaign. Had Buell relied on local resources to feed the horses and mules in the Army of the Ohio, he might not have placed such a tremendous burden on Louisville and Nashville quartermasters, especially since more than two-thirds of the tonnage Buell demanded was forage for animals. Still, reliance on local resources would have necessitated two conditions: first, that local forage existed, and second, that he was willing to rely on it. Although relying on Southern civilians to provide food for his soldiers might have undermined the loyal sentiment that had apparently prevailed in northern Alabama before his arrival, requisitioning forage for animals would have caused less distress among the locals.[35]

Buell, however, had no intention of relying liberally on the local citizens for requisitions, even for animals. To draw extensively on the locals for forage would upset the discipline of his army and might lead to pillaging. Forceful requisitions might attract the wrath of those loyal to the Confederacy. Because he held the view that a mild policy would maintain the loyalty already present and might even win Southerners sympathetic to the Confederacy to the Union cause, Buell extended constitutional guarantees to Southerners whenever and wherever he could. Ironically, in his attempt to keep his army safe from the exterior elements, it steadily deteriorated from within as the morale of the soldiers weakened.[36]

Buell, however, did attempt to make use of some of the region's resources, by taking and purchasing considerable quantities of bacon and cattle. Building and repairing bridges required lumber, and Buell attempted to open the sawmills between Huntsville and Stevenson to provide lumber for pontoons and a bridge floor. Still, the Buell Commission would later consider Buell's efforts misguided, since all this had to do with securing the means of getting to Chattanooga rather than getting there quickly.[37]

On July 8 Buell received the first indication that the president was not pleased with his advance. "The President telegraphs that your progress is not satisfactory," wired Halleck, "and that you should move more rapidly. . . . I communicate his views," he closed, "hoping that your movements hereafter may be so rapid as to remove all cause of complaint, whether well founded or not."[38] Halleck certainly shared the president's frustration, though he did not reveal his personal feelings. According to one contemporary, "it would have hardly been becoming in one who had taken thirty days to move an army, unopposed, twenty-five miles . . . to chide his subordinate after setting him such an example."[39]

Halleck's telegram merely highlighted what was already obvious to Buell, his soldiers, and his superiors: his march toward Chattanooga was pathetically slow—so slow, in fact, that Bragg was uncertain of its objective. In his defense before the commission, Buell argued that he wanted to conceal the object of his campaign until he was ready to launch it. Apparently, he wanted to be at the gates of Chattanooga at full strength with his supply lines intact before descending on the city. In July 1862, though, Buell was offended by Lincoln's dissatisfaction, since he thought that his logistical nightmare had been the chief cause of the delay and had been properly explained to his superiors. "I regret," Buell responded three days later, "that it is necessary to explain the circumstances which must make progress seem slow." He knew what Halleck had intended for him but continued to believe that reaching Chattanooga quickly would be useless if his army were not in condition to fight when it got there.[40] "The advance on Chattanooga must be made with the means of acting in force," he said; "otherwise it will either fail or prove a profitless and transient prize." Furthermore, Buell did not want his operations to jeopardize his army "nor its honor nor trifle with the lives of loyal citizens." Stating that the arrangements were being pushed forward as industriously as possible, the general added: "The disaffection of the President pains me exceedingly."[41]

The president's displeasure indicated that Buell was not operating in harmony with the expectations of the administration or of

Halleck. Lincoln's disapproval also reflected the degree to which Buell had subordinated political desires to military operations. His operations always seemed more important than the administration's desires. This attitude had foundation. In March, when Lincoln appointed Andrew Johnson the military governor of Tennessee, Buell had protested that such an appointment was unnecessary and debilitating to what he had managed to accomplish during his occupation of Nashville. He had done very little to support Johnson, and the former Tennessee senator never forgot it. Johnson and Buell had resented each other since the previous fall, when Johnson had demanded that Buell advance into east Tennessee. The fact that Buell continued his policy of conciliation when Johnson clearly did not support it simply made him a target of severe criticism. To Lincoln, Johnson warned, "I said to you repeatedly in the fall, General Buell is not the man to redeem East Tennessee."[42]

Although Buell was not aware of the degree to which Johnson and, by July, other midwestern Republicans had come to resent him, he was aware that the war had changed significantly since his capture of Nashville in late February. After all, his occupation of the Tennessee capital had provided the impetus for the appointment of a military governor, which reflected the administration's desire to restore the Union government on Tennessee soil and depart from limited war. Buell was also aware that in March Congress had passed resolutions that forbade commanders to return slaves to their masters, which he ignored. If those examples were not enough to convince him that the war had changed and that he needed to accommodate these political changes, the obvious paralysis of his operations during the summer should have persuaded him to depart from his soft-war views.

If Buell needed reassurance that his industry in coping with the overwhelming problems of moving his army east was appreciated, Halleck provided at least a gesture of encouragement on July 12. He advised Buell to be more patient with the amateurs in Washington, who had "no conception of the length of our lines of defense and of operations," especially since "the disasters before Richmond [had] worked them up to a boiling heat." He closed by assuring Buell that his movements would be "properly explained" to the president. Four days later, Halleck was appointed general in chief of the armies and became one of those impatient authorities in Washington.[43]

McClellan's failed attempts to get at Richmond in the summer of 1862 cast new light on the war in the West in general and on Buell in particular. Political leaders and newspapermen were no kinder to Buell than they had been to McClellan. The longer his campaign continued, the more critical the press became. The editor of the *Indianapolis Daily Journal* questioned the whereabouts of Buell's army. "He has . . . the best appointed and best drilled army in the West," wrote the editor, "and for all the country knows of him, he might as well be in the middle of Brazil."[44] The editor of the *Daily Nashville Union* declared Buell the "master of inactivity" because of his snail-like pace across northern Alabama.[45]

By this time, soldiers and officers had become disheartened as well by Buell's solicitous treatment of the population in his attempt to pacify them. Some soldiers could simply not understand why Buell continued to protect Southern civilians when it was evident that these same people had assisted the Confederates by giving them food, water, and information. Major Keifer had written scathing letters to his wife about Buell's conciliation and slowness since the fall of Nashville. Regarding the general's conciliation policy and delay, he complained that under Buell's command, "the most contemptuous rebel in this country has more claims upon his time and is entitled more of his consideration than any officer in his army." He declared, "We will rejoice to get away from his command. I . . . fear that unless more magnanimity is shown among our generals, we might just as well hang up the fiddle for this war." Three days later, Keifer wrote: "We still hope and pray that we get out of Buell's command.—(Buell is either a weak imbecile man, or a *secession* sympathizer.)"[46] Although Keifer's sentiments certainly did not reflect the view of the entire army, a significant portion of the soldiers had become similarly disheartened.[47]

Although the Chattanooga campaign assumed more prominence after Lincoln ordered McClellan from the Virginia peninsula, its problems eclipsed its importance. On July 12 Buell received the good news that the railroad was repaired and that a trainload of supplies would be on the way to Stevenson the following day. Finally, Buell would be able to put his army back on full rations and move to Chattanooga with renewed strength. The completion of the bridge repairs at the Elk River meant that the Nashville and Chattanooga Railroad was open to Stevenson. For Buell, however, good news always seemed to have a false sense of optimism. Sunday, July 13, might as well have been Friday, for Buell's luck could not have been worse. On that day, Nathan Bedford Forrest, who had been hovering around McMinnville, swooped down on Murfreesboro, destroying the depots containing all government supplies that could not be transported and wrecking the Nashville and Chattanooga Railroad bridges in the immediate vicinity. The news was bad indeed. "We are living from hand to mouth," Buell's chief of staff James B. Fry telegraphed to the Nashville adjutant on the fourteenth.[48] The repair crews had barely completed their work near Murfreesboro when Forrest struck again near Nashville on July 21. He wrecked the bridges over Mill Creek, and Buell's troops remained on half rations. Again the Union repair gangs went to work, and within a week they had the railroad ready to operate. The first train pulled into Stevenson from Nashville with 210,000 rations on July 29. Another train followed the next day, and the troops went back on full rations—but it was too late.[49]

The ominous cloud that had hung over Buell's army since it began the campaign burst on July 20 when General Grant, writing from Corinth, warned Buell that Braxton Bragg was headed toward Chattanooga. Eight days later, Brig. Gen. William S. Rosecrans confirmed Grant's suspicions. The final determination came from General McCook, who informed Buell that Bragg had arrived at Chattanooga on the twenty-ninth and made preparations to concentrate his 35,000 troops and then cross the river. What Lincoln, Halleck, Johnson, and Keifer had feared had now become a reality.[50]

With the news that Bragg had reached Chattanooga, Buell faced the anticipated chiding from the administration. "There is great dissatisfaction here at the slow movement of your army toward Chattanooga," Halleck wrote from Washington. Buell responded that it was "difficult to satisfy impatience."[51] To add to his frustration, Buell learned that John Hunt Morgan had struck the tunnel at Gallatin on the Louisville and Nashville Railroad on August 12, essentially isolating Nashville and rendering the railroad from Louisville to Nashville useless for over three months. This crippled Buell's supply line and consequently his efforts to concentrate his forces to strike at Bragg. Buell's army continued to deteriorate because of its paralyzed state. Sickness and the shortage of forage and food took their toll. By mid-August the stationary Union army had thoroughly exhausted the countryside of forage and provisions. Bragg, by contrast, had restored morale to his soldiers, saying that the army had "improved in health and strength and has progressed rapidly in discipline, organization and instruction."[52]

With the news of Bragg's concentration with Kirby Smith's army at Chattanooga, Buell wrote, "I shall march upon Chattanooga at the earliest possible day, unless I ascertain certainly that the enemy's strength renders it imprudent."[53] Finally, Buell was excited into action, but it was too late. He would eventually get the chance to fight Bragg, but it would not be in Tennessee; it would be in the Bluegrass state two months later.[54]

The campaign to Chattanooga probably taught Buell more about unlimited war than he could ever have imagined. He learned at the hands of Nathan Bedford Forrest and John Hunt Morgan. Still, the logistical problem of protecting 300 miles of railroad proved only as crippling to the Army of the Ohio as Buell allowed it to be. The trouble with the Chattanooga campaign was Buell's continued emphasis on securing the means of getting to Chattanooga rather then concentrating on Halleck's objectives. From the beginning of the campaign, Buell's march was "like holiday soldiering," with the average day's march beginning at dawn and ending long before noon. Major Keifer considered Buell's policy of "*Watch* and *Wait*" frustrating and debilitating almost to the point of treachery.[55]

The idea that it might be good to beat Bragg to Chattanooga certainly bothered Halleck more than it did Buell. After six weeks of campaigning, Buell came within striking distance of the Confederates but never struck. His offensive campaign became a defensive one. On August 18, in an attempt to get Buell to use his troops more effectively, Halleck told Buell that the dissatisfaction in Washington at his "apparent want of energy and activity" was so strong that Lincoln had ordered Buell removed. Halleck, however, had managed to convince the president that Buell should not be removed at that time, no doubt because "Old Brains" feared that he could not find a suitable replacement.[56] The following day, Buell moved his headquarters to Dechard, which placed his army at the central point of his line extending from Jasper to McMinnville. He was as uncertain of Bragg's movement as Bragg had been of Buell's march to Chattanooga. Bragg considered combining with Kirby Smith's army, fighting Buell south of Nashville, and then invading Kentucky.

Smith, however, chose to move north independently and left Bragg in the position of keeping Buell from capturing Chattanooga or pursuing Smith into Kentucky. By the end of August, Bragg determined to follow Smith, keeping his army between Smith's and Buell's and heading for either Nashville or Lexington. The Union campaign to Chattanooga was finished, and the Confederate campaign into Kentucky began.[57]

Clearly the evidence supports Buell's claims of logistical difficulties in carrying out the Chattanooga campaign. Still, Buell became a victim of his own philosophy of war. In arguing that his goal was not just to get to Chattanooga but to be in a favorable position upon arrival, he illustrated one of the hallmarks of his command—emphasizing preparation over movement. Buell was nothing if not thorough, and securing the logistics of getting to east Tennessee would allow him to maneuver his army into position, perhaps without risk or fighting. Buell had convinced himself that despite its vulnerability, the railroad was the only way to move an army in an offensive campaign.

Of course, there was considerably more to Buell's campaign than just the logistical problems of supplying his army via the railroad. Buell worried about an incomplete occupation of east Tennessee. An incomplete occupation would not sustain political restoration and would jeopardize otherwise innocent civilians when the Union army had to leave. Had Buell not been so determined to secure the means of sustaining a permanent occupation, he might have considered more seriously the desires of his superiors. But as a thorough military practitioner, Buell tried to prepare for every contingency. At a time when the president was judging generals by the standard of victory, Buell would have to prove himself capable of success as the test of merit.[58]

Another consideration that surfaced during the commission's hearings had to do with Buell's failure to catch Bragg and evidence that Buell believed his army to be inferior to Bragg's. During his cross-examination of Gen. Lovell H. Rousseau, Buell made several references to the superior discipline of the Confederate army and its steadiness under fire. Although Rousseau did not wholly agree with Buell's assessment, he did agree with Buell's conclusion that discipline often determined success on the battlefield. This reinforced Buell's contention that the conditions of the summer had unraveled the discipline of his army and rendered it inferior to Bragg's. He simply failed to realize that he was responsible for his army's condition and, consequently, its inferiority.[59]

At the core of Buell's reluctance to move swiftly into east Tennessee was the fact that his actions might compromise his beliefs about waging war itself. Fundamental to those beliefs was the protection of the constitutional rights of citizens—including Southerners and slavery. Therefore, Buell extended his policy of conciliation with every mile the army marched through northern Mississippi and Alabama. In this, Buell played the politics of pragmatism and idealism—practical in its application, idealistic in its expectation. Buell did not want to alienate the citizenry, so he refused to live off the countryside or the people more liberally. He thought that this might prevent his army from incurring the wrath of the citizens and might enable him to secure necessities that might otherwise have been concealed or destroyed. "Wars of invasion," Buell wrote, "always difficult, become tenfold so when the people of the invaded territory take an active part against the invading army." He added, "These considerations are of such importance to success that there is no exception to the rule of securing the neutrality if not the friendship of the [enemy's] population."[60]

Buell believed that his army was an extension of good government and extended the olive branch whenever and wherever he could. In this he remained consistent to his belief in a limited war for limited goals, even when it became evident that the federal government had moved beyond such constitutional restraints, and even when many of his soldiers opposed him. He wanted to restore the antebellum Union rather than wage war as a contest that would bring considerable social change to the slaveholding South. He refused to think that his policy of conciliation had contributed to such a condition. And despite being stuck out in Mississippi and Alabama, Buell was aware that the war had shifted; Johnson's appointment as military governor signaled an expansion of war aims, and Congress's passage of the second Confiscation Act in July signaled a change in the conduct of war. The problem was that Buell was in a vulnerable position in the campaign when war turned hard.[61]

In the end, for Buell, perception proved more of a curse than a blessing. If he appeared a confident and disciplined commander who maintained the respect of his troops, it merely belied a commander with an incomplete idea of the kind of war the Union was fighting. From its inception, the Chattanooga campaign had little chance of succeeding, not because of the logistical difficulties of relying on the railroad, but because Buell had become convinced that, for the safety of his army, it was necessary to rely on the railroad as the only means of securing his objectives of waging a limited war. If getting to Chattanooga represented anything to Buell, it represented departing from his philosophy of war. Thus, while Buell held firm to his attitude about waging limited war, the Union was applying a new criterion to generals who proved unsuccessful. "The government seems determined to apply the guillotine to all unsuccessful generals," Halleck wrote in the summer of 1862. "It seems rather hard to do this when the general is not at fault; but, perhaps, with us now, as in the French Revolution, some harsh measures are required." In the fall of 1862, Buell, like McClellan, suffered the effects as Lincoln removed him from command.[62]

Chapter Five

In Defense of Fighting Joe Hooker

Stephen W. Sears

Maj. Gen. Joseph Hooker gets a uniformly bad press from Civil War historians. "Fighting Joe" invariably lags toward the bottom of any ranking of commanders of the Army of the Potomac, clumped together with John Pope and Ambrose Burnside. The old whispers that he was drunk at Chancellorsville, his one battle as army commander, are whispered anew. Alternatively, if it is allowed that he was in fact sober at Chancellorsville, his fault was going teetotal upon assuming his new responsibilities; it would have been better for the army if he had downed a few whiskeys when the fighting began in the Virginia wilderness. As T. Harry Williams puts it, "The sudden shutting off of his familiar stimulant was bad for Hooker. He depended on whiskey to brace his courage."[1]

But the historians' primary charge against Joe Hooker is that, drunk or sober, when he was confronted by Robert E. Lee at Chancellorsville, he lost his nerve and thereby lost the battle. James McPherson describes the scene metaphorically: "Like a rabbit mesmerized by the gray fox, Hooker was frozen into immobility." Authorities point to firm documentation for their case—an admission

Adapted from Stephen Sears's forthcoming book, *Controversies and Commanders of the Civil War: Dispatches from the Army of the Potomac* (Boston: Houghton Mifflin, 1999).

of his loss of nerve by Hooker himself. In their acclaimed studies, Shelby Foote, Bruce Catton, and Kenneth P. Williams all quote the general's confession. Hooker's biographer Walter H. Hebert adopts the confession as a chapter title: "Hooker Loses Confidence in Hooker." A profile of Hooker in *American Heritage* trumpets, "He was close to winning the Civil War when he suffered an almost incredible failure of nerve." In final sanctification, Hooker's words are given voice in Ken Burns's 1990 television epic *The Civil War*.[2]

Is it any wonder, then, that Fighting Joe Hooker's military reputation has fallen into low repute? What could be worse than an army commander losing his nerve in the midst of a battle? In fact, there is something worse—that general confessing his failing. For the historian seeking to document how the Union lost the battle of Chancellorsville, here is the clear and simple answer, in the clear and simple words of the commanding general himself. And so in the books and the articles and the biographical studies—and on television—Joe Hooker has become fixed forever, as if in amber, as the general who lost his nerve.

It was not always thus. The revelation of Hooker's confession came nearly half a century after the event, and not all that many of his wartime comrades were still alive to hear of it. Joe Hooker was always tremendously popular with his men—a popularity at least the equal of McClellan's—and he was well known and admired as the general who fed his troops just as well as he led them. When he assumed command of the Army of the Potomac in January 1863, Hooker was regarded, deservedly, as the fightingest general in that army. On the peninsula, in the Seven Days, at Second Bull Run and Antietam and Fredericksburg, he had proved to be a leader who showed no fear of going in with his men (he was wounded at Antietam) and revealed no lack of decision in the heat of the fighting. Nor did the Chancellorsville defeat drive Hooker off the Civil War stage. In the Chattanooga campaign that fall, he seized Lookout Mountain in spectacular fashion, and on the road to Atlanta the following spring, his Twentieth Corps did more hard fighting for Sherman than any other outfit.[3]

Hooker remained popular and admired and respected after the war. Although crippled by strokes suffered in 1865 and 1867, he was active in veterans' affairs and visited the old battlefields and closely followed the early efforts at compiling histories of the war. He died, just shy of his sixty-fifth birthday, in 1879. A quarter century later, on Boston's Beacon Hill, an equestrian statue of Joseph Hooker, native son of Massachusetts, was unveiled with appropriate ceremony. Naysayers did not interrupt the proceedings.

Theodore A. Dodge, a fledgling historian of the war, was made uncomfortably aware of the admiration in which Hooker was held after he delivered a lecture on the battle of Chancellorsville to a Boston audience in 1885. On that occasion, Dodge found not a few faults with Hooker's generalship at Chancellorsville, although he did not accuse him of drunkenness or of losing his nerve. Not long afterward, at a reunion of veterans of the Third Corps, Hooker's old outfit, Dodge found himself the object—indeed, the victim—of an angry resolution: "Loyalty to the memory of our beloved commander, Major-Gen. Joseph Hooker, makes it a duty, on this occasion, to protest against unjust and uncalled-for criticisms on his military record as commander of the Army of the Potomac." In the words of poor Dodge, who was in attendance, "the bulk of the time devoted to talking on this occasion was used in denunciation of the wretch, in other words, myself," who had had the temerity to find fault with Fighting Joe.[4]

This is not to say that military historians of the late nineteenth century tiptoed around the subject of Chancellorsville. Dodge's attack was the sharpest delivered against Hooker, but it was certainly not the only one. After all, there was no gainsaying that he had been soundly defeated, despite having a two-to-one manpower edge over Lee, and that Jackson's surprise attack—Stonewall's last march—had victimized Hooker in dramatic fashion. As commanding general, the responsibility for the defeat was undeniably his. Hooker had been out-generaled by Lee—in which category, of course, Hooker had plenty of company. Chancellorsville was General Lee's fifth campaign in less than a year, a brief span to have taken the measure of four Union army commanders.

Although not recognized at the time—and not recognized by latter-day historians, either—Joe Hooker managed to have his say in the nineteenth-century debate over his generalship at Chancellorsville. He did so in an indirect way. Hooker wrote little after the war—there was no memoir, for example—and not a great deal during the war. Although he claimed that his report on Antietam (as printed in the *Official Records*) was written within two months of the battle, it was in fact written fifteen years later. He filed no reports for Second Bull Run or Fredericksburg, and none for Chancellorsville. As for Chancellorsville, he liked to point out that his extended testimony before the Joint Congressional Committee on the Conduct of the War in 1865 was for all intents and purposes his official report of the battle. Since his testimony, in today's parlance, was a "prepared statement," thirty-nine pages long, we can grant him his point.[5]

Hooker opened his second Chancellorsville campaign in 1876 with a letter to a Pennsylvania professor named Samuel Penniman Bates, who the year before had published a history of the battle of Gettysburg. He "rejoiced to learn," said Hooker, that Professor Bates was "at present engaged in writing a history of the campaign of Chancellorsville," and he felt "extremely anxious that its narrative should be made up *impartially* to all concerned *and truthfully* as it concerns history." At the time, the only published study of Chancellorsville was the view from the Confederate side by Jedediah Hotchkiss and William Allan—a book that Hooker volunteered to correct in detail for Bates's benefit. The general explained that he had "some manuscripts in my possession which I should like to lay before you before your work is completed." These dealt in particular with "the part Gen. Howard and his command played in the battle." As Professor Bates was soon to discover, mention of the name Oliver Otis Howard, who had commanded the Eleventh Corps at Chancellorsville, invariably caused General Hooker to see red.[6]

This letter was the first of fifty-six that Hooker wrote to Bates over the course of the next three years, the last one written just three weeks before Hooker's death in 1879. Bates had responded eagerly to Hooker's overture, especially to his offer of documents. The *Official Records* volumes on Chancellorsville were a dozen years in the future, so what the general was offering was a Civil War historian's dream come true. Having thus set the hook, the general reeled in his catch. He sent Bates long discourses defending his role in all the controverted points of the campaign. He traveled to the battlefield with the professor, a visit that Bates would later record for the readers of *Century* magazine's "Battles and Leaders" series. He read and carefully critiqued each of Bates's chapters as he finished them, making sure, among other things, that the professor was clear on

Joseph Hooker

Joe Hooker's acerbic views of such battlefield lieutenants as the Eleventh Corps' Howard, the Sixth Corps' John Sedgwick, and the cavalry's George Stoneman.

Although modern-day reviewers have characterized Bates's writing as turgid and discursive, his book is acknowledged to be "not uninformed." In point of fact, it offers the only clue we have to Joe Hooker's thinking and his decisions at several crucial points in the fighting. Hooker did not live to see the book into print—it was not published until 1882—but he seems to have been satisfied that his view of the Chancellorsville struggle would be represented. "So much *twaddle* has been written about this battle," he complained in one of his last letters to Bates, but he remained hopeful: "A day of reckoning however is close at hand, and that is all I want." Perhaps at last Fighting Joe Hooker's day of reckoning is upon us, but the path from then to now has been long and rocky.[7]

What in due course would send Joe Hooker's military reputation plummeting was nothing more sinister than a footnote in John Bigelow, Jr.'s *The Campaign of Chancellorsville*. Bigelow (as the book has come to be known) meets the description of a weighty tome. Published in a limited edition of 1,000 copies by Yale University Press in 1910, it is an oversized, imposing volume containing 528 pages, 47 maps and plans, and the draping of authority. The footnote, giving Maj. E. P. Halstead as source, appears in Bigelow's concluding chapter titled "Comments," where he describes what he terms "Hooker's irresolution in this campaign"; clearly Bigelow intended it to document that irresolution. The footnote relates an incident that took place "a couple of months" after Chancellorsville, during the march toward Gettysburg. The Army of the Potomac had just crossed the Potomac in pursuit of Lee, and army commander Hooker was riding with Abner Doubleday, who headed a division in the First Corps, when Doubleday turned to him and asked, "Hooker, what was the matter with you at Chancellorsville? Some say you were injured by a shell, and others that you were drunk; now tell us what it was." Hooker answered, frankly and good-naturedly: "Doubleday, I was not hurt by a shell, and I was not drunk. For once I lost confidence in Hooker, and that is all there is to it."[8]

It is safe to say that, since 1910, virtually every author writing about Chancellorsville or about Joe Hooker or about the change of command in the Army of the Potomac just before Gettysburg, or indeed writing any general military account of the period or any study of the Union high command, has quoted or paraphrased or cited this exchange. These authors all appear to have done so without a second thought, so imposing is Bigelow's reputation.

Give it a second thought, however, and even on the face of it there is an odor to this incident. For example, Hooker is said to have replied that, no, he was not injured by a shell at Chancellorsville. Yet in fact he was quite seriously injured when a wooden pillar of the Chancellor house, against which he was leaning, was hit by a Confederate solid shot. In the weeks after the battle, he had often spoken of this injury as a factor in his defeat, and for him to deny it ever happened is not credible. His confession is even less credible. Joe Hooker, it is true, was likely to say all manner of surprising and outrageous things, but never in disparagement of himself. Quite the contrary. He had made sure that it was widely known that it was his generals who had failed at Chancellorsville; he might have to accept the ultimate responsibility, but they were really to blame for the lost campaign. For Joe Hooker to admit to a subordinate (and within hearing of that subordinate's aide hovering nearby) that he had lost his confidence, his nerve, in the midst of battle is simply not believable.

Look closely at the reteller of this tale, E. P. Halstead, and it all quickly comes unraveled. Halstead had served on Doubleday's wartime staff, and in 1903—forty years after the alleged event—he included this conversation between Hooker and Doubleday in a letter describing the First Corps' role at Chancellorsville. Bigelow acquired the letter as research for his book. When the movements of Hooker's headquarters and of the First Corps' headquarters are tracked for this period, it is clear that they were dozens of miles apart, with never an opportunity for the two generals to meet like this. Indeed, they were never near enough to meet at *any* time on the march north from the Rappahannock and before Hooker left the army command. For good measure, the rest of Halstead's letter is a grossly inaccurate account of the First Corps' actions at Chancellorsville.[9]

Halstead's tale is not all that uncommon for Civil War historiography at the turn of the century: an elderly staff officer with at best a clouded recollection of some long-ago campfire speculation, or with at worst an urge to create a role for himself—in this case, a footnote—in the history of this war of the past. Of course the two principals were dead and unavailable to confirm or deny. Civil War bookshelves, alas, are crowded with memoirs and recollections of events that never happened, retailed by old Yanks and old Johnnies seeking a little sliver of notice in what had been the greatest experience of their lives.

With this slanderous cliché discounted, where does it leave us in evaluating Joe Hooker's generalship? It is useful to look first at what in the nineteenth century were termed the qualities for moral leadership. This was more than morality per se; it meant the whole of a man's character for leading in war. It needs to be understood, in this connection, that Joseph Hooker came into the Civil War, at least in the eyes of certain of his contemporaries, as not quite a gentleman. The antebellum army was a petty aristocracy, putting a high premium on social conformity, and with his rough edges, Joe Hooker was no model of conformity.

His biographer explains that during his posting in California in the 1850s, "Idleness led Hooker along the usual path to the devil's workshop." He played cards for money, he drank, and he pursued female companionship on a fee-for-service basis. Hooker's raffish California reputation preceded him into the Civil War. General McClellan would write that in 1861 he gave a briefing on Hooker to Mr. Lincoln: "I told him that in the Mexican War Hooker was looked upon as a good soldier but an unreliable man, & that his course in California had been such as to forfeit the respect of his comrades— that he was then a common drunkard & gambler."[10]

It is true enough that Hooker enjoyed a game of cards played for money, but that he was a common drunkard is another matter. There is good evidence that the reputation of a drinker that attached to Joe Hooker was more perceived than real. John Hay, Lincoln's wartime secretary, made a perceptive comment on the subject. In his diary, Hay described dining one evening in Washington with a group that included the general. "Hooker drank very little," he wrote, "not more than the rest who were all abstemious, yet what little he drank made his cheek hot and red & his eye brighter. I can easily see how the stories of his drunkenness have grown, if so little affects him as I have seen." This would explain the contradictions in the contemporary evidence—Hooker *appearing* to have drunk to excess when in reality he drank no more (and probably less) than the average general. It also belies the imputation, made first by the vindictive Gen. Darius Couch, that Hooker was an alcoholic who found his courage in a bottle and lost it if he stopped drinking. There are too many adamant and wholly reliable eyewitnesses to Hooker's sobriety—among them Gen. George Meade, artilleryman Charles Wainwright, and intelligence chief George Sharpe—for anyone today to believe otherwise. Joe Hooker did not abuse alcohol, nor was he dependent on it.[11]

Nevertheless, the undercurrent of tales about Hooker's drinking, originating from his California days, persisted right through his war service, apparently unquenchable. Some who saw him lying comatose after his injury at Chancellorsville, for example, spread the gossip that he was dead drunk. After the battle, George Armstrong Custer made sure that his old commander, General McClellan, knew what was behind the report of Hooker's wounding by a shell. "If anything," Custer wrote, "prevented him from succeeding, it was a wound he received from a projectile which requires a cork to be drawn before it is serviceable." Congressional investigators could find no basis for such charges. The *New York Tribune* put its best correspondent, George Smalley, on the story. "I asked everybody likely to know," Smalley reported, "and not one witness could testify to having seen General Hooker the worse for whiskey." But the gossip was too deeply rooted to disappear.[12]

Another dimension of the general's moral character acted on the gossips like pure catnip. On January 31, 1863, soon after Hooker took command of the Army of the Potomac, artillerist Charles Wainwright entered in his diary, "I am asked on all sides here if he drinks. Though thrown in very close contact with him through six months, I never saw him when I thought him the worse for liquor." Then he added, "Indeed, I should say that his failing was more in the way of women than whiskey." Blue-blooded Charles Francis Adams, Jr., grandson and great-grandson of presidents, is often quoted on this latter failing of Hooker's. During that winter of 1862–1863, sniffed Captain Adams, "the headquarters of the Army of the Potomac was a place to which no self-respecting man liked to go, and no decent woman could go. It was a combination of bar-room and brothel." During this period in Washington, it was said, the general's carriage might be found of an evening drawn up outside one or another of the city's better-known brothels; indeed, a section of Washington's Second Ward thickly packed with brothels was known—and continued to be known for many years afterward—as "Hooker's Division."[13]

In contrast to the tales of Hooker's drunkenness, there seems to be little doubt that the general patronized prostitutes, although Adams's contention that Army of the Potomac headquarters was little better than a brothel must be taken at a large discount. Age forty-eight and unmarried when he took command of the army, Hooker made no particular secret of his habit. The one myth in this connection is that the slang term for a prostitute derived from his name. In fact, "hooker," meaning prostitute, long predated the Civil War, originating probably from streetwalkers "hooking" or snaring their clients.[14] This did not prevent insiders in Washington from winking and snickering at the nice conjunction between the general's name and the general's proclivity. Some dismissed the matter with a shrug. Others regarded it as evidence of his moral unfitness for high command.

One other burden Joe Hooker brought with him from his days in California was a mutually embittering relationship with Henry W. Halleck. For the general in chief of all the North's armies and the general commanding the largest of those armies to be at loggerheads was an awkward situation, to say the least; certainly it was one more burden that President Lincoln had to bear. Halleck was characteristically guarded on the subject, saying only that Hooker was aware "that I know some things about his character and conduct in California, and, fearing that I may use that information against him, he seeks to ward off its effect by making it appear that I am his personal enemy." Hooker, characteristically, was not at all guarded about their dispute. During their days together in California, he explained, Halleck joined a law firm specializing in land claims, and Hooker, trying to protect the interests of acquaintances, charged Halleck to his face with "schemes of avarice and plunder. . . . Indeed I indulged in still harsher language." Whatever the truth of the matter, it sounds like something Joe Hooker would say, and in a loud voice. He insisted that Halleck carried a grudge against him right into the war. It was Halleck, he said, who had persuaded Lincoln to award command of the Army of the Potomac to Burnside in November 1862 rather than to him.[15]

Two and a half months later, when Lincoln replaced Burnside with Hooker after the Fredericksburg disaster, this time he made the decision alone, without consulting General Halleck; he recognized Halleck's predisposition. Hooker's sole condition for accepting the appointment was his insistence on an arm's-length relationship with the general in chief. Neither the Army of the Potomac "nor its commander expected justice at his hands," Hooker told the president. On all substantive matters he would deal only with Lincoln, and so it was until the finish of the Chancellorsville campaign. Halleck complained that he was the last person in Washington to know what was going on with the Army of the Potomac.[16]

Until Hooker retreated back across the Rappahannock, ending his Chancellorsville adventure, he was allowed to operate the Army of the Potomac with a free hand. He could ignore the general in chief with impunity. But as Lee's army shifted northward and became an invading force, Lincoln began drawing in the reins on his army commander. The divide between Hooker and Halleck became a major factor in the growing crisis. "It was no use for me to make a request," Hooker said, "as that of itself would be sufficient cause for General Halleck to refuse it." The president sought to smooth the path between the two with a letter to Hooker marked "private." "If you and he would use the same frankness to one another, and to me, that I use to both of you," Lincoln wrote, "there would be no difficulty. I need and must have the professional skill of both, and yet these suspicions tend to deprive me of both. . . . Now, all I ask is that you will be in such mood that we can get into our action the best cordial judgment of yourself and General Halleck."[17]

It was to no avail, of course. Neither Halleck nor Hooker would blink, and in due course they clashed, disastrously for Hooker, over the garrison at Harpers Ferry. Hooker wanted the garrison for his army, Halleck refused him, and Hooker filed his resignation in protest. It was accepted and Joe Hooker was gone—gone forever—from the army he had become so much a part of. Hooker noted bitterly that his successor, General Meade, was allowed to do as he wished with the Harpers Ferry garrison. In his valedictory to the Joint Congressional Committee on the Conduct of the War, Hooker leveled a broadside at Halleck. "If the general-in-chief had been in the rebel interest," he testified, "it would have been impossible for him . . . to have added to the embarrassment he caused me from the moment I took command of the army of the Potomac to the time I surrendered it."[18]

For historians persuaded by Bigelow's footnote that Joe Hooker had lost his nerve at Chancellorsville, it was but a short step to the conclusion that he welcomed the chance to relinquish army command in the face of the new test looming ahead. General Hooker, wrote T. Harry Williams, "was looking for an excuse to get rid of his command. He was afraid of Lee." But once the Bigelow footnote is deleted, the matter takes on a different cast.

It is widely acknowledged that Hooker's march north from the Rappahannock was carried out with considerable skill. It was Hooker who dispatched cavalry to the town of Gettysburg as the most likely point of concentration for the Confederates, and his moves shadowing Lee seem to have been taken with considerable confidence. This was in spite of the fact that he was in constant friction with the general in chief and was the recipient of a warning from Lincoln: "I must tell you that I have some painful intimations that some of your corps and division commanders are not giving you their entire confidence." Indeed, it seems that the real purpose behind Hooker's resignation was merely to precipitate a showdown with Halleck. Hooker's comment on the change of command, although written later, appears to be a true reflection of his feelings in the summer of 1863. The "wavering and vacillating" of some of his lieutenants did bother him, he admitted. "However," he wrote, "this would have been a source of no regret, could I have commanded, *as I wished to,* at Gettysburg, but the fates were against me."[19]

In contrast to the McClellan era, Lincoln's relationship with Hooker as army commander had been comfortable and open. The president was remarkably candid with his general when appointing him to the command, and Hooker responded with full reports of his intentions and details of his plans. He also respected, and acted on, the president's suggestions. Whatever Joe Hooker's failings—and Lincoln was very much aware of them—this man would fight. He might be rash, he might intrigue for promotion, but on his record he would fight. It will be remembered that the president had said of another general, Ulysses S. Grant, under a cloud after Shiloh, "I can't spare this man; he fights."[20]

At first, after Chancellorsville, Lincoln gave Hooker the benefit of the doubt. He was not disposed, he said, to throw away a gun just because it misfired once. In any case, it would look bad to the country if the administration continued to relieve generals after every battle. What finally changed the president's mind, as much as anything else, was the outspoken complaints against General Hooker by the Potomac army's high command. It did not sit well with these corps commanders when Hooker blamed some of their own—specifically, Howard, Sedgwick, and Stoneman—for the Chancellorsville defeat. A generals' revolt had been a major factor in Burnside's overthrow; now the same fate befell Joe Hooker—ironically, one of the originators of high-command discontent in this army.

When Lincoln warned Hooker about his dissident generals, he observed that the effect of such a revolt on the army would be "ruinous." With a showdown battle sure to be fought any day somewhere in Maryland or Pennsylvania, it was vital that there be harmony among the generals who had to direct the fighting. The dissidents made it clear to Lincoln that Meade was their choice, Hooker had commended Meade as his best corps commander. With John Reynolds having taken himself out of contention for the high command, Meade's appointment was made without debate. Joe Hooker would have no second chance against Robert E. Lee; the fates, as he said, were against him.[21]

Amidst all the controversy that has swirled about this larger-than-life figure, all the gossip and debate about his moral character, it is easy to overlook how well Hooker was prepared for army command when compared with most of his fellows. The primary training ground for the Civil War officer had been the Mexican War. Much has been said of Lee's scouting missions on the march to Mexico City, Jackson fighting his guns at Chapultepec, McClellan's bravery under fire, and other such exploits. Yet beyond the indelible experience of serving under enemy fire, the tactical lessons of Mexico were mostly those of the smoothbore era. The age of rifled armaments—Springfields and Enfields and Parrotts—ushered in by the Civil War was something new under the sun for the American soldier.

What could be gained from the war with Mexico, however, was the experience of military administration—how to run a command, and how to serve as chief of staff to no less than five generals. None was a professional; each relied on Major Hooker to run his command for him. This involved, in addition, leading troops in combat often enough to earn him three brevets for gallantry. When Hooker met

Lincoln for the first time, after First Bull Run, he blurted out, "I was at Bull Run the other day, Mr. President, and it is no vanity in me to say that I am a damned sight better general than any you had on that field." He may have spoken brashly, but he had the credentials to back up his brashness. And he did back it up.[22]

There is something refreshing about such candor, and there is something refreshing about Joe Hooker. By all accounts, he was open and warm and disarmingly sincere in his personal relationships. "A gallant and chivalrous soldier," Gen. Alpheus Williams said of him, "and most agreeable." To be sure, Hooker talked far too much and too indiscreetly and with too much brag, but what he said, upon examination, often sounds suspiciously like the truth. His boast to Lincoln that he was a better general than any the Union had at First Bull Run is an example. Look at some of the Union names on that battlefield—McDowell, Heintzelman, Keyes, Hunter—and one is inclined to agree. When he said that Ambrose Burnside had a brain the size of a hickory nut, he may not have been far off the mark. Hooker liked to boast, before Chancellorsville, that he had the finest army on the planet, and considering the sorry state of the army that he had inherited from Burnside, and how he had restored it to life, there was truth there, too. In the midst of the Chancellorsville fight he issued an address to his army, saying, "our enemy must either ingloriously fly, or come out from behind his defenses and give us battle on our own ground, where certain destruction awaits him." This would be much derided, yet at the time of its issue it was a perfectly accurate statement of the case—and, if the truth be acknowledged, "certain destruction" ought to have been Lee's fate.[23]

Joe Hooker was outspoken enough to wear his ambition on his sleeve. He sincerely believed that he was a better general than George McClellan (and he was) and that his fighting record rated him the command in McClellan's place. He had no doubt at all that he was a better general than Ambrose Burnside (and without a doubt he was), and he unblushingly campaigned for Burnside's spot. The Army of the Potomac, rooted and grown to maturity in Washington, was the most politicized of Civil War armies, which fact Hooker understood perfectly; to get ahead in that army, one had to have friends in high places. It was necessary and vital that he work at that. General Halleck, head of the army, was his enemy and the roadblock to his advancement, but Hooker hoped to neutralize Halleck by cultivating members of Congress and the two cabinet members he regarded as the most influential—Secretary of War Stanton and Secretary of the Treasury Chase. Others might call this intrigue; Hooker called it pragmatism.

The one friend in high places who understood Hooker best was, of course, Abraham Lincoln. His famous letter of January 26, 1863, handed to Hooker along with his appointment as Army of the Potomac commander, weighed the general's assets and liabilities in blunt but kindly fashion. After fifteen months of frustration trying to reach and reason with General McClellan, Lincoln, commander in chief, was determined that this general understand exactly what was expected of him. The letter's candor also owed much to the Lincoln-Hooker arrangement to shunt Halleck to the sideline in the forthcoming campaign; if Hooker insisted on dealing only with the president, it was best that he be clear on where he stood with the president. Hooker calmly accepted Lincoln's criticism that "you have taken counsel of your ambition" in undercutting Burnside, "in which you did a great wrong to the country," for he believed that the accusation was spread by Burnside himself as vengeance for losing the army command. Hooker was quoted as saying, "That is just such a letter as a father might write to his son," and it "ought to be printed in letters of gold." He was careful to preserve the letter, arranging for its publication in Professor Bates's book on Chancellorsville and in the *Official Records*.[24]

Hooker took hold of the army command like he had been born to it, and Lincoln had every reason to be pleased with his new general. Hooker's talents as a military executive, talents honed in the Mexican War, seem to have come as a complete surprise to his contemporaries. In just two months he turned the Army of the Potomac around, to universal amazement. He cut the number of deserters on the rolls from more than 25,000 to fewer than 2,000. He introduced much-needed reforms in the daily running of the army and saw to it that the men were well fed, well clad, and well housed. This resulted in an enormous leap in morale. At the time of Hooker's appointment, Capt. Henry Livermore Abbott, a proper Bostonian, dismissed the new commander as "nothing more than a smart, driving, plucky Yankee, inordinately vain & . . . entirely unscrupulous." Six weeks later Abbott was writing, "I must give Hooker the credit of saying that this step is the very best for the army that could be taken." The *New York Times* editorialized that the Army of the Potomac "is about as much Hookerized as it was at one time McClellanized."

These administrative changes and reforms were so solidly grounded that in the aftermath of the Chancellorsville defeat in May 1863, there was nothing like the virtual collapse of the army that had followed Burnside's defeat at Fredericksburg the previous December. A Massachusetts soldier summed it up by insisting, "The morale of the Army of the Potomac was better in June than it had been in January," and he recalled "nothing of that spirit of insubordination and despondency." To Joe Hooker's lasting credit, if he led the Potomac army to defeat at Chancellorsville, he left it strong enough to survive and win at Gettysburg. In that sense he might be better remembered as "Administrative Joe" than "Fighting Joe." [25]

A second aspect of Hooker's generalship—one largely unappreciated by historians—was his dedicated effort to finding a new way to fight once he was in command and got his army to the battlefield. Throughout his fighting record, from Williamsburg on the peninsula under McClellan to Fredericksburg under Burnside, Hooker had been in the forefront of frontal attacks. At Williamsburg his division suffered almost 1,600 casualties in an unsupported frontal attack. In the Seven Days battles he defended against enemy frontal attacks. At Second Bull Run he led a frontal attack, on Pope's orders and under protest, and pronounced it "a useless slaughter." At Antietam he lost a third of his corps in a head-to-head slugging match with Stonewall Jackson. At Fredericksburg, in a fury at Burnside's tactics, he assaulted Marye's Heights, "lost as many men as my orders required me to lose," and suspended the attack. It was obvious that the rifled musket and the rifled cannon had made storming tactics tragically costly. There had to be, Hooker thought, a better way.[26]

The particular problem Hooker faced in the Chancellorsville campaign was to mount an aggressive offensive, yet not throw his army against an entrenched enemy as Burnside had done—and in fact, the enemy was far better entrenched than it had been at Fredericksburg. All Hooker's planning, all his maneuvering at Chancellorsville, was designed, first, to force Lee out of his entrenchments and, second, to press on Lee the choice of either attacking the Federals or giving up the Rappahannock line and falling back on

Richmond. And after three days of brilliant maneuvering, Hooker achieved exactly that position.

Then came the familiar story, with everything going sour for Fighting Joe. There was more than ample justification for each of the charges he leveled against his lieutenants. Howard, Sedgwick, and Stoneman in particular were dismal failures on this battlefield. There were flukish failures of communications. Hooker made important tactical errors. Yet in spite of all these failings and missteps, the battle was winnable for the Union during the furious fighting on the morning of Sunday, May 3—until the moment General Hooker was hurled unconscious to the front porch floor of the Chancellor house by a solid shot from one of Porter Alexander's rifled pieces firing from Hazel Grove.

Without Hooker's loss-of-nerve confession to explain his Chancellorsville defeat, this battlefront injury assumes major importance. It was 9 A.M. when Hooker went down. For three hours that morning he had been managing the contest like the Fighting Joe of past battles—personally posting his infantry and his guns, rushing reinforcements to threatened points, riding his lines to encourage his troops. He was in his element. Whatever else had gone wrong, one thing had gone right and was happening according to Hooker's original plan—the Confederates were being forced to use storming tactics on this battlefield. The night before, after Jackson's flank attack on the Eleventh Corps, Gouverneur Warren was briefed by Hooker on how he planned to meet the enemy's renewed assault on May 3: "Genl. Hooker," Warren explained, "made his dispositions accordingly and intends to flank and destroy Jackson."[27] That remained his aim: let the enemy fully commit his forces in attack, then counter with a flank assault using his reserves. On the porch of the Chancellor house, Hooker was too far forward for safety—Alexander had learned from prisoners that the house was Hooker's headquarters, and he took it under fire deliberately—but it offered a commanding view of the field, and Hooker was always a general who led from the front.

The morning had been an unrelenting struggle of attack and counterattack, tilting first to the Confederates, then to the Federals. At nine o'clock the tilt was Confederate, but to achieve that, Jeb Stuart—who had replaced the wounded Jackson in command of that wing of the army—had committed his last reserves. Hooker's reserves were still ample, and at the moment he was hit he was being handed a call for reinforcements to meet Stuart's charge. The solid shot hit the wooden porch pillar, split it lengthwise, and (in Hooker's words) hurled half of it "violently against me . . . which struck me in an erect position from my head to my feet." He lay unconscious for between thirty and forty minutes. At first it was assumed that he had been killed. When he was found to be breathing, Dr. Jonathan Letterman, his medical director, expressed doubt that he would revive. When at last Hooker regained consciousness and tried to mount his horse to show himself and reassure the troops, he collapsed and vomited. In a daze, he was carried to the rear. "The blow which the General received seems to have knocked all the sense out of him," a staff man told his family. "For the remainder of the day he was wandering, and was unable to get any ideas into his head." Gen. Abner Doubleday wrote that Hooker "suffered great pain and was in a comatose condition for most of the time. His mind was not clear, and they had to wake him up to communicate with him."[28]

These are the classic symptoms of severe concussion. For the rest of the day the commanding general drifted in and out of awareness; he probably suffered periods of amnesia. The question here is why Darius Couch, the senior general on the field, did not immediately take the command. The answer lies in the absence of Dan Butterfield from field headquarters. Butterfield, Hooker's chief of staff, was directing the army's left wing around Fredericksburg. In his place temporarily on the other wing, with Hooker at the Chancellor house, was James Van Alen. Brigadier General Van Alen was a Sunday soldier, a wealthy New York political appointee with no particular skills whom Halleck had recently palmed off on Hooker's headquarters. Van Alen had no idea what to do in this crisis, and apparently no one told him. Dr. Letterman, who was authority for the fact that Hooker was incapable of command and ought to be replaced, seems to have been reluctant to take any action without a decisive chief of staff to lead the way. General Couch was eventually called to the scene, but by then, Hooker had regained consciousness and, superficially at least, appeared to be uninjured. As Couch put it, "I went about my own business."[29]

Hooker collapsed soon afterward, and it was at least half an hour before he was rational enough to call Couch back. It had been more than an hour since Hooker was first struck down, and in that time the battle reached its crisis and then slid rapidly into the Confederates' hands. Every call to headquarters for reinforcements from Union commanders on the firing lines had been met by silence. The high command was struck mute. Even now there might have been a chance for victory—Reynolds's First Corps and Meade's Fifth had hardly been engaged all morning—but it would not be risked. Meade pleaded the case, and Hooker refused him. He turned command over to Couch, with orders to pull back to a new line to protect the army's Rappahannock crossings. Hooker's impaired mental faculties were focused narrowly on one object—to save the army. His plan seemed a shambles. His reasoning was clouded. Over the next days his mind began to clear, but even then he could think of nothing more than inviting an attack by Lee against his fortified lines. Then, after yet another communications failure, Sedgwick and the Sixth Corps recrossed the Rappahannock prematurely, and Hooker was done. He recrossed the river with the rest of the army. Joe Hooker's grand campaign, begun with such high hopes, ended not with a bang but with a whimper.

Less than two months later, Potomac army commander Hooker met the same fate as his four predecessors. The question in Washington now became what to do with him. In contrast to the earlier four, Lincoln was active in supporting a fighting role for Fighting Joe Hooker. "I have not thrown Gen. Hooker away," he told Meade, and attempted to promote a corps command for Hooker in the Army of the Potomac. Meade managed to evade this possibility. "It would be very difficult for Hooker to be quiet under me or anyone else," he remarked in a private letter, and there was truth to that. It is hard to imagine the irrepressible Joe Hooker meekly playing the subordinate in the army he had once commanded.[30]

The solution was found when it was decided to send reinforcements to Rosecrans in the western theater in the form of the Eleventh and Twelfth Corps from the Army of the Potomac. These two corps had never been at home in the Potomac army—especially the Eleventh Corps, with unhappy experiences at both Chancellorsville and Gettysburg—and the army was glad to see them gone. This offered the answer to the Hooker problem—let him command the two orphaned corps.

When the command structure in the West was reshaped, Hooker found himself increasingly an outcast. Grant, put in overall command in the western theater, seemed to resent Fighting Joe being forced on him from Washington and hoped to be rid of him. General Grant, it was reported to Secretary Stanton, felt that Hooker's "presence here is replete with both trouble and danger." Hooker's strong showing in taking Lookout Mountain during the Chattanooga campaign did not persuade Grant, who in his recollections was dismissive of Hooker's so-called battle above the clouds. "It is all poetry," he said contemptuously. Hooker said defiantly, "I find I am regarded with a great deal of jealousy by those filling high places here," but he believed that his soldiership, as he called it, would carry him through: "I have never yet seen the time that there was no place for a man willing to fight."[31]

In the spring of 1864, now under William Tecumseh Sherman, Hooker marched on Atlanta in command of his two corps consolidated as the newly formed Twentieth Corps. He could take no comfort from having to report to Sherman. Sherman, who had served with Hooker in the California days, wrote even before Chancellorsville: "I know Hooker well and tremble to think of his handling 100,000 men in the presence of Lee."[32] Presumably, Sherman thought that Chancellorsville confirmed his prediction. Like Grant, he felt that he had to tolerate Hooker because he was the president's choice. In any event, Hooker directed his corps effectively all during the advance to Atlanta's outskirts. Indeed, the Twentieth Corps did most of the fighting on this march and suffered by far the most casualties—over 5,000.

In the battle for Atlanta, Gen. James B. McPherson, commanding the Army of the Tennessee, was killed in action. The natural choice seemed to be to name Maj. Gen. John A. Logan, who had succeeded McPherson during the fighting as senior officer on the field, as permanent commander of the Army of the Tennessee. But Sherman passed over Logan as army commander because he was not a West Pointer, naming Oliver Otis Howard instead.

Of all the corps commanders under Sherman, Hooker had the most seniority and the most experience—experience in, among other things, commanding an army. He believed that he was entitled to McPherson's command. To give it to Howard, his former subordinate and the man he believed above all others to be responsible for the Chancellorsville defeat, he took as an insult on Sherman's part, and a carefully calculated insult at that. Hooker's resignation was prompt. "Justice and self-respect alike require my removal from an army in which rank and service are ignored," he explained.[33]

So ended Fighting Joe Hooker's service in the Civil War. How might he be summed up? Of two things we can be sure—he was not a drunk, and he never lost his nerve in battle. Once these canards are out of the way, it may be possible to paint him in more realistic colors. In that essential role of an officer—to take care of his men— he was paramount. No general on either side was better at that than Joe Hooker. No general in the Army of the Potomac had a better combat record. In every battle in which he was engaged—except one—his performance has to be rated at least creditable and at best excellent. He was rough-edged and not much of a gentleman, and he talked too much and too loudly. He did not bother to disguise his ambition, and he did not suffer fools gladly. As to the battle for which he will always be remembered, Joe Hooker is entitled to be heard. "You may like to know my opinion of the battle of Chancellorsville," he wrote to Professor Bates. "I won greater success on many fields in the war, but nowhere did I deserve it half so much." Sitting in judgment after Chancellorsville, Lincoln said, "I have not thrown Gen. Hooker away." Nor should we.[34]

Chapter Six

Misused Merit: The Tragedy of John C. Pemberton

Michael B. Ballard

His heart was never in the Civil War, and his level of talent was not sufficient to meet his superiors' expectations of him. Such was the dilemma that confronted and eventually overwhelmed John Clifford Pemberton after his country divided and went to war in 1861.

Born in 1814 to a Philadelphia, Pennsylvania, Quaker family, he had walked away from the nonviolent tenets of the Friends' faith.[1] Influenced by his father's friendship with military hero Andrew Jackson, Pemberton, through Jackson, received an appointment to the U.S. Military Academy in 1833.[2]

Pemberton's years at West Point demonstrated that he had neither the soul nor the mind of a warrior. His best marks were in drawing, and his best times were partying, with both female guests and fellow cadets. He did excel at currying favor with the academy's commandant, and that no doubt worked in his favor when he was nearly expelled during his senior year for dereliction of duty.[3] Pemberton finished twenty-seventh out of fifty in the class of 1837; he had accumulated 163 demerits during his four years at West Point.[4]

Following graduation, Pemberton was commissioned second lieutenant in the Fourth U.S. Artillery. He also dallied with the idea of becoming a husband. His family protested, and ultimately he ended the relationship, enlisting his father's help to break the news

141

to the young lady in question. Lieutenant Pemberton thus displayed marks of immaturity and an unwillingness to take charge of his own responsibilities.[5]

Pemberton's first combat experience came in the Second Seminole War in Florida. Actually he participated in little fighting, for he soon used the stroking abilities he had honed at West Point to lobby, albeit unsuccessfully, for an adjutant position under a colonel. Later he did become head of an ordnance depot and landed an administrative post at a fort. Though he may have cozied up to superior officers in order to get jobs, Pemberton excelled at such duties. By the time he left Florida, he had earned a reputation as a solid staff officer.[6]

The young Pennsylvanian continued to gain staff experience in the milieu of service at various army posts in the South, Midwest, and Northeast until the outbreak of the Mexican War in 1846.[7] By that time he had met and fallen in love with Martha "Pattie" Thompson, a Norfolk, Virginia, girl whom he would marry after his return from Mexico.[8] His union with her would cause him great anguish about choosing sides in the Civil War.

Aside from his fateful love affair, Pemberton had undergone other experiences that did not portend well for his future as a general in the Confederate army. Service at isolated forts had hardened him. He was no longer the carefree cadet of West Point days. He occasionally clashed with recruits and fellow officers, frequently over mundane matters, setting a pattern that would continue throughout the remainder of his military career.[9]

The Mexican War was a proving ground of sorts for young West Point alumni who would experience their first combat in a conventional conflict. John Pemberton's experience was very positive and indicated an excellent future. He was on the field at Palo Alto, but his first real fight occurred at Resaca de la Palma during Zachary Taylor's campaign. He performed ably in a hotly contested part of the battlefield and experienced a rush of adrenaline that convinced him that he had made the right career decision.[10]

His enthusiasm waned as the war dragged on. As Taylor led his army further into Mexico, Pemberton followed his usual pattern of meeting the right person and landing a better job. He became aide-de-camp to Gen. Williams Jenkins Worth, a quality combat veteran who, despite being rash, abrupt, inflexible, and self-centered, was in other ways a worthy role model. Unfortunately, some of Worth's negative qualities rubbed off on, and at times dominated, the personality of John Pemberton.[11]

Worth cited Pemberton for "alacrity, zeal and gallantry" at the battle of Monterey. Later, after Worth's division had been reassigned to Winfield Scott's expedition against Mexico City, Pemberton received a promotion to brevet captain for "gallant and meritorious conduct" at the battle of Molino del Rey.[12] By the time his service in Mexico ended, Pemberton had established himself as a solid soldier. However, he still had not proved himself as a combat leader. His preferences and strengths in Mexico had been in the administrative area. He was, and always would be, a staff officer at heart. The inclination had been evident in Florida and had solidified in Mexico.

After the war, Pemberton married Pattie, and they began their family. Pemberton drew duties in several areas of the country, returning for a time to Florida and serving at posts near New Orleans, in New York, and out west. In 1850 he was promoted to the regular rank of captain. Although he occasionally went out on patrols, especially during Indian trouble in the West, Pemberton's duties were mostly administrative, and though he was disappointed that he had not been able to get an assignment in Europe, he was relatively content. But civil war loomed on the horizon, and when it came, it would turn John Pemberton's world upside down. He and his family were at the remote outpost of Fort Ridgely, Minnesota, when he was recalled to Washington in early 1861.[13]

As war became a matter of when rather than if, Pemberton agonized over what he would do. Initially, he decided to remain with the North unless Virginia, Pattie's home state and a state he had grown fond of during a brief antebellum tour of duty there, left the Union. His Philadelphia family breathed a sigh of relief, but their anxiety soon returned.[14]

As the boom of guns at Fort Sumter echoed across the South, Virginia left the Union on April 17. Pemberton's older brother Israel hurried to Washington to dissuade his sibling from resigning from the U.S. Army. John wavered and did not follow through on his threat to head South once Virginia seceded. He remained in the army, obeyed orders, and listened to Israel's exhortations. The decisive words, though, came from Pattie, who was in Norfolk with the children. "Why do you stay?" she inquired, assuring him that Confederate president Jefferson Davis would have a place for him in the Southern army. Davis was in Montgomery putting together a new government, and whether he had made any promise regarding John Pemberton is not known. Whatever the case, the pressure from his beloved wife led to a decision to resign on April 24. The Philadelphia Pembertons were disappointed but not surprised and had no option but to accept John's decision and hope for the best.[15]

Pemberton's decision to turn his back on the army that had been his career for almost three decades was the toughest of his life. Despite claims of his apologists to the contrary, he was not a fanatical supporter of the Southern cause. Had he been, he would not have hesitated to go South once war came and Virginia joined the Confederacy. John Pemberton was no fire-eater, no states' rights dogmatist. In his mind, he had only two choices: he could sit out the war with its possibilities of rapid promotion and battlefield glory, hardly a pleasing option for a career officer, or he could fight for Pattie's homeland. His strong relationship with his wife settled the issue. At the same time, there seems little doubt that Pemberton's heart was not in this conflict that threatened to destroy the Union. When he turned his back on the land of his nativity, he became a traitor in the North and a suspect Yankee in the South. He had placed himself in a most uncomfortable position, and his low-key service in Virginia during the early months of the war indicates that he recognized the benefits of anonymity.[16]

Originally joining the provisional Army of Virginia, Pemberton later went into the regular Confederate army. By June 17, 1861, he held the rank of brigadier general in the artillery corps. This rapid rise in rank could be attributed to several factors. Pemberton habitually practiced the blandishment of superior officers, and Pattie's family had some influence. At what point Pemberton may have met Jefferson Davis is not known, but Davis's future actions indicated that he liked this Pennsylvanian. Also, Pemberton had originally reported for duty to Gen. Joseph E. Johnston, whom he had probably met in Mexico. At this point in the war, Johnston apparently had a good relationship with Pemberton.[17]

Despite his high rank, Pemberton remained unobtrusive. Through the summer and fall of 1861, he was in Norfolk, first supervising an artillery instructional camp and then directing his artillery brigade

John C. Pemberton

in operations around the Smithfield-Suffolk region west of Norfolk. When the first great engagement of the war took place at Manassas, Pemberton was supervising the placement of guns along the James River.[18] He may well have been content to serve out the war in this area close to Pattie's home. There is no surviving correspondence to indicate that he sought other duty. But other duty soon sought him. He was about to begin his journey into Civil War infamy.

The first phase of that journey began soon after Robert E. Lee assumed command of the defenses along the South Carolina and Georgia coasts. Lee needed brigadiers, and the War Department ordered John Pemberton to South Carolina, where Lee had set up headquarters in the Charleston area.[19] He was probably chosen because of his experience with coastal defenses in Virginia. Pemberton obeyed the orders, perhaps with some trepidation. A Pennsylvania-born general could not have been anxious to assume a post in the state that had been the cradle of secession.

As long as Lee remained in South Carolina, Pemberton continued to stay in the background as he had in Virginia. He no doubt observed Lee; his later actions indicated that he had been influenced by Lee's strategic ideas. For example, Lee concentrated on key areas of defense rather than scattering his limited resources along outlying areas of the coast. Lee also constructed an interior line of defense far inland out of range of Federal gunboats, and he used trains to move troops where needed. Lee, the man and the soldier, impressed the irascible Governor Francis Pickens of South Carolina. Pickens found Lee to be a quiet, dignified man and a "thorough and scientific officer."[20] As he later demonstrated in his relationship with Jefferson Davis, Lee knew how to handle people, especially civilian officials. Whoever followed Lee in South Carolina would face a formidable task.

When Lee was recalled to Richmond to advise Davis during the peninsula campaign in early 1862, fate, and the Confederate War Department, looked to John Pemberton to take on that task. Why Pemberton was chosen is a difficult question to answer. Why did Jefferson Davis, no matter how much he may have liked Pemberton, think that a Northern-born general could handle a commander's position in rabidly Confederate South Carolina? A possible explanation is that Davis and his advisers did not think that the situation in South Carolina and Georgia was urgent, and at this point, it was not. Therefore, it may have seemed a safe risk to assign command to an unproven commander. It is possible, too, that Davis thought that placing a Pennsylvanian in command in South Carolina might be a good propaganda move to embarrass the North.

Pemberton had done nothing spectacular since coming to the state, but he must have impressed Lee. In February 1862 Pemberton was promoted to major general. By date of appointment, he out-ranked the other brigadiers present, so his promotion was in a sense logical. But there was more to it than that. It seemed apparent that Pemberton was being groomed to take Lee's place. On March 4 Pemberton assumed temporary command, and ten days later it be-came permanent.[21]

In many respects, Pemberton proved to be a good man for the job. The tasks of the command primarily required bureaucratic skills, which he possessed and had honed through his many years in the army. Lee, too, had been a staff officer, and perhaps it was this aspect of Pemberton's work that led Lee to agree to leave his post in command of his senior lieutenant. In many ways, Pember-ton's first taste of command was a staff officer's dream—and night-mare. One of his first acts was to reorganize the districts within what had become known as the department of South Carolina and Georgia (for a brief time, parts of Florida would be added to the department).[22] There was no apparent need for the reorganization; it was probably just too much of a temptation for a general with a staff officer mentality.

Other more immediate issues inundated Pemberton, and he and his staff handled most of them quite deftly. These included secur ing construction material for boats and railroads, getting funds from Richmond to pay his soldiers, obtaining ordnance and food, keep-ing his forces at an adequate strength in the face of frequent demands for reinforcements elsewhere in the Confederacy, building adequate fortifications when neither he nor any of his staff had engineering experience or skills, making politically sensitive decisions on such issues as martial law and the use of slave labor, and devising strat-egies such as developing his interior rail lines, blocking waterways, and restricting his defensive lines to defend his department against an ever-increasing presence of the Federal navy.[23]

Although Pemberton exhibited quality administrative leader-ship in handling many of these tasks, it soon became apparent that he lacked Lee's adroitness in handling government officials. Governor Pickens was the titular head of state government and had considerable influence, but an organization called the South Carolina Executive Council, on which Pickens served, had been set up as a war measure and had a heavy hand in directing the state's affairs. The council consisted of the governor, lieutenant governor, and three men elected by South Carolina's secession convention.[24]

Pemberton never understood, as did Lee, that powerful political leaders must be cultivated and kept informed about military decisions. He made his decisions and rarely volunteered explanations, often not commenting at all until pressed by the council. A case in point was Pemberton's decision to abandon several outlying areas along the coast. Rather than scatter his forces, he sought, as Lee had done, to concentrate them for more effect. Pickens, no doubt acting with the approval of the rest of the council, complained to Lee in Richmond that the inner defenses were too thin for Pemberton to pull the troops in from the outer defensive works. Also, when the troops left, people living in those areas would be at the mercy of the Yankees. Pemberton should have at least held off to give those who wanted to evacuate time to do so.[25]

Lee had one of his aides pen a message of fatherly advice to his successor at Charleston. "It is respectfully submitted to your judgment whether, in order to preserve harmony between the State and Confederate authorities, it would not be better to notify the governor whenever you determine to abandon any position of your defenses, in order that he may give due notice to the inhabitants to look out for their own security."[26] Pemberton further undermined his credibility when he deceived himself into believing that Fort Pulaski near Savannah, Georgia, could hold out against Federal attacks. Lee had suspected that the fort's demise was inevitable and had concentrated on strengthening the interior lines around Savannah. Pemberton visited the fort on April 10, gave assurances that it would hold, and was subjected to a great deal of embarrassment when it fell the next day.[27] Misreading military situations would haunt Pemberton even more in his next command.

For the present, he continued under a cloud of suspicion that he was not up to meeting the demands of his job. He finally decided to move his headquarters to Charleston from the small town of Pocotaligo. In Charleston he could more closely supervise the constriction of his defensive lines. Shortly before he moved, he suffered yet another blotch on his public image. When a Confederate steamer's officers and men all went ashore in violation of regulations, the ship's slave crew absconded with the steamer and its five cannon and escaped into Union lines.[28]

At times, Pemberton seemed to go out of his way to feed the growing distrust of him by politicians and the general public. This was especially true in his handling of questions regarding the defense of Charleston. He proposed the dismantling of some of the forts defending the city, including Fort Sumter, the symbol of secession and the Confederate cause. Those forts might be taken by the enemy and their guns turned on the very streets they were built to defend. In suggesting the destruction of Sumter, Pemberton clearly showed that he was totally out of touch with political reality.[29]

Charleston's mayor grew concerned that abandoning the outer coastal defenses might open the way for the Federal navy to enter Charleston Harbor. He pointedly asked Pemberton if Charleston would be defended or abandoned to the enemy. Pemberton refused to commit himself based on a hypothetical situation, but he later commented that if future events should warrant the withdrawal of his troops, he would withdraw them.[30]

Pickens pleaded with Pemberton to take a firm stand. Even if the fight meant reducing the city to rubble, Pickens wrote, that would be preferable to giving up Charleston without a desperate struggle. "We can afford to lose our city, but not our honor."[31] Unlike Lee, Pemberton had no understanding of or sympathy for Southern honor; he simply would do what the military situation dictated.

At this point, Lee again wired Pemberton, this time with more strongly worded advice. Pickens had kept Lee informed of the Charleston controversy, and Lee scolded Pemberton for the latter's negativism. Savannah and Charleston both had to be strongly defended; Charleston was especially important as a supply artery. Pemberton must make known his resolve to fight it out "street by street and house by house as long as we have a foot of ground to stand upon."[32] Lee no doubt intended to make Pemberton understand the importance of building morale and sustaining optimism. Future events would suggest that Pemberton took Lee's words all too literally.

Federal pressure along the coast exacerbated the tension between Pemberton and South Carolinians. Designed primarily to keep Pemberton from sending reinforcements elsewhere, Union operations kept Charleston in an almost constant state of panic. On June 16, 1862, Confederate forces met and defeated Federal troops on James Island in the battle of Secessionville. The battle proved to be another defining moment for Pemberton, who made no effort to go to the front. Ever the staff officer and administrator, he stayed at headquarters monitoring the situation. Clearly, he was still no warrior.[33]

The victory at Secessionville did not deter a growing movement, led by Governor Pickens, to get Pemberton replaced. Lee and Jefferson Davis received a steady flow of complaints about Pemberton's leadership.[34] He did "not possess the confidence of his officers, his troops, or the people of Charleston. Whether justly or unjustly, rely upon it the fact is so."[35] Famous South Carolina diarist Mary Boykin Chesnut noted that "Pemberton said to have no heart in this business, so the city cannot be defended." Another diarist observed of Pemberton's problems, "as he is a Pennsylvanian, [he] engenders suspicion. . . . Everybody has lost confidence in Pemberton and many even suspect treachery, though it cannot be proved of course."[36]

Aside from politicians and other civilians, Pemberton had problems with a troublesome subordinate general, Roswell Ripley, and soldiers who felt that Pemberton was inviting defeat by continuing his strategy of constricting defensive lines. Like many Mexican War veteran officers, he did not think highly of volunteer soldiers, and he did little to cultivate good relations with the men in the ranks.[37]

As Pemberton's status in South Carolina deteriorated, Lee advised Davis that a new commander must be found. Confederate Adjutant and Inspector General Samuel Cooper came to the same conclusion after visiting Pemberton. Cooper thought that Pemberton had done a good job, yet "with such an opposition as constantly surrounds him it would be difficult for any commander situated as he is to effect much." Davis hesitated to act, but on August 29 he named P. G. T. Beauregard to replace Pemberton.[38] The news produced a smattering of support for him, but Pemberton was glad to be moving on to whatever the future might hold. He made it clear that he wanted to return to Virginia, perhaps to a low-profile assignment. His self-confidence had sunk to a low ebb; he wrote to Richmond that he was sure that Beauregard would prove to be "far more capable" in South Carolina.[39]

John Pemberton's time there had been illuminating. His administrative skills had served him well, but it had become obvious that he did not have Lee's talent for dealing with people. Lee had managed to gain the respect, admiration, confidence, and affection of civilians and soldiers alike, whereas Pemberton had failed in all four areas. Cadet Pemberton would probably have fared better than hardened career soldier Pemberton. Also, Lee was destined for battlefield greatness, but Pemberton had shown no affinity at all for the front. The fact seemed simple enough; he had been promoted and assigned above his capabilities in several areas. He probably realized that he had taken on too much; certainly as he entrained for Virginia he had no inkling that he would be thrust into a similar or possibly more difficult situation. Unfortunately for this forlorn Confederate Yankee, Jefferson Davis had other ideas.

On October 1, 1862, Pemberton received what he must have considered later to be an ominous order to take command of "the State of Mississippi and that part of Louisiana east of the Mississippi River." With the new job came another promotion, to lieutenant general.[40] This new assignment offered monumental challenges far greater than he had faced on the Atlantic coast.

Unlike the South Carolina command, which contained no urgent Union target, Pemberton's department of Mississippi and east Louisiana contained a major Federal objective—the Mississippi River town of Vicksburg. Since the outbreak of hostilities, combined Union army-navy operations had been working to clear the river of Confederates. Northern control of the Mississippi would split the Confederacy and restore unfettered commercial shipping to and from midwestern states. By the time Pemberton arrived in Mississippi on October 9, the major river towns of New Orleans, Baton Rouge, and Natchez south of Vicksburg had been surrendered. North of Vicksburg, Federal forces had won a major victory at Island Number 10 near the Kentucky-Tennessee border and had forced the surrender of Memphis. That left Vicksburg as the last great obstacle. Strongly fortified, the town stood on high bluffs along a sharp hairpin turn in the river. Union President Abraham Lincoln had the strategic insight to understand that Vicksburg was the key to Union victory on the Mississippi.[41]

In light of the obvious significance of fortress Vicksburg to the Confederate cause in the western theater, the question loomed then and now: why was the command given to John Pemberton? A Mississippi acquaintance of Jefferson Davis would later claim that during a personal conversation with Davis, the latter confided that he had a high opinion of Pemberton and that both Lee and Cooper, consulted by the president separately, had named Pemberton as their choice.[42] If this account is valid, the endorsement of Pemberton by Davis, Lee, and Cooper is truly incredible. Did they think that what had happened in South Carolina was an aberration?

With no other known accounts of the decision-making process, one can only speculate on the rationales that resulted in Pemberton's assignment in Mississippi. Angered by South Carolina's criticism of one of his favorites, Davis may well have decided to give Pemberton another important command as a way of taunting critics. Those same critics had often given Davis a hard time. The president could also, with some validity, argue that Pemberton had done a good job in South Carolina. Despite the criticism, most of Pemberton's former district was still in Confederate hands. Davis characteristically focused on the positive when it came to his friends, no matter how much the negatives might taint future performances.

Lee's role may be more instructive. By the time Pemberton left South Carolina, Lee had taken command of the Army of Northern Virginia, had won the peninsula and Second Manassas campaigns, and had escaped with a drawn battle at Sharpsburg. During these early months of command, Lee made it clear that he did not want problem generals in Virginia. Many such Confederate officers who started their service in the Virginia theater would eventually end up in other areas.[43] This may account for Lee supporting Pemberton. Lee also was Virginia-focused and resisted any proposal for sending his best generals west.

As for Cooper, after his visit to Charleston, he may have felt that Pemberton had been treated unjustly and deserved another chance. Whatever their motives, if these three men honestly thought that Pemberton could get the job done, they grossly miscalculated his ability. Moreover, they never seemed to appreciate fully, until it was too late, the significance or complexities of the challenges that awaited any commander of the Vicksburg area.

The Mississippi command would have challenged a commander of supreme ability. Myriad waterways offered the Union navy several possible approaches to Vicksburg. The Confederates had very little in the way of a navy to contest those approaches. Various roads, though admittedly not very good ones, gave Federal commanders several possible invasion routes. For Confederate forces, railroads were a blessing and a curse. Two ran north and south and one east and west, the latter connecting Meridian and points east with Vicksburg. They were vital to supplying Pemberton's army and providing flexibility for troop movements, but their length made them vulnerable to Union destruction or use as a supply line for General Grant's invading force in north Mississippi.[44]

Pemberton did not have numbers to match Grant, and with a few diversions, Grant could so scatter Pemberton's forces as to make them almost impotent.[45] Grant understood that and would put such a strategy to effective use. Obviously, Pemberton faced great challenges in protecting Vicksburg and in keeping his army supplied.

As the Vicksburg campaign progressed, the command structure in the West further compounded Pemberton's problems. Joseph E. Johnston, severely wounded during the early stages of the peninsula campaign, had permanently lost command of the Virginia army to Robert E. Lee. President Davis therefore appointed Johnston to command the western theater. Johnston's command included most of the territory between the Blue Ridge Mountains in North Carolina and the Mississippi River. He would be the immediate superior of both Pemberton and Braxton Bragg, who commanded the Army of the Tennessee. Pemberton continued to report directly to Richmond as he had done before Johnston's appointment. Bragg also occasionally bypassed Johnston, leaving the latter angry but powerless to remedy the situation without the support of Davis and Cooper.[46]

Johnston also had no control over the trans-Mississippi. Commanders there did not have to obey Johnston's wishes for them to cooperate with Pemberton. Davis refused to intervene, and the result was very little coordination between Confederate forces on opposite sides of the Mississippi.[47]

Not fully recovered from his severe wound, Johnston accepted the assignment with trepidation. Consequently, his heart was never in the Vicksburg campaign, at least not in it the way Richmond wanted it fought. Johnston would give up geographic points in favor of combining Pemberton's and Bragg's armies.[48] Davis would have none of it, and Pemberton would soon find himself trying to juggle his orders to appease both his immediate superior and his commander in chief. Pemberton sided with Davis; he had learned through his South Carolina experience that Richmond ultimately ruled. But the president and the War Department had created a dysfunctional command system and had placed an insecure general in the midst of it. It was surely a situation with disastrous potential.

Pemberton's actions during his initial days in Mississippi were equally foreboding. Despite the great pressure that Grant was putting on Confederate forces in north Mississippi, pushing south with the idea of taking Jackson and then moving west to Vicksburg, Pemberton preferred to spend time behind his desk in Jackson. There he sought to get his department in order through piles of paperwork, while occasionally checking on the battlefront. Also, unlike in South Carolina, he had developed a decent working relationship with the governor of Mississippi, John J. Pettus. Certainly Pemberton was no slacker; passersby often observed him working late into the night. One of his staff noted that confusion had reigned in all departments before his boss's arrival, but that order had gradually been restored thanks to the general's leadership. But Pemberton's frequent absences from the front were another indication that he was no battlefield commander. If anyone in Richmond found this disturbing, there is no record of it.[49]

As Grant pressed on, Pemberton pulled his army slowly southward to prevent Union troops from turning vulnerable flanks. His forces had retreated all the way to Grenada before salvation finally came. One of Pemberton's officers suggested a raid on Grant's supply base at Holly Springs. Given his ever-lengthening supply line, the destruction of this base might force Grant to retreat into west Tennessee. That Pemberton had not thought about such an option himself says much about his tactical and strategic abilities, but at least he had the gumption to order the raid.

Led by his predecessor, Earl Van Dorn, Confederate cavalry swooped down on Holly Springs on December 20, destroyed huge piles of Union food and ordnance, and escaped. A disgusted Grant retreated as Pemberton had hoped, and the north Mississippi campaign ended.[50] But a concomitant campaign was still alive. William T. Sherman had taken a large force down the Mississippi from Memphis to attack Vicksburg. The idea was to link up with Grant, but then came Holly Springs. Sherman should have abandoned his part of the plan, but he decided to forge ahead and attack entrenched Confederates along bluffs overlooking Chickasaw Bayou just north of Vicksburg. Pemberton, who was enjoying himself reviewing troops with visitors Jefferson Davis and Joseph E. Johnston, hurried to Vicksburg after receiving news of Sherman's approach. Actually, reports of Sherman's move down the Mississippi had begun arriving shortly after Van Dorn's raid, but Pemberton had virtually ignored them. A general with a noncombative, nonaggressive nature, Pemberton had a penchant for ignoring intelligence reports that indicated that the enemy was on the offensive.

At Vicksburg, Pemberton stayed away from the front during the battle of December 27–29. Wearing the self-imposed mantle of staff officer, he ordered reinforcements from north Mississippi to Vicksburg and funneled them to the Chickasaw front, where his subordinates Martin Luther Smith and Stephen Dill Lee orchestrated Sherman's defeat. Pemberton's staff-officer role was yet another warning ignored in Richmond.[51]

Of course there was cause for celebration. Grant and Sherman had been repulsed. Pemberton thus far had excelled in reorganizing his department, and he had kept the enemy at bay. But his battlefield successes had been as much the result of Grant's failure to guard his supplies properly and Sherman's impetuosity as of anything Pemberton had done. Despite the victories, Pemberton had developed a strictly defensive state of mind. As a result, and despite his disappointment, Grant had been allowed to set the pace of the campaign. He had not so much seized the initiative from Pemberton; rather, Pemberton had handed it over. The tenacious Grant was not one to give it back, and as the new year of 1863 approached, he began a season of diversions that left his opponent looking anxiously this way and that in a state of constant reaction to Grant's moves.

Grant put his troops to work digging a canal across from Vicksburg that would have diverted the Mississippi away from the city's fortified bluffs. The canal had been tried before, and as before, the project failed, as did a similar project called the Duckport Canal. Grant also tried cutting a path through various waterways to reach the Red River below Vicksburg. The Red emptied into the Mississippi, so such a route would make Vicksburg superfluous. But this gambit, known as the Lake Providence expedition, also failed.[52]

Two other expeditions also failed, but they underscored two glaring Pemberton weaknesses. The Yazoo Pass operation, an attempt to reach the Yazoo River via rivers flowing south from northwest Mississippi, resulted in a repulse by Confederates at Fort Pemberton near Greenwood. During the course of this successful campaign, Pemberton agitated William Loring, an aggravating general of the Ripley stripe and another eastern-theater reject. Loring complained bitterly because Pemberton would not send him more guns and men. Pemberton had few soldiers and little ordnance to spare, and he considered Loring's request unnecessary. Loring, along with one of his lieutenants, Gen. Lloyd Tilghman, formed an anti-Pemberton clique. Tilghman, an old Pemberton friend, was still bitter about a run-in he had had with the commander in north Mississippi. For the remainder of the Vicksburg campaign, dissent would grow among Pemberton's generals, and there is no evidence that he ever did anything to address the problem. Rather than build an effective team, he simply immersed himself in paperwork, leaving his command structure at times in an almost anarchical state.[53]

That state was clearly in evidence during another Grant scheme, the Deer Creek (also known as Steele's Bayou) expedition by David Dixon Porter, commander of the Union navy at Vicksburg. With Grant's blessing, Porter hoped to bypass Confederate works on Yazoo River bluffs above Vicksburg. By negotiating a series of waterways, Porter intended to reenter the Yazoo above Confederate artillery emplacements, threaten Fort Pemberton upriver, or go downriver to shell rebel works. Instead, Porter almost got trapped in the narrow waterways and was fortunate to keep his boats from falling into Confederate hands. Pemberton, anchored to his Jackson desk, was not on hand to take charge. The capture of Porter's boats would have been a significant turning point in the Confederates' favor, but Pemberton's generals in the area were more concerned with stopping Porter than with aggressively attacking him. The mentality of the commanding general was filtering down to his subordinates, with predictable results. Pemberton had become so absorbed in work that should have been delegated to his staff that he ignored the duties of leadership, and a golden opportunity slipped by when Porter's fleet steamed safely back into the Mississippi .[54]

General Grant noted his rival's weaknesses and kept up the pressure. A Federal foray inland from Greenville convinced Pemberton that Grant had given up a direct assault on Vicksburg and was going to try north Mississippi again. But by far the most spectacular and effective plan Grant devised was a cavalry raid from northwest Mississippi through the heart of the state and on to Baton Rouge. Led by Benjamin Grierson, the raid entranced Pemberton, who focused all his attention on stopping the Yankee horsemen who destroyed much rebel property, including railroads. Grierson and his men escaped practically unscathed, and while a frustrated Pemberton fumed over the raid, Grant was making a decisive move.[55]

After his series of failed efforts to approach Vicksburg, Grant had decided to move his army south down the Louisiana side of the Mississippi and cross below Vicksburg. Porter's boats ran the gauntlet of Confederate cannon to meet the army and ferry it across. Despite numerous warnings from his scouts and generals, and despite the obvious giveaway that something was afoot when Porter's boats steamed past his batteries, Pemberton continued to track Grierson until it was too late. During Sherman's Chickasaw Bayou campaign, Pemberton had ignored warnings but salvaged a victory. Now he ignored warnings and gave Grant the edge he needed to break the Vicksburg stalemate. Temporarily thwarted by rebel batteries at Grand Gulf, Grant moved his landing point farther south to Bruinsburg, where he crossed, and on May 1 he won the battle of Port Gibson, which gave him a vital foothold.[56]

With no direct rail line from Vicksburg to Port Gibson over which to send reinforcements, Pemberton had to sit by and watch his outnumbered troops fight well but ultimately lose to Grant's superior numbers. Had Pemberton paid attention to reports coming into his office from his most competent general, John Bowen, he would have had time to concentrate forces and possibly beat Grant back into the river. Trying to recover, Pemberton revealed the degree to which he had lost control of himself and the campaign. He sent an urgent message to commanders in the Jackson-Vicksburg area to proceed at once; he forgot to tell them where to go.[57]

With Grant now threatening the south flank of Vicksburg, Pemberton pulled his men toward the city and set up a defensive perimeter, entrenching along the bluffs of the west bank of the Big Black River. This was sound strategy and might have worked had not the flawed western Confederate command system intervened.[58]

Joseph Johnston, in the dark for several days about what had happened at Port Gibson because Pemberton was reporting directly to Richmond, now began to take an active and, for the Confederacy, unfortunate role in the campaign. First he advised Pemberton to forget Vicksburg and unite his forces to defeat Grant at the Mississippi. The orders came too late, for Grant was now driving inland. Meanwhile, Davis sent Pemberton word that Vicksburg and Port Hudson (a Confederate stronghold on the Mississippi above Baton Rouge) must be held at all costs. In Johnston's mind, holding Vicksburg was not as important as uniting forces to defeat Grant; Davis disagreed, and Pemberton was caught in between.[59]

Grant's army, meanwhile, won another battle at Raymond, and Grant, hearing of Johnston's arrival at Jackson, decided to attack the Mississippi capital city before turning west toward Vicksburg. Johnston, more timid than his orders, concluded that he was too late to do anything, ordered Pemberton to march toward Jackson to catch the Federals between the two Confederate forces, then abandoned Jackson after offering only token resistance. He still wanted Pemberton to unite with him, but Johnston retreated north to Canton, leaving Grant between his small force and Pemberton's. Trying to appease both Johnston, who wanted him to move, and Davis, who wanted Vicksburg protected, Pemberton marched his army away from the Big Black bluffs to hit Grant's supply line. Such a move would keep his army between Vicksburg and Grant. The march to the Raymond road from Edwards, Mississippi, near the Big Black was a comedy of errors. Logistical support had been botched, and ineffective scouting had delayed the advance.[60]

As Pemberton carried out his plan, he received word that Johnston had evacuated Jackson and the latter's most recent message ordering a junction of Confederate troops. Grant, presented with a copy of Johnston's message by a Federal spy, intervened as Pemberton tried to carry out the order, and the resulting battle of Champion Hill proved to be the decisive conflict of the campaign.[61]

Champion Hill was the first and only battle in which John Pemberton commanded an army. All the aspects of his personality that prevented him from being a good field general, and all the seeds sown by his mistakes thus far, combined for the predictable disaster. Disgruntled generals, especially Loring and, to a lesser degree, Bowen, ignored his orders. Pemberton's staff—like their boss, inexperienced at controlling a large army in battle—did not perform well. Pemberton remained confused and uncertain the whole day, just as he had been through much of the campaign. Some of his lieutenants fought well, but the lack of command coordination doomed their efforts. Pemberton could not retreat to his office and analyze the situation and write out orders. Decisions had to be made quickly, instinctively, and forcefully, and he simply was not up to the task.[62]

When it became apparent that the day was lost, Pemberton ordered a retreat back to the Big Black. Loring's division got cut off, and as Pemberton kept waiting for word from his protagonist, Grant launched an assault that sent Pemberton's army reeling across the Big Black and into Vicksburg (Loring managed to escape Grant's grasp and join Johnston at Canton).[63] As Pemberton waited with his army in Vicksburg for Grant's approach, another message from Johnston arrived ordering the evacuation of the city. But Pemberton, more attentive to Davis's orders than those of his immediate superior, decided to try to save Vicksburg. He had learned his lesson in Charleston. After two attacks on rebel works failed, Grant settled in for a siege. Johnston marked time, more interested in debating the size of his army with Richmond than in relieving Pemberton. No appreciable help came from the Mississippi, and in the end, Pemberton had no choice but to surrender the city he had tried so hard to protect.[64]

Pemberton chose, he later claimed, to give up the fight on July 4 to get better terms. This only fueled the criticism of him, which had been growing ever since Grant crossed the Mississippi and was now practically hysterical. The name Pemberton became anathema throughout the South. President Davis defended his general but was unable to find him another suitable command. Ultimately, Pemberton settled for a reduction in rank and reassignment in the eastern theater, where he served out the remainder of the war quietly. As a result of Johnston's published criticisms of him, he demanded but never received a court of inquiry. The feud lasted into the postwar years. Johnston published his memoirs, but Pemberton, though writing defenses of his actions, a part of which was published by his grandson in a 1942 biography, never got his story out to the degree that Johnston had. He died on a hot July 13 in 1881, his death barely noticed in the South for which he had sacrificed so much. His passing probably would not have gained much attention anyway but was certainly overshadowed by the ultimately successful assassination attempt on President James Garfield.[65]

The Confederacy never recovered from the loss of Vicksburg. Pemberton's army was paroled but would not fight again as an army. The Union navy had uncontested control of the Mississippi, and vital supply lines from the trans-Mississippi were cut off from the rest of the Confederacy.

Whether the disaster to Confederate arms could have been avoided is a question that cannot be answered. But there can be no doubt that the Confederate government sent the wrong man to the Vicksburg theater. John Pemberton had much merit as a staff officer who could organize and direct noncombat affairs of a military department. He had no merit at all as a field general who was required to create public confidence and an effective command structure, motivate soldiers, and deftly handle tactical and strategic challenges. His actions in South Carolina and Mississippi clearly demonstrated these facts, yet Jefferson Davis and his cohorts blindly placed this beleaguered general in a vital command. The results were devastating, both for the Confederacy and for John Clifford Pemberton.

Chapter Seven

"If Properly Led": Command Relationships at Gettysburg

Brooks D. Simpson

Eleven days after the death of Thomas J. "Stonewall" Jackson, Robert E. Lee decided that it was time to answer a letter from one of his division commanders, John Bell Hood. Hood had not been at Chancellorsville; his men had been engaged in operations in southeast Virginia. Lee had missed both the division and its commander, believing that had his whole army been united at Chancellorsville, he would have crushed the Army of the Potomac. But that was wishful thinking. In the wake of Jackson's death, it was time to contemplate future operations. Already Lee was advocating an invasion across the Potomac into the North. "I agree with you in believing that our army would be invincible if it could be properly organized and officered," he told Hood. "There never were such men in an army before. They will go anywhere and do anything if properly led."[1]

Across the Rappahannock, the commander of the Army of the Potomac's Fifth Corps, George G. Meade, was clearly unhappy with Joseph Hooker's management of his soldiers at Chancellorsville. "He was more cautious and took to digging quicker even than McClellan," Meade noted, "thus proving that a man may talk very big when he has no responsibility, but that it is quite a different thing, acting when you are responsible and talking when others are"—something brought out by what would happen in Pennsylvania less than two months later. After calling his corps commanders together for advice, Hooker disregarded the majority recommendation to stay and fight; in days to come, Hooker would try to blame others, including Meade, for that decision, although Meade favored staying in place. Meade thought that Hooker's job was safe, for unlike his predecessors, he was not plagued by subordinates seeking to overthrow him. That prediction proved unfounded, though it was Hooker's own request to be replaced that brought matters to a climax and resulted in the elevation of none other than Meade to the top spot.[2]

Thus, as both Robert E. Lee and George G. Meade well knew, much depended on the quality of generalship. Generations of writing about the conduct of military operations during the American Civil War reflect a near obsession with the decisions generals made or should have made. Yet generals do not exercise command in grand isolation. Superiors must work with subordinates to carry out a plan of battle, and often it is the implementation of a plan, not its conception, that is the difference between success and failure. Subordinates must be willing to take initiative when circumstances warrant a deviation from the original plan. One sign of a great general is the ability to improvise on the battlefield in response to unanticipated opportunities, situations, and enemy reactions. Superior officers often consult with their subordinates about what to do, although in the end, ultimate responsibility rests on the commander's shoulders. It is the duty of a good subordinate to execute the plan of battle as if it were his own and to exercise appropriate discretion when necessary. Staff officers must act as the eyes and ears of their chiefs and do their part in putting a plan into action, both by their own actions, such as reconnaissance and assessment of the situation, and by facilitating communications between superiors and subordinates. All too often, assessments of generalship focus on an individual general, allocating praise and blame among officers, when in reality it is better to think of command in terms of a team whose success depends in part on each player doing his part to contribute to the overall outcome.

The battle of Gettysburg offers a rich opportunity for students of command to ponder exactly how the performance of the team of top commanders at the army and corps levels shapes the course of battle and contributes to its result. For Lee and his three infantry corps commanders, James Longstreet, Richard S. Ewell, and Ambrose P. Hill, it proved a difficult battle to fight, in part due to the nature of the interaction among them. In contrast, although all was not perfect harmony between Meade and his corps commanders, as a whole, their performance was superior to that of their counterparts and was a marked improvement on previous experiences, where friction between generals had greatly contributed to failure on the battlefield in a series of clashes that helped make the reputation of Lee and his generals. Thus, the story of the battle can in part be understood if we examine why *both* command teams did not follow the form established over the past year, in which rebel generals cooperated to outwit and usually defeat their slower, more contentious counterparts. The discussion that follows is confined to the battle itself. Although one can explore with profit the impact of command relationships on the campaign as a whole, contemporaries, scholars, and students alike have concentrated much of their attention on the three days of bloodshed in the fields and ridges surrounding a small Pennsylvania town and road hub.[3]

It is natural that most critics of generalship at Gettysburg have focused their attention on the performance of Robert E. Lee and his corps commanders, including cavalryman James Ewell Brown "Jeb" Stuart. In part, this is due to the rather lively debate among several of the battle's rebel participants who sought to ascertain who among them was responsible for Confederate defeat—thus revealing their assumption that the Army of the Potomac was little more than a passive obstacle or a puzzle waiting to be solved by intrepid Confederates. The history of this debate has contributed to a massive outpouring of books and more recently its own flourishing historiography, to the point where most scholarly discussions assessing Confederate command performance commence with the almost obligatory tour of the historiography of postwar writings. The most important result of such work has been the critical assessment of the trustworthiness of various accounts on which historians base their interpretations.[4]

From such discussions it is clear that something was awry in the relationship between Lee and his corps commanders, as well as with Lee's own ability to assess circumstances and frame an appropriate response. For the latter, one can choose from a plethora of explanations, ranging from bad health to the excitement of battle approaching bloodlust to an almost mystical commitment to seek a decisive battle at this particular moment. Lee himself wondered whether he was physically up to the demands of his position, arguing that his ailments prevented him "from making the personal examination and giving the personal supervision to the operations in the field which I feel to be necessary. I am so dull that in making use of the eyes of others I am frequently misled." Had the Confederates triumphed, one would not dawdle long over such questions. Still, it stands to reason that in a battle where Lee was not at his best, how he worked with his corps commanders would assume even greater importance. However, at Gettysburg, Lee enjoyed problematic relationships with each of his subordinates, two of whom had never exercised command at the corps level prior to this campaign. In turn, this disharmony did much to shape how he fought the battle. He made decisions that are rightly subject to scrutiny and criticism, but what makes Gettysburg stand out as exceptional is how he and his commanders developed and implemented a plan of attack.[5]

Much has been made of the fact that Stuart was nowhere near the battlefield on July 1, supposedly leaving Lee "blind" with respect to the deployment and movement of enemy forces. Although Lee had several brigades of cavalry at his disposal, he did not employ them for reconnaissance, and in any case, Stuart was far more able at managing such operations, making his absence all the more damaging. Lee himself later complained that Stuart's absence, by depriving him of intelligence, "deceived him into a general battle."[6] This seems somewhat of an overstatement, for while Lee's movements through June 28 were shaped in part by a lack of information about the general location of the Union army, his decision to concentrate his forces on June 29 and 30 after learning that the Army of the Potomac was north of its namesake river reflects his anticipation that he was about to engage the enemy. Surely a general who was unclear about enemy intentions might have exercised more caution as he approached the foe. To complain as he did on July 1 that he was "not prepared to bring on a general engagement" reflects poorly on his ability to adjust to circumstances, all the more so because, if we are to believe Isaac Trimble, Lee had as early as June 27 anticipated fighting at Gettysburg.[7]

If Lee was not ready to fight a major battle on July 1, he should have objected when Ambrose P. Hill informed him of the planned reconnaissance in force for July 1, precisely because he did not know

Robert E. Lee

what awaited him. Instead, Lee approved the move, although he added that he was not yet ready to fight—as if everything would wait until he was ready, an assumption strangely akin to one held by his former Union counterpart, George B. McClellan. If Gettysburg proved anything, it was that even the mighty Marse Robert could not always impose his will on events.[8]

Stuart's absence, compounded by Lee's failure to utilize the cavalry available to him (odd for a man who had once headed a cavalry regiment), helps one understand the opening stages of the battle, but it does little to explain how Lee responded once he arrived on the field. Whatever his preferences about a general engagement, once he came upon the battle proper, he decided to take advantage of the convergence of two of his corps to pitch into the Union's First and Eleventh Corps north and west of the town. It was well within his power to break off his attack, establish a defensive perimeter, and await reinforcements. Hill and division commander Henry Heth may have commenced a meeting engagement against his will, but they did not force him to continue it. Indeed, what he saw before him seemed an ideal opportunity to defeat the enemy in detail—the very concept he had outlined to Trimble on June 27.

Lacking detailed information about the location of enemy forces, Lee might have proceeded with more caution and circumspection. He issued orders in ignorance of the terrain south of the town and the location of Union reserves. One should not assail Lee for not knowing what he had no means of ascertaining, but it is worth wondering why Lee acted as he did when he knew that he was ignorant of important facts. He apparently did not know that Ewell's two lead divisions had encountered only two of the three divisions of the Eleventh Corps, for corps commander Oliver O. Howard had left a third division in reserve on Cemetery Hill; the Twelfth Corps was within a short distance of the field. Compounding these difficulties was Lee's thinking about how best to follow up on the afternoon's success. His famous order to Richard S. Ewell —to take Cemetery Hill "if he found it practicable" without bringing on a general engagement—reeks of ambivalence. Ewell would not know if he was bringing on a general engagement *unless* he attacked Cemetery Hill. Lee could not have it both ways. What makes Lee's order even more vulnerable to criticism was his later admission that he knew that Ewell suffered from "want of decision" long before Gettysburg and had even discussed the matter with Ewell. Why, in light of this knowledge, Lee issued orders worded to maximize Ewell's opportunity to exercise his own discretion is hard to explain.[9]

Ewell's hesitation that afternoon is far more understandable. Only two of his divisions were on the field that day, and they had spent much of it marching under a hot July sun. Part of Robert Rodes's division had been treated rather roughly by Union brigades along Oak Ridge, while much of Jubal Early's success on the Union right was due to the nature of the road network, which allowed him to converge on a poorly deployed Union division. Nevertheless, it, too, had found itself in a pretty fair firefight. The town itself, its streets clogged with soldiers, hampered pursuit: Ewell would have to shift his forces eastward if he was to attack Cemetery Hill. Perhaps he could already see Union preparations to defend that hill; it would take some time to find out whether the wooded slopes of Culp's Hill to the east shielded more defenders. Lee's admonition about not bringing on a general engagement carried more weight with him than it did with Heth or Hill (in fact, it seems a rather crass double standard to criticize Heth and Hill for ignoring Lee's warning and assail Ewell for heeding it). If he waited for the arrival of Edward Johnson's division, he would give the Yankees an opportunity to catch their breath and hurry up reinforcements, but he risked a great deal if he simply ordered Early and Rodes to press forward without regrouping in an assault that necessarily would have used the town itself as a staging area.

In spite of these considerations, Ewell at first wanted to renew the offensive before nightfall. Only when he found out that Lee would not use Hill's men to support an assault did he begin to have serious second thoughts. Those brigades already on the field were scattered; Johnson remained in the distance. As he regrouped, Ewell knew that the Yankees were doing the same. At the same time, reports reached him of Union units approaching town from the east. Here, if anywhere, the lack of cavalry proved critical, for Ewell decided to post two brigades to guard his flank. By the time Johnson's men arrived, Ewell had turned to Culp's Hill as a more promising objective, having heard reports that the summit was not occupied—reports that proved to be mistaken. Nightfall cut short that opportunity, if in fact there was one.

Several factors help explain why Lee failed to exercise command effectively on July 1. He had not yet sorted out in his own mind what he wanted to do: while he wanted to drive the Yankees from the field, he was still wary of the possibility of a general engagement in light of his ignorance about the location of the remainder of Meade's army. Although he did not anticipate the form or the intensity of the meeting engagement on the ridges west of Gettysburg that morning, he was on the field in time to direct the afternoon's operations. Because Hill was not feeling well, it was up to Lee to take charge. Confederate successes offered new challenges and opportunities, but Lee's response demonstrates that he was still not sure what to do. His orders to Ewell may have embodied his preference to give his subordinates discretion, but it is puzzling, in light of what Lee already knew about Ewell, that he was surprised when Ewell decided against an attack—and Ewell was in a much better position to judge whether such an attack was wise. Why, if Lee thought that one more push would win the day, did he hold back Maj. Gen. Richard Anderson's division? Why did Lee demand of Ewell what he did not ask of himself—to take the risk of a general engagement by pressing forward with the resources at hand?[10]

By the morning of July 2, Lee had settled on an intention to attack the Army of the Potomac before it could concentrate south of Gettysburg. However, his implementation of this intention was badly flawed and poorly thought out. If he wanted to strike before Meade could bring up his entire army, he needed to do so immediately, instead of sending Longstreet on a long flank march; when it became obvious that Longstreet would not open his attack until midafternoon, Lee should have reassessed his options. Instead, he clung to the curious notion that information gleaned from an early-morning reconnaissance would provide an accurate portrayal of Union deployment several hours later, and that Meade would not distribute his reinforcements as they arrived—and Confederate accounts make it clear that they saw the arrival of the Third Corps along the Emmitsburg Road early that morning. As the Confederates had earlier intercepted a Union dispatch reporting the approach of the Fifth Corps, it was reasonable to assume that by now all but the Sixth Corps had arrived. It remains unclear how much Lee knew of the Union order of battle on July 2, especially as his men had yet to make contact with the Fifth and Sixth Corps (careful observation would have revealed the presence of the Second, Third, and Twelfth Corps, for their positions were visible), but with every hour the likelihood of their arrival on the field increased. The later redeployment of the Third Corps appears to have come as a surprise to Lee; no record exists of the impact, if any, of the firefight between Union sharpshooters and Hill's men at midday, although the incident in itself should have called into question his understanding of the Union position. Rather, Lee and Longstreet engaged in some last-minute improvising when it became evident that circumstances had changed somewhat, but Lee failed to rethink the premises of his plan, and Longstreet appears to have resigned himself to it, having failed to persuade Lee to change his mind.

Central to the finger-pointing debate that followed about Long-street and Lee on July 2 is the question of exactly when Lee decided to have Longstreet attack, what he thought it would achieve, and how Longstreet should deploy his men. Talk of a "sunrise assault" is clearly inconsistent with the historical record, in part because Lee's staff officers did not conduct a reconnaissance of the area in the vicinity of Peach Orchard until the dawn hours of July 2. As Edward Porter Alexander later remarked, "I am impressed by the fact that the strength of the enemy's position seems to have cut no figure in the consideration [of] the question of the aggressive; nor does it seem to have been systematically examined or inquired into—nor does the night seem to have been utilized in any preparation for the morning."[11] As Lee's decision on the morning of July 2 to consult with Ewell about the advisability of an attack on the Union right suggests, the commanding general's thinking about what course to pursue was still incomplete as precious minutes ticked away. Complicating a reconstruction of what happened and when are conflicting narratives, each shaped by a desire to argue a case in light of what subsequently happened, and the lack of contemporary documentation in the form of orders and records. Longstreet insisted that he did not receive orders to move until 11 A.M.; other accounts insist that at that time Lee was dissatisfied because Longstreet had not yet moved his men into position. The confusion and conflicts between various witnesses expose the failure of Lee and Longstreet and their respective staffs to work together toward a common end.

The performance of James Longstreet on July 2 remains the subject of one of the liveliest debates among military historians, Confederate buffs, and Gettysburg aficionados. Some of the general's most fervent critics have made their case as if the matter was a personal one, churning out briefs for the prosecution that resemble the heated contributions of fiction writers Jubal Early and company. One theme that dominates discussion is whether Longstreet was wiser than Lee in proposing a sweep around the Union left; however, contributors to the debate do not always confine their speculations to the information available to both generals at the time Lee overruled his lieutenant. Longstreet's proposal was more of an idea than a plan: no one had scouted out possible routes of march or ascertained anything about the Union position. In light of what Lee knew at the time, and what he believed to be the situation on the morning of July 2, it was reasonable for him to assume that an attack on the Union left, *if it were possible to make,* would bring great results. Whether it was also reasonable for him to assume that Longstreet could get into position in a timely fashion is another question altogether, for Lee's insistence that Longstreet conceal his line of march from the Yankees in an effort to replicate Jackson's flank march at Chancellorsville meant that it would take some time for Longstreet to deploy his forces. If Lee had expected Longstreet to attack any time before noon on July 2, that reflects poorly on Lee's knowledge of the condition and positioning of the divisions of Hood and Maj. Gen. Lafayette McLaws. Soldiers of both units had marched all night, and Hood arrived on Herr Ridge as signs of daybreak appeared (so much for the sunrise attack argument). Had Lee wanted to engage Meade earlier, he should have used Richard Anderson's division to commence the fighting.[12]

Longstreet did not carry out Lee's plan with alacrity or enthusiasm. Perhaps he was wise in waiting for the arrival of Evander Law's brigade—a suggestion Lee accepted—but in what followed, the corps commander appeared grumpy and at times pigheaded in his sullen obedience to orders. As his aide, Moxley Sorrel, put it, "There was apparent apathy in his movements. They lacked the fire and point of his usual bearing on the battlefield." In marked contrast stands William T. Sherman's response to Ulysses S. Grant's plan of campaign against Vicksburg the previous spring: Sherman disapproved of Grant's plan, freely complained about it, yet did what Grant told him to do. Some three weeks after the battle, Longstreet expressed a similar concept of duty: "I consider it a part of my duty to express my views to the commanding general. If he approves and adopts them, it is well; if he does not, it is my duty to adopt his views, and to execute his orders as faithfully as if they were my own."[13]

At Gettysburg, Longstreet did not follow his own concept of duty. It appears that he believed that he possessed the power to talk Lee out of a command decision, as indeed he had on earlier battlefields; surely, as Lee demonstrated at Chancellorsville, he was willing to listen to his lieutenants and follow their advice. During the afternoon of July 2, Longstreet honored the letter but not the spirit of Lee's directive, and never more so than when he nearly snapped John Bell Hood's head off when Hood, after a hasty examination of the ground south of Big Round Top, asked Longstreet to revise the plan of attack. Perhaps Longstreet was right in replying that Lee's plan must be followed; perhaps Lee was not willing to tolerate yet another plea for an adjustment, in the belief that Longstreet was trying to subvert his authority.[14]

In their eagerness to pin blame on Longstreet, Lee's staff officers remained comparatively silent about their own activities that day, and wisely so, for Lee was never worse served by his staff than on July 2. Capt. Samuel R. Johnston's reconnaissance of the Union position between Peach Orchard and the Round Tops was a lamentable and misleading disaster; the supervising officer, William N. Pendleton, was even more useless. Their report claiming that there were no Union forces in the vicinity of Peach Orchard and Little Round Top was remarkable for its inaccuracy—and in any case, there was no reason to believe that the situation would remain the same. All this should have become apparent by noon, when Hill's men fired on Hiram Berdan's sharpshooters near Pitzer's Woods, and painfully so when Daniel Sickles advanced his two divisions, but it did not. The historical record suggests that the first time the Confederates were aware of Sickles's position was when McLaws came under fire as he moved into position that afternoon. Just as disastrous was the poor staff work on Longstreet's line of march that fateful afternoon. Lee's staff officers should have identified a route of march in accordance with Lee's preferences for concealment (or reported that it would be difficult to do); the ensuing countermarches did not escape the observations of the signalmen on Little Round Top, although it appears that they were somewhat confused by what they saw.

The shortcomings of Lee's staff work were of critical importance precisely because the deployment of the Army of Northern Virginia on July 2 hampered Lee's efforts to coordinate operations. In making his way from army headquarters by the seminary to Ewell's headquarters at Benner's Hill, Lee necessarily lost touch with Hill and Longstreet; in returning to his headquarters, he effectively lost touch with Ewell and Longstreet. The ailing Hill had little to do with the unfolding plan. In some cases, such a central location might seem ideal for coordinating operations, but the view of the Union position from Lee's headquarters was a misleading one, and Lee seems to have done little in the way of actively coordinating the actions of his corps commanders. Lee could not be everywhere at once, and for several critical hours on the afternoon of July 2, it appears that he was not anywhere. Nor does it seem to have occurred to him that as time passed without any sign of an engagement, the situation might be changing in ways that would have a material effect on his plan. Perhaps Lee was more than a little overconfident that the Army of the Potomac would simply stay in place until he was ready to act—an assumption that, oddly enough, had paid off before. Why no one thought to have someone watch the area around Peach Orchard for signs of Union movement prior to the arrival of Longstreet's men is rather curious.[15]

In short, the operations of the Army of Northern Virginia at Gettysburg from dawn to midafternoon on July 2 reflect poorly on that army's high command and staff. There was more than enough blame to go around that day, and the exercise in finger-pointing that followed was an unworthy one (especially when some of the original participants were not part of the deliberations that day). Moreover, it is a serious mistake to confuse what might have happened had Longstreet attacked earlier with what did happen. By midafternoon, Lee knew that the circumstances he believed existed on the morning of July 2 were no longer operative. He had ample opportunity to reassess his plan of attack. It can be inferred from several accounts of discussions between Longstreet and Hood just before Hood advanced, as well as other narratives, that Lee was somewhere in the vicinity of McLaws's division when Hood and McLaws deployed opposite Sickles's men, and that Lee, while sticking to his original concept, altered its implementation by allowing Hood to lead off. As Alexander observed, Lee "yielded to Longstreet's request to wait for Law's brigade; and the delay caused by Longstreet's infantry being taken in sight of Round Top seems to have entirely escaped his attention, & that of all his staff. He was present on the field all the time, & was apparently consenting to the situation from hour to hour." Great generals improvise in response to changing circumstances. On this day, Lee was not a great general. Knowing what he knew (or should have known) at the time, he nevertheless persisted in following a plan based on assumptions that no longer applied.[16]

The fight that followed soon passed from the hands of Lee and Longstreet to division, brigade, and even regimental and battery commanders. Hood's division fought as independent brigades after its commander fell; as McLaws's men surged forward, they moved out of his hands. Later, several of Anderson's brigades came temptingly close to Cemetery Ridge, but no one was around to exploit the opportunity. It was as if Lee and his subordinates had overlooked the importance of reserves. In the end, the Confederate attack achieved much, but not enough, and gained what it did at a sizable cost.

In compliance with Lee's orders, Ewell initiated a barrage on Cemetery and Culp's Hills but did little to prevent Meade from detaching forces to shore up his crumbling left. The gaps left by those redeployments, in turn, offered the Confederates their best chance of victory on Culp's Hill that evening. Far more puzzling is the botched handling of operations against Cemetery Hill, where the Confederates might have enjoyed their best chance for victory on July 2 if they had crushed the salient occupied by battle-worn soldiers from the First and Eleventh Corps. Yet it is unfair to hold Ewell solely responsible for what happened, for Lee, despite his reservations about Ewell's fitness to exercise sufficient initiative, did not monitor operations in his sector. However, Ewell did not coordinate the attacks of his division commanders, with the result that neither Early nor Johnson was able to exploit initial opportunities, while Rodes remained quiet. In targeting both Culp's and Cemetery Hills, Ewell rendered it more difficult to take either, for the two divisions that attacked did so in ways that foiled any efforts to render support to their comrades. Once more, bad management contributed to battlefield failure, although the terrain heavily favored the defenders.

Critics of Hill and Ewell on July 1 and of Ewell and Longstreet on July 2, speaking as they do with the benefit of hindsight and the tendency to shape counterfactual speculation in line with their own preferences, would do well to recall that it was Lee's command style to extend to his subordinates great latitude. As the British observer Arthur J. L. Fremantle noted, "It is evidently his system to arrange the plan thoroughly with the three corps commanders, and then leave to them the duty of modifying and carrying it out to the best of their abilities." There was a touch of religious fatalism to this approach. Lee later told a Prussian officer, "I think and work with all my powers to bring my troops to the right place at the right time." Once he had done this, "I leave the matter up to God and the subordinate officers." These sentiments, quoted with increasing frequency by recent scholars, are not the whole story, for Lee obviously believed that there were strings attached to his bestowal of initiative on his subordinates—he expected them to fulfill his vision with only minor variations. If Lee wanted Ewell to attack Cemetery Hill on July 1, he should have said so—or even taken the time to ride over and decide on the spot what to do. If Lee was unhappy with Longstreet on July 2, he should have supervised his subordinate's moves more closely. Instead, he remained curiously passive, even after Longstreet's two divisions went into action, for he returned to his headquarters as the attack commenced and sent only one rather vacuous message to his warhorse. One of the ironies of the action of July 2 is that Lee twice let Ewell have his way, failing either to shift the Second Corps or to have it lead off in attack, while he remained impervious to Longstreet's arguments, demonstrating that how much latitude and trust he extended to his subordinates was relative and depended on the situation.[17]

The most famous Confederate counterfactual scenario concerning operations on July 1 and 2 asks whether things would have been different if Stonewall Jackson had been present. What if Jackson had been in Hill's shoes on the morning of July 1? What if he had been in Ewell's place that afternoon in the wake of the rout of the Eleventh Corps? What if Jackson and not Longstreet had been in charge of the assault against the Union left on July 2? Such counterfactual queries betray the problematic nature of the enterprise. Does the inquiry stipulate what happened to Jackson at Chancellorsville? Was he seriously wounded, or did he escape friendly fire altogether? In the latter case, one must ponder whether the course of events at Chancellorsville would have been far different. Had Jackson remained in command, Lee might have moved more vigorously to assault Hooker's fortified position, with sad consequences for the Confederates. If Jackson were badly wounded, would that have affected his generalship? Sometimes sustaining a serious battlefield wound alters one's subsequent behavior, and if Jackson had to use painkillers for relief, the result might have affected his judgment. Would Lee have reorganized the Army of Northern Virginia into three corps if Jackson had been able to exercise command? If not, then the opening stages of the engagement on July 1 would have assumed a different form, for no longer could three corps approach Gettysburg as they did. If Lee would have reorganized his army in any case, who would have headed the third corps? The "Jackson" of such speculation can displace Hill or Ewell, but not both. In short, if one is to engage seriously in such a rewriting of history, one must also conclude that only under a special set of circumstances would the events of July 1 have unfolded as they did where they did if Jackson had been present—rendering these rather timid what-ifs moot.

Rather, when one examines the accounts of Gettysburg that feature a longing reference to the impact of Jackson's absence, one discovers that the "Jackson" of such accounts is an abstract construct, designed to fulfill the fantasy of its creator by flawlessly and successfully executing whatever course of action the narrator finds in hindsight to have been ideal. Invoking "Jackson" circumvents the exploration of the impact of command relationships by assuming that perfect harmony existed between Lee and Jackson and that Jackson could always be trusted to realize his superior's vision of victory, both by following orders and by taking the initiative in response to unanticipated circumstances and opportunities. With "Jackson" present, in fact, any general could win. Moreover, "Jackson" can bounce from position to position, from situation to situation: he can take Hill's place in the morning of July 1, then assume Ewell's position that afternoon, and finally stand in for Longstreet on July 2. "Jackson" possesses such properties precisely because Jackson was dead. If someone were to point out that Winfield S. Hancock would have handled matters better than did Daniel Sickles on July 2, a sage commentator would point out that Hancock could not be two places at once, so his contributions elsewhere could no longer be taken for granted. Jackson dead is a much better general than Jackson alive, for "Jackson" can do it all.[18]

But Jackson was not at Gettysburg. Lee's expectation that two generals who were exercising corps command for the first time in a major battle would rise to the performance of an experienced Jackson is much more of a commentary on Lee than on Hill or Ewell. After all, Jackson's early experiences as a corps commander were far from flawless. If, as Longstreet's critics claim, Lee complained that Longstreet was slow on the battlefield, one must ask why Lee did not take matters in hand. If, as even Lee remarked, Ewell was prone to indecisiveness, one must wonder why Lee allowed him to indulge that weakness on July 1, or why he allowed Ewell to talk him out of renewing the attack on the Union right or shifting his corps to another sector of the field on July 2, instead leaving Ewell on his own in a position where, due to the terrain and the exterior lines of the Confederate position, it would be hard to supervise him while tending to matters elsewhere. Lee knew the shortcomings as well as the strengths of his corps commanders, yet he managed affairs on the battlefield at Gettysburg as if he were ignorant of them. By the morning of July 2, he had seen signs of Ewell's hesitation and Longstreet's dismay, yet he failed to adjust his outlook accordingly. When Lee himself indulged in pondering what would have happened had Jackson been present at Gettysburg, he unwittingly revealed his own limits as a commanding general, for by conjuring up "Jackson," the ideal subordinate, he sidestepped the need to examine his own actions at the battle. It is perhaps fortunate for Lee's reputation that he did not live to write his account of the operations of his army, for the observations he offered about the battle in retrospect suggest that he would not have been above pointing fingers at others, thus diminishing his image as a man who accepted responsibility.

Never was the collapse of the Confederate command structure more evident than on July 3. Lee's initial plan was for Ewell and Longstreet to renew their attacks on the flanks of the Union position. However, fighting broke out on Culp's Hill as dawn approached, and by midmorning the Confederate threat to that portion of the Union line had subsided. It was just as well, for Lee's understanding of affairs on his right was flawed, to say the least. The Fifth and Sixth Corps (along with what was left of the Third Corps) had secured the area between the southern portion of Cemetery Ridge and the Round Tops, with horsemen providing flank security to the south and west. Even with George Pickett's fresh troops, Longstreet would have found it difficult to make much headway, and the attackers would not have enjoyed the artillery support they had on July 2. Lee did not appreciate the strength of the Union position that morning and did little to educate himself on that topic.

Compounding Lee's difficulties was Longstreet's persistence in pressing for a sweep around the Union left. Whatever merit one might attach to his preference for such a plan on July 2, by July 3 the moment had passed. The Army of the Potomac was now reunited: any movement undertaken by Longstreet with Hood's and McLaws's divisions could not be concealed from Union forces on the Round Tops, depriving the Confederates of the element of surprise. At best, Longstreet might have used Pickett's fresh division to undertake such a march. It had arrived too late on July 2 to participate in that day's actions, but neither Lee nor Longstreet had seen to it that it was placed in a position whence it could join the battle early on the morning of July 3 pursuant to either general's original intentions. In any case, Longstreet appears to have undertaken detailed planning for such a movement without prior consultation with Lee, because the commanding general vetoed it as soon as he learned of it as the skies around Gettysburg began to lighten in the early-morning hours of July 3.

Both generals seemed to have been operating in a fog that morning, primarily because of what they planned to do with the divisions of Hood and McLaws. Both commands had been badly battered in the fighting on the second: three brigade commanders had gone down, and a fourth had assumed command of Hood's division in place of that severely wounded general—a cumulative turnover of 50 percent. To rely on them for a major combat role on July 3 was not clear thinking; to believe that Longstreet could take them out of position preparatory to another assault once dawn had arrived was equally questionable—and such a redeployment would have opened up new opportunities for Meade. Much more serious was Longstreet's failure to move Pickett up during the early hours of July 3 in preparation for renewing operations at daybreak.

It is symbolic of that morning's confusion and muddled thinking that the evidence on what Lee and Longstreet wanted to do is fragmentary and contradictory. As William G. Piston has pointed out, between July 1863 and January 1864, Lee offered three different explanations of what he intended to do on July 3, and certainly (if perhaps unintentionally) misrepresented what happened that afternoon. Nor do we know much about what communications passed between Lee and Longstreet during the night of July 2, although the two generals did not meet.[19]

Longstreet's own report, not contradicted by Lee, mentioned the flanking option but failed to indicate its authorship; his later writings implied that it was his own idea. Although Lee rejected Longstreet's proposal, he also decided against renewing the action of July 2, in part because Pickett's men were not yet in place to support the renewal of the offensive against the Union left.[20] This initial confusion paled in comparison with what followed. Lee decided to blast a hole through the Union center on Cemetery Ridge. A massive artillery barrage would presumably pulverize the position; then an infantry assault would overwhelm what remained. Longstreet once more expressed his doubts about the wisdom of the plan. Lee brushed them aside and placed Longstreet in immediate charge of the operation, cobbling together an assault force from Pickett's division and what remained of Heth's and Maj. Gen. William Dorsey Pender's commands from the first day's action. James J. Pettigrew had taken over for the wounded Heth, and Isaac Trimble, who had been unattached, replaced Pender. Pettigrew's combat experience was limited: this was the first battle he had fought in Lee's Army of Northern Virginia. Trimble had not seen action since Second Manassas, where he had been wounded; Pender's command was new to him. Pickett had last seen action at Fredericksburg, although his last serious battlefield experience was at Gaines's Mill, where he was wounded. In short, these were not the ideal units for such a demanding mission, but the battle had left them as the best of an ailing lot. Lee was improvising command relationships right and left; it might be expecting a great deal to assume that orders would be issued and executed flawlessly.[21]

Everyone knows what happened next. Could the result have been any different? Lee thought so. As what remained of the nine main attack brigades straggled back to Seminary Ridge, Lee reportedly acknowledged that what had happened was his fault, but his subsequent comments suggested that in taking responsibility he was not accepting all the blame. Both he and others argued that if the attack had been properly supported, it would have succeeded, which raised the question of who was responsible for failing to plan for adequate support. Moreover, the exact meaning of "properly supported" was not always clear. Initially, Lee and one of his aides, Walter Taylor, argued that although Pickett's men did their job, the six brigades from the Third Corps did not. In part, this was due to a faulty understanding of what exactly happened on Cemetery Ridge. Taylor, who was by Lee's side during the attack, reported that Pickett's men actually seized the ridge—a gross exaggeration of the temporary penetration achieved by at most a thousand Confederates, and one that overlooked the presence of significant Union reserves on the ridge's east slope, concealed from Lee's line of vision.[22] Over time, however, other critics looked to those forces that did not take part in the charge: Edward Porter Alexander, for example, argued that both Richard Anderson's division and Cadmus Wilcox's brigade might have joined in the attack. Those Confederates even more hostile to Longstreet lumped in Hood and McLaws, a suggestion recently echoed by Emory M. Thomas; Alexander went so far as to suggest that perhaps Ewell's corps could have spared eight more brigades had it been "drawn to the right."[23]

In some cases, such criticism is easy to counter. Had Longstreet pulled McLaws and Hood out of line, the result would have freed a considerable portion of the Union army, including the fairly fresh Sixth Corps, for redeployment. Indeed, these two battered divisions accomplished much simply by pinning the Fifth Corps and part of the Sixth Corps in place. Besides, as Lee had already agreed with Longstreet's reasoning on this point, he (and not Longstreet) would have to shoulder the blame for this decision. Much the same applies to Alexander's suggestion about Ewell, although one might observe that Robert Rodes's division might have been put to better use on both July 2 and 3. Besides, only so many men could have been massed in one area and used effectively: think of the tempting targets they would have offered Union gunners. As for Anderson and Wilcox, as even Alexander admitted, it was not clear who was responsible for their deployment—and Wilcox did step into the fray, only to veer southward and be cut up by Union defenders. However, as Alexander adds, Lee was present during the charge; "certainly he & his staff officers also were all about in my vicinity, during the morning, & if there was one thing they might be suppos[e]d to take an interest in, it would be in seeing that the troops which were to support the charge were in position to do it. Why else should they have been around there & what else had they of more importance to look after during all that time?"[24]

That later commentators could have expanded on the original sense in which Lee referred to the failure of Pettigrew and Trimble to support Pickett reveals once more the confusion among Confederate commanders about what was to be done and who was to do it. In fact, the assault was poorly planned, and Pettigrew's and Trimble's divisions were unfairly made the scapegoats (although surely some brigades did not perform well). That the attack was not otherwise supported must in the end be placed at Lee's feet; it is difficult to see how the attack as made could have succeeded in doing anything more than making a temporary lodgment in the Union line, unless the Yankees simply panicked and broke, creating a headlong rout.

Five years after the battle, Lee reflected on the reasons for the Confederate defeat at Gettysburg. Although he asserted that he had not invaded Pennsylvania in search of a decisive battle, and that the engagement at Gettysburg had been forced on him by circumstances, he attributed the outcome to the failure of his generals to launch coordinated and simultaneous attacks. One might imagine that the Confederates could have scored a triumph on July 2 if they had launched major attacks on both flanks, but to manage such an effort successfully is among the most difficult tasks of command. As Alexander pointed out, "To read military history is calculated to make one think that it should be stated not as a difficulty but an impossibility. [T]hat is the thing which always looks beforehand very simple and easy, & always proves afterward to have been impossible, from one of a hundred possible causes."[25]

According to Lee, Stuart's absence led him to stumble into battle, and *"the imperfect, halting way in which his corps commanders* (especially Ewell) *fought the battle"* led to defeat. Had Jackson been there, he mused, things might have been different. One can sympathize with Lee for cataloging the mistakes of others, but the general forgot to reflect on his own shortcomings during those three days. Gettysburg was Lee's worst battle, and one of the reasons was his flawed handling of his subordinates. Believing Ewell to be indecisive, he gave the Second Corps commander an opportunity to demonstrate it on July 1 and then blamed Ewell for the result. Yet he allowed Ewell and his division commanders to talk him out of several worthwhile options for July 2, while rejecting out of hand Longstreet's more reasoned skepticism about a plan of attack on July 2 and 3. Why he chose to indulge Ewell and override Longstreet remains an interesting question. Nevertheless, he did not adequately supervise Longstreet on July 2, and he was ill served by his staff; however dissatisfied he may have been with Longstreet's performance, he placed his warhorse in charge of the July 3 assault and did nothing to improve on the result. Others have singled out Longstreet as the culprit in the case, and it is clear that the commander of the First Corps was not a cooperative subordinate. Lee, however, singled out Stuart, Ewell, and Pettigrew's men as responsible for his failure to win a decisive victory. Lee never attributed the result to the nature of the Union position or the performance of his counterparts, betraying arrogance, not the fabled audacity for which he is so often celebrated. After the battle he observed, "I know how prone we are to censure and how ready to blame others for the nonfulfillment of our expectations. This is unbecoming in a generous people, and I grieve to see its expression." One wishes that he had honored that sentiment in his postwar comments. There was more than enough blame to go around.[26]

Long after the end of the Civil War, in response to the heated debates between Confederates as to who was responsible for the result at Gettysburg, George Pickett reportedly observed that perhaps the Yankees had something to do with it. The wisdom of this remark might appear self-evident, but it is not always apparent that others heed it. In fact, its application is much broader than even Pickett intended it, for in some fashion, the Yankees also contributed to many of Lee's earlier successes. It was with understandable envy that Joseph E. Johnston noticed after Fredericksburg that no one ever presented him with such an easy victory as Ambrose Burnside offered Lee. What, then, was different at Gettysburg?

In the year preceding the eve of the battle of Gettysburg, the Army of the Potomac had proved to be a flawed fighting machine, primarily because its generals could not work together. George B. McClellan essentially turned over the conduct of battlefield operations during the Seven Days battles to his subordinates, preferring to attend to shifting his supply base to the James River. Fitz-John Porter performed admirably in such circumstances. The risks were far more evident at Savage's Station and White Oak Swamp, where corps commanders failed to work together. Much more damaging was the feuding between John Pope and his subordinates at Second Manassas, where the failure of the army and corps commanders to work together offered Lee perhaps his best chance during the war to destroy his opponent. At Antietam, McClellan remained passive at key moments and failed to coordinate attacks on the Confederate center and right; afterward he preferred to saddle his friend Burnside with the blame for failing to engage the Confederates earlier in the day. Such disharmony did not go unnoticed. Arriving in Washington on the eve of Second Manassas, Charles F. Adams, Jr., gathered story after story about friction between Union generals and concluded that the struggle in Virginia had become "discordant numbers against compact strategy." Nearly three months later, in the wake of McClellan's removal, Adams remarked that "the Generals are jealous and ambitious and little, and want to get a step themselves, so they are willing to see him pulled down."[27]

These rivalries and jealousies played right into Lee's hands. The success of his offensive operations depended not only on cooperation among his own generals but also on a lack of a coordinated response (Chancellorsville); on the defensive, his survival depended on the tendency of Union generals to launch piecemeal attacks without proper support (Fredericksburg, Antietam). Once in a while, as at Second Manassas, both elements were essential to victory. In order to conquer the Yankees, Lee sometimes divided his own forces, but he always sought to exploit divisions in the high command of his opponent. In fact, he counted on the predictability of the generals of the Army of the Potomac in mapping out his plans. As he told James Longstreet after McClellan's removal, "I fear they may continue to make these changes till they find some one whom I don't understand."[28]

The result damaged and embarrassed the Union's most celebrated field army. The court-martial of Fitz-John Porter was merely the most visible sign of the consequences of such feuding. Nor were its sources solely internal. Several times in 1862, Abraham Lincoln had consulted with McClellan's subordinates on the condition of the army and the outlook for military operations. After one such meeting in January 1862, the president had gone so far as to appoint corps commanders, and his review of the army's condition in July and October 1862 offered them the opportunity to contradict McClellan's estimate of the army's strength and opportunities. It was thus perhaps inevitable that by 1863 subordinates began to make it a habit of informing the president of the supposed shortcomings of their superiors. After Fredericksburg, several generals complained about Burnside's handling of the army; in turn, Burn-side wanted to clean house, bringing matters to a head in the form of his own replacement. Joseph Hooker, whom Lincoln had admonished because of his willingness to backbite, found himself beset by critics after Chancellorsville.

Of course, friction between Union commanders and subordinates was not confined to the Army of the Potomac. Ulysses S. Grant and John A. McClernand battled each other for well over a year, and that rivalry shaped key portions of the campaign against Vicksburg. William S. Rosecrans had a talent for irritating both superiors (Grant) and subordinates (Thomas J. Wood); the latter led to perhaps the key Union misstep at Chickamauga when Wood, chafing under previous admonishments from Rosecrans, mindlessly obeyed a flawed order framed in ignorance of the battlefield situation, leading to a Confederate breakthrough. And Lincoln's talent for meddling was clearly evident in the Grant-McClernand squabble, although many of the Union generals in the West later claimed that distance from Washington led to greater harmony between commanders. However, these problems did not have a long-term impact on the Army of the Tennessee and the Army of the Cumberland (although a rivalry between these two field armies would always exist). First, army commanders in the West, especially Grant, proved far more adept in handling these problems. Grant clearly outmaneuvered McClernand; at other times he persevered despite friction (as with George H. Thomas at Chattanooga, where he stayed by Thomas) or headed off potential problems by acting decisively (as when he cut short Charles S. Hamilton's efforts to derail James B. McPherson's career). Second, with the exception of Chickamauga, Confederate commanders proved unable to take advantage of the opportunities presented by such friction to strike decisive blows. At best, Union disharmony in the West constrained the effort to seek decisive victory.

In contrast, the Army of the Potomac suffered from three problems. First, Lee and his generals usually took advantage of Union command problems and made their opposing numbers pay for their mistakes—thus highlighting the friction among Union generals by demonstrating its costs. Second, rather than act to contain existing friction, Union generals usually compounded it, leading to mistake after mistake on the battlefield. Although Stonewall Jackson's assault on the Eleventh Corps at Chancellorsville was dramatic, it was not nearly as decisive as Hooker's mishandling of his army between May 3 and May 6. At Fredericksburg, Burnside's determination to hit Marye's Heights again and again was shaped in large part by his misunderstanding of what was happening on the Confederate right. In turn, miscommunication and downright pigheadedness largely explain why Union commanders failed to exploit their early success that day against Jackson's corps. Third, the very proximity of the army to Washington offered far more frequent opportunities for contacts between generals, political leaders, administration officials, and the president. Lincoln never visited the headquarters of either the Army of the Tennessee or the Army of the Cumberland, but between July 1862 and June 1863 he visited McClellan twice (July and October), Burnside once (November), and Hooker twice (April and May). Nor did Union generals in the West (aside from McClernand) make it a practice to visit Washington, as did several of their Potomac counterparts. As a result, meddling and wire-pulling escalated and more often involved direct contact between generals and high-ranking officials. Each of these factors fed on the other two, creating a difficult situation for any commander of the Army of the Potomac.

Why, then, did the Army of the Potomac not fall apart at Gettysburg? What was different about this battle? The performance of the army's generals was not flawless, and in a few instances, command decisions opened opportunities for the Confederates to deliver damaging blows. The eagerness of historians to praise John Buford's handling of his horsemen obscures the fact that the Union cavalry as a whole could have been doing a much better job in fixing the position and movement of enemy forces. Especially notable was the failure to locate Longstreet's corps, for Meade confessed to Halleck late on the first day of battle that he did not know where Longstreet was—which led him to believe that perhaps he was fighting only two of Lee's three corps. On July 1 Oliver O. Howard and his subordinates, especially Francis C. Barlow, failed to work together in establishing a position north of the town, leading to Barlow's faulty and uncorrected deployment on the knoll that now bears his name. At the same time, Twelfth Corps commander Henry W. Slocum's failure to move energetically from Two Taverns to Gettysburg, some six miles away, deprived Howard of much-needed reinforcements that afternoon. On July 2 Sickles, in charge of the Third Corps and acting on his own liberal interpretation of Meade's instructions, deranged the entire Union left flank; equally inexcusable was Buford's decision to withdraw his two brigades from the left and cavalry commander Alfred Pleasanton's failure to send replacements. And Meade contributed his share of mistakes on July 2, neglecting affairs on his left flank far too long (for he already knew that Sickles could prove a troublesome subordinate) and endangering his hold on Culp's Hill when he shifted forces piecemeal to shore up his left. It is not clear who was responsible for the failure to fortify Cemetery Ridge on either July 2 or July 3 (in contrast, George S. Greene gets far too little credit for his actions on Culp's Hill on July 2, for his earthworks proved invaluable in holding the position). Surely the penetration achieved by Ambrose R. Wright's brigade on July 2, however short-lived, should have pointed out the necessity of preparing the position; and if Meade anticipated an attack on Cemetery Ridge on July 3, he certainly failed to prepare for it, even though it was just several hundred yards west of his headquarters. Finally, Judson Kilpatrick's stubbornness led to a series of bad decisions involving Union horsemen on July 3 that might have had more serious costs had Pleasanton not acceded to a request to leave one of Kilpatrick's brigades (George Custer's Michigan troopers) on the Union right, where it helped repel a Confederate cavalry assault that afternoon.

Aside from Kilpatrick's fiasco, which produced tragic results but did not have an impact on the course of the battle, each of these mistakes could have established the starting point for a disaster. Why, then, did no disaster follow? In each case, although the Confederates did not pass up the opportunities these errors offered them, they did not exploit them as fully as they might have in the past. Although shortcomings in Confederate leadership contributed to the result, Union generals did not compound the problems with additional significant errors, allowing the army to recover from a series of initial setbacks. By leaving part of his corps on Cemetery Hill, Howard provided retreating Union forces with a rallying point that gave Ewell cause to pause. Instead of panicking when Longstreet opened his attack on July 2, Meade and his generals moved quickly to rectify the situation and establish a new line; the same applies to their response to the attack on Culp's Hill and Cemetery Hill that evening. On July 3, Henry Hunt's handling of his artillery and the actions of Meade and Winfield Scott Hancock in reinforcing the center doomed the Confederate attackers, making it seem as if the failure to fortify the position was the deliberate baiting of a trap. In short, although Union command decisions at Gettysburg were far from mistake free, for once the army did not compound its initial errors but overcame them.

Even what in retrospect appears to have been the most serious error of the battle—the handling of the Union left on July 2, especially the redeployment of the Third Corps to the Emmitsburg Road, leaving a single division to cover the ground between Peach Orchard and the base of Little Round Top—may have had its benefits, although Sickles surely engaged in a massive distortion of historical truth when he claimed that such was his intent. By wrapping his corps around Peach Orchard, Sickles disrupted Lee's original vision of an attack sweeping toward Cemetery Ridge; instead, the bloody struggle that followed succeeded in wearing out the Confederates and sapping their strength. It remains one of the more intriguing what-ifs of Gettysburg to ponder what would have happened if Sickles had remained in his initial position along Cemetery Ridge, although one might posit that had Longstreet followed the attack plan, his right flank would have been exposed to a terrible cross fire and counterattack, had Sickles had it in him to order such an assault.

The responses of Union generals to dangerous situations revealed a willingness to cooperate on the battlefield. Instead of battling each other over who was in charge late on the afternoon of July 1, Hancock and Howard worked together to establish a defensive position just south of Gettysburg. On July 2, Hancock earned his sobriquet "the superb" by feeding reinforcements into Wheatfield and the fields northwest of the Round Tops, while the initiative of chief engineer Gouverneur K. Warren, brigade commanders Strong Vincent and Stephen Weed, a host of regimental colonels (the most prominent of which would be Joshua Chamberlain, although Patrick O'Rorke of the 140th New York also deserves credit), and artillerist Charles Hazlett saved Little Round Top. Cooperation forged through previous relationships proved critical here: Warren, Hazlett, Weed, and O'Rorke knew one another rather well, having fought together on other fields. And even if Hunt and Hancock disagreed over the best way to handle the artillery on July 3, together they did much to beat back the Confederate attack, while Meade positioned reserves to limit whatever damage the Confederate assault might inflict.

Meade's performance at Gettysburg proper has often been overshadowed by the controversy over his failure to launch a counterattack on July 3 or his inability during the next ten days to pursue Lee vigorously and bring him to battle once more. The Pennsylvanian deserves a far better fate. He assumed command under trying conditions; he found it virtually impossible to reshape his staff until after the battle, when he sent Butterfield packing. Yet he consulted with his commanders, entrusted certain generals with key tasks, kept everyone working together far more than had been the case in the past, and did a good job of shuttling reserves to threatened points. Unlike Hooker, who disregarded the advice of his generals at Chancellorsville, Meade listened and responded in such a fashion as to make everyone responsible for the decision. Just days before he replaced Hooker, Meade criticized his superior for "keeping his corps commanders, who are to execute his plans, in total ignorance of them until they are developed in the execution of orders." He would not repeat that mistake. What some critics later cited as a sign of his weakness and indecision was actually an attempt to create harmony and unity. Whatever his shortcomings, they paled in comparison to those of his predecessors. As General in Chief Henry W. Halleck observed in a letter to Grant, "Meade has thus far proved an excellent general, the only one in fact who has ever fought the Army of the Potomac well. He seems the right man in the right place."[29]

One senses that one reason for Meade's success at Gettysburg was that the vast majority of his corps and division commanders liked him and wanted to help him out. They understood that he had not sought the job. Everyone believed that this time the consequences of failure might well be disastrous. After the conclusion of the campaign, when Meade came under criticism for his failure to bring Lee to battle again north of the Potomac, Howard took the unusual step of defending his superior in a letter to Lincoln—unusual in that in the past, such letters from corps and division commanders were designed to tear down army commanders, not build them up.

This spirit of cooperation did not long survive the battle itself. Maj. Gen. Henry W. Slocum and his division commanders thought that Meade had slighted the performance of the Twelfth Corps in his report; chief of staff Daniel Butterfield, Sickles, and later First Corps division commander Abner Doubleday assailed Meade in a series of vicious attacks, showing far more aggressiveness with the pen than they ever had with the sword. None of these men saw service with the Army of the Potomac after September 1863. But even among Gettysburg's heroes, the moment seemed to have passed, exemplified by Warren's comment in 1864 that he would be damned if he cooperated with anyone.[30] The circumstances of the moment—including the common assumption that the next defeat the Army of the Potomac suffered might well be its last—created an atmosphere of crisis, and this time most of the army's leaders met the challenge. As Douglas Southall Freeman noted, "The Army of the Potomac fought well in every battle where the blunders of rash or incompetent commanders did not paralyze or counteract the effort of the men."[31]

In his own way, Lee anticipated what would happen when he learned that Meade had replaced Hooker. Much of his past generalship had been shaped in part by an appreciation of the qualities of his counterpart in command of the opposing army. His actions during the Antietam campaign reflected a rich contempt for McClellan that some later historians attempted to conceal by reciting Lee's charitable comments about him. Even as he acknowledged that Hooker's opening move at Chancellorsville was brilliant, his response indicated that he thought that Hooker would fold when it counted. Ambrose Burnside did not threaten him, and his feelings about John Pope transcended professional disdain. Meade might not be a genius, and he had assumed command under difficult circumstances; nevertheless, Lee observed, "General Meade will commit no blunder in my front, and if I make one he will make haste to take advantage of it." It would have been wise to act on that premise.[32]

The course of the battle of Gettysburg, like any battle, was the product of the interplay of many variables. Decisions made and implemented at the level of army, corps, and division command were critical to the outcome. Moreover, speculating about what might have been at Gettysburg reflects one's understanding of what came before—and perhaps incorporates a belief that what happened before would happen again. That approach fails to take into consideration what had changed and the circumstances under which the two armies confronted each other in July 1863. To speculate, for example, what would have happened if Stonewall Jackson had been alive and well and in command may seem appealing, especially to those who harbor a rooting interest in Confederate victory, but it is a futile and ultimately counterproductive exercise in counterfactual logic and reflects an unwillingness to accept that things had changed.[33] Lee and his generals approached the battlefield with the assumption, born of arrogance as well as of success, that their opponents would cooperate in their own destruction. The Confederate commanders, especially Lee, took the unusual and the extraordinary for granted; Lee betrayed this when he later admitted that he had expected too much of his men.

Gettysburg was different. Defeat exposed weaknesses in Confederate command structure and style; this time they would not be overlooked in the celebration of a battlefield success due in part to the deficiencies of the Yankee generals. Despite several missteps, Union commanders worked together, understanding for once that they were engaged in a common cause. Although he was far from flawless, Meade's steady generalship offered Lee few opportunities and constrained his ability to exploit the ones he seized. The performance of Union generals at Gettysburg, in addition to the circumstances of the battle itself, left Lee and his subordinates with a much-reduced margin for error that demanded a flawless execution of a well-conceived plan of attack for success. Neither Lee, Longstreet, Hill, nor Ewell were up to that challenge. In victory, one can let much pass; it is usually left to losers to point fingers.

Conclusion

And so these generals went down to defeat, despite high hopes and strong promise for a better outcome. Unless we remember the strong and apparently well-founded expectations of their government and their peers for victory, we will often fail to understand the significance of their defeats. The question is not how bungling incompetents lose battles and campaigns, but rather how men of excellent qualifications—even proven winners like the leadership of the Army of Northern Virginia—can sometimes fail to achieve success.

The failures of the generals examined in the foregoing chapters stemmed from causes numerous and varied and defy simple explanation. That in itself is the first lesson to be learned. Obvious as it may seem, we who pursue military history must remind ourselves that the protagonists in the great dramas we study faced situations of immense complexity in which there might well be only a single solution that would bring victory but dozens of potential errors that could produce disaster. If we study a general's winning strategy, tactics, and so on, we would do well to bear in mind that he had to do myriad other things right in order to get into a position to make such winning decisions. When a general fails, there are likely to be a great many contributing causes as well, not all of them things that were subject to the general's control.

Some factors, however, show up repeatedly in the stories of the various unsuccessful campaigns chronicled in this book. Albert Sidney Johnston, George McClellan, Joseph Hooker, and John C. Pemberton faced as their foes men who proved to be the ablest generals the opposing side had to offer. Although defeating a great general might not be impossible, it is certainly far from easy. Facing such opponents drastically reduced the margin of error enjoyed by each of these men. Yet this observation hardly explains the lot of those generals who failed. The question is why they failed while their opponents went on to become great generals.

Another common factor was difficulties with subordinates, superiors, or both. Albert Sidney Johnston's case is perhaps the most striking example. He received inadequate support from Jefferson Davis until fairly late in the campaign, both in dealing with the recalcitrant Polk and in providing an appropriate share of the Confederacy's admittedly meager resources in men and weapons. He also suffered great difficulties with his subordinates. Tilghman proved slow to obey orders. Polk refused to do so at all. Beauregard muddled the plans for the Shiloh attack, and Floyd was a hopeless poltroon.

A similar pattern is borne out in the experiences of the other generals dealt with here. Joseph E. Johnston had a notoriously bad relationship with Davis and came to feel that his second in command in Virginia, Gustavus Smith, had let him down. Another subordinate, James Longstreet, badly mangled Johnston's plan for the battle of Seven Pines. McClellan's frustration with the authorities in Washington is almost proverbial. Hooker blamed subordinates Howard and Sedgwick for his disaster at Chancellorsville. Pemberton came to hold Johnston responsible for the loss of Vicksburg and was poorly served by his own subordinates Tilghman and Loring. Several members of the high command of the Army of Northern Virginia at Gettysburg spent considerable time and effort after the battle, and especially after the war, trying to fix blame on one another for the loss suffered there. Their blame shifting was unappealing, as such exercises usually are, yet a number of their claims had at least some basis in reality.

Clearly, when a military operation fails, there are usually at least several individuals whose performances can be pointed to as having been inadequate and having thereby contributed to the outcome.

Yet even though it may be just to apportion a share of blame to the various subordinates or superiors who helped a general lose, it does not help us determine why that general failed. Even the hapless A. S. Johnston had opportunities for action that might have headed off at least some of his subordinates' miscues. Much the same could be said of many of the other subjects of this study. Furthermore, the fact is the winning efforts of their opponents often featured appalling blunders and lapses of duty on the part of one or more responsible individuals. Somehow, though, the winners managed to prevail anyway. In the encounter between two opposing generals, one of them was able to cope with—or avoid—such mishaps to a greater degree than the other, and the question to ask in considering the losing general is why he was not that one.

To the extent that such matters are open to generalization, it might be fair to say that frequently the losing general showed a lack of ability to adapt. The paradoxical logic of war places a general opposite an enemy of nearly equal if not greater cunning and strength whose goal is to thwart that general's every action. This means that he can almost never proceed toward success in the logical equivalent of a straight line—devising a plan, implementing it systematically, and carrying it through in a methodical manner to victory. Every reaction of the enemy to that plan requires a readjustment, perhaps even the discarding of the original plan and its replacement by another one that is better adapted to the new circumstances.[1]

Nor is success or failure in war likely to be incremental. Small disadvantages, once they occur, often cannot be canceled out by equally modest gains posted somewhere else along the front, as if the two-way struggle of a campaign were an exercise in balancing a bookkeeper's ledgers. Instead, such small beginnings of enemy ascendancy require much larger adjustments to the original plan, or else they become the precursors of a major defeat that will cancel out all the previously gained advantages, as Lee's success in the Seven Days battles canceled out all of McClellan's hard-won strategic advances.[2] The winning general may well be the one who most quickly and skillfully adapts his plans to the changing situation while still maintaining a clear vision and steadfast aim toward the ultimate political objectives that his country requires.

No Civil War general epitomized this flexible tenacity better than Ulysses S. Grant, although Lee provided a comparable example of it in his much different circumstances. Many of the generals dealt with in the foregoing pages displayed a notable lack of the ability to adjust and adapt to and to cope with changing circumstances.

Albert Sidney Johnston was one of the most respected officers in the pre–Civil War U.S. Army, a man who had achieved considerable success mostly in the peacetime administration of troops. His previous wartime experience had included little or no planning, though undeniably much courageous leadership. He had commanded the forces of the Republic of Texas at a time when no major campaigns were fought. Later, his Second U.S. Cavalry had chased Indians on the plains, but he had faced no opposing general. Like nearly all American officers at the outset of the Civil War, he was new to the business of directing an army in an active campaign against a comparable foe. For him, as for other Civil War generals, the question would be how well he could adjust and adapt to the challenges of the new position as well as to the movements of the enemy. In Johnston's case, it is significant that the general who defeated him, Grant, was nearly twenty years his junior and had enjoyed far less success within the established prewar system. Grant's prewar failures did not necessarily reveal greatness—many prewar failures no doubt turned out to be wartime failures as well—but perhaps they made him quicker to adjust when prewar logic no longer applied. Johnston, for his part, seems to have been slow to realize how different his volunteer officers were from peacetime regulars and how much personal supervision that would require. Furthermore, his cordon defense, with forces parceled out along a line that ran from Arkansas to the Appalachians, though effective in bluffing Federal commanders for a time, was also interestingly similar to the way in which one would deploy a cavalry regiment's ten companies to shield the far-flung Texas frontier from the depredations of the Comanches. At each step in the campaign—with the exception of the first few hours of the assault at Shiloh—Johnston was just slightly behind Grant in adapting to the new circumstances both were encountering, and that made the difference. Johnston was learning and might have gotten up to speed later in the war, but he was not afforded that opportunity.

A similar pattern, to one degree or another, can be observed with several of the other unfortunate generals in this volume. Don Carlos

Buell proceeded across northern Alabama as if there were no possible countermove his enemy could have made and then was slow to adjust when his enemy responded in a way he had not expected. He was further tested in his ability to adapt when his country's war aims—and, correspondingly, the acceptable methods for waging the war—changed during the course of his campaign. The hardest indictment against him as a general is that he saw how the situation was changing and refused to alter his approach accordingly.

McClellan tried to adapt his plan of campaign to the unexpected need to await McDowell's arrival overland via Fredericksburg, yet the result was a not particularly viable hybrid of his ideas and those of Lincoln and Halleck—his army's flank left dangling and isolated north of the Chickahominy. Probably a much more fundamental adjustment was necessary, an acceptance that the slow and methodical approach to Richmond from the east was, for political reasons, no longer practical. As in the case of Buell—and for some of the same reasons—McClellan's problem was in part an unwillingness to adapt to the conditions imposed on him by his civilian superiors.

Joseph Johnston has become notorious among historians for his often-expressed desire for the enemy to approach and attack him frontally in an impregnable position. Unfortunately for his military career, his enemies were rarely willing to cooperate. When an enemy implemented some new movement to get around Johnston's defensive lines or reduce them by siege, he showed little recourse but to retreat to another impregnable position and hope that the enemy would be more obliging next time. Whether because of fundamental inadequacy as a general or because of personality conflicts and political problems, Johnston failed to adapt successfully to the varying challenges put to him by resourceful enemies.

Other cases are classic examples of that problem. It has long been held that Hooker showed all the aggressive resourcefulness of a deer caught in the headlights when Lee failed to respond as he had anticipated to what was undeniably a superbly well-conceived turning movement. As Sears argues, perhaps Hooker's movements actually represented the carrying out of his plan to the point that he had calculated would bring success. But it did not. After the setback on the right flank—precisely the sort of thing Grant would shrug off the following year on that same ground—Hooker again seemed slow to adjust. To give Fighting Joe his due, however, his ultimate failure to adjust may have come as a result of being stunned by a close encounter with a Confederate roundshot.

In an even more classic example, Pemberton seemed stunned before he ever came under fire. Sometimes he appears to have been born that way. So slow and inadequate was his adjustment to Grant's radically innovative and unexpected campaign against Vicksburg that Ballard reasonably concludes that Pemberton was by nature unqualified for field command. Still, his experience is a prime illustration of the fact that an intelligent man and a skillful organizer may be unable to adapt rapidly and successfully to an opponent's movements and the demands of wartime generalship.

Confederate leadership at Gettysburg can also be viewed in terms of a failure to adjust. Lee apparently failed to adjust his style of command to the loss of Jackson and the elevation of two new and untried corps commanders. Stuart did not adjust to the improved quality of the Federal cavalry. Longstreet would not adapt his own tactical and operational concepts to those of his commander. And as a group, the leadership of the Army of Northern Virginia did not adapt successfully to the improved quality of Union leadership. Lee correctly predicted prior to the battle that "General Meade will commit no blunder in my front." Yet the tactic he attempted against Meade was essentially the same that had brought success against Hooker two months before. There is no more striking example of the fact that in warfare, the same action is not likely to produce the same result when repeated. The enemy will act and react, constantly changing the equation of what will yield success. The successful general will probably be the one who is more effective at learning, adapting, and innovating so as to gain and keep the initiative while always maintaining a clear, sharp, intense focus on his overall goal.

Of course, it would be an oversimplification to claim this as the sole ingredient of successful generalship. The foregoing chapters make unmistakably clear that commanding an army in a Civil War campaign was an extremely complicated task and that failure could be produced by almost infinite combinations of circumstances, including, but probably not limited to, failures of subordinates or superiors, lack of resources, and an exceptionally good performance on the part of the enemy. A general might fail—through lack of adaptability or other causes—and thus produce the failure of his campaign, but usually there was more to it than that. In examining the unsuccessful general himself, we may well ruminate on the possible factors in his performance that affected the final outcome. Yet viewing the campaign as a whole, we would do well to remember that failure or success was the product of many factors, of which the general's role was an important one, but not the only one.

Contributors

Steven E. Woodworth is a member of the History Department of Texas Christian University. His books *Jefferson Davis and His Generals* and *Davis and Lee at War* were both winners of the Fletcher Pratt Award of the New York Civil War Round Table. He also edited *The American Civil War: A Handbook of Literature and Research.*

Alan Downs is a member of the History Department at Georgia Southern University. He has written several articles, and his first book, a study of Joseph E. Johnston, is forthcoming.

Ethan S. Rafuse's publications include contributions to *Civil War Times Illustrated, Oxford Companion to American Military History, Journal of the Abraham Lincoln Association,* and over three dozen book reviews and encyclopedia entries. He is presently a doctoral candidate at the University of Missouri–Kansas City, writing a dissertation on George B. McClellan, and he teaches history and political science at Johnson County (Kans.) Community College.

Stephen D. Engle teaches history at Florida Atlantic University. His publications include biographies of Franz Sigel and Don Carlos Buell.

A prolific author, Stephen W. Sears has written a number of impressive Civil War books, including *Landscape Turned Red: The Battle of*

Antietam, To the Gates of Richmond: The Peninsula Campaign, George B. McClellan: The Young Napoleon, and, most recently, *Chancellorsville.* His essay that appears as Chapter 5 is adapted from his forthcoming book *Controversies and Commanders of the Civil War: Dispatches from the Army of the Potomac.*

Michael B. Ballard is an archivist at Mississippi State University, as well as a respected Civil War historian. His many publications include *A Long Shadow: Jefferson Davis and the Final Days of the Confederacy* and *Pemberton: A Biography.*

Brooks D. Simpson, a member of the History Department of Arizona State University, has written *Let Us Have Peace: Ulysses S. Grant and the Politics of War and Reconstruction, 1861–1868* and *America's Civil War,* as well as numerous other publications, including an edition of the Civil War letters of William Tecumseh Sherman.

Notes

Introduction

1. Charles P. Roland, *Albert Sidney Johnston: Soldier of Three Republics* (Austin: University of Texas Press, 1964), 298–307.
2. Roland, *Albert Sidney Johnston*, 307.

Chapter One. When Merit Was Not Enough

1. Charles P. Roland, *Albert Sidney Johnston: Soldier of Three Republics* (Austin: University of Texas Press, 1964), 6–259; Richard Taylor, *Destruction and Reconstruction*, ed. Charles P. Roland (Waltham, Mass.: Blaisdell, 1968; originally published 1879), 232; Jefferson Davis, *The Rise and Fall of the Confederate Government*, 2 vols. (New York: Appleton, 1881), 1:309, 2:67; Dunbar Rowland, ed., *Jefferson Davis, Constitutionalist, His Letters, Papers and Speeches*, 10 vols. (Jackson: Mississippi Department of Archives and History, 1923), 8:232, 9:206, 270, 292.
2. Roland, *Albert Sidney Johnston*, 265–66, 277; Davis, *Rise and Fall*, 1:407–8; U.S. War Department, *War of the Rebellion: A Compilation of the Official Records of the Union and Confederate Armies*, 128 vols. (Washington, D.C.: Government Printing Office, 1881–1901), 3:530; 4:193–94, 416–17, 430, 531 (hereafter cited as *OR*; all references are to series I unless otherwise noted); Stanley Horn, *The Army of Tennessee: A Military History* (Indianapolis: Bobbs-Merrill, 1941), 55–60.
3. Roland, *Albert Sidney Johnston*, 271–72; *OR*, 4:531; Lloyd Lewis, *Sherman: Fighting Prophet* (New York: Harcourt Brace, 1932), 182–207; John F. Marszalek, *Sherman: A Soldier's Passion for Order* (New York: Free Press, 1991).
4. Horn, *The Army of Tennessee*, 69–70; *OR*, 7:849–50, 855, 862–63, 872, 10 (pt. 2): 379, 52 (pt. 2): 256–57; George B. Crittenden to Davis, November 12, 1862, papers received by the Confederate Adjutant and Inspector General's Office,

National Archives, microfilm M-474, roll 13, frames 495–501; Davis, *Rise and Fall*, 2:19–22.

5. On Polk's role in ending Kentucky neutrality, see Steven E. Woodworth, "'The Indeterminate Quantities': Jefferson Davis, Leonidas Polk, and the End of Kentucky Neutrality, September 1861," *Civil War History* 38 (December 1992): 289–97.

6. *OR*, 52 (pt. 2): 115.

7. Horn, *The Army of Tennessee*, 76–77; *OR*, 7:710–11.

8. Thomas Lawrence Connelly, *Army of the Heartland: The Army of Tennessee, 1861–1862* (Baton Rouge: Louisiana State University Press, 1967), 79–85; *OR*, 3:739, 4:481, 491–92, 513–14, 517, 539, 7:699–700, 705, 710–11, 779, 813, 817–18, 52 (pt. 2): 239, 245–46; Horn, *The Army of Tennessee*, 76–77; William Eric Jamborsky, "Confederate Leadership and Defeat in the West," *Lincoln Herald* (Summer 1984): 57; Jopseh H. Parks, *General Leonidas Polk, C.S.A., the Fighting Bishop* (Baton Rouge: Louisiana State University Press, 1960), 188, 195; Benjamin Franklin Cooling, *Forts Henry and Donelson: The Key to the Confederate Heartland* (Knoxville: University of Tennessee Press, 1987), 58–59.

9. *OR*, 7:831, 833, 835, 839; Parks, *Leonidas Polk*, 206; Cooling, *Forts Henry and Donelson*, 85.

10. Cooling, *Forts Henry and Donelson*, 85.

11. Horn, *The Army of Tennessee*, 80–83; Cooling, *Forts Henry and Donelson*, 101–6.

12. Carl von Clausewitz, *On War*, ed. Anatol Rapoport (New York: Penguin, 1968), 164.

13. *OR*, 7:880; Roland, *Albert Sidney Johnston*, 295.

14. *OR*, 7:225, 880, 52 (pt. 2): 274.

15. *OR*, 7:255; Cooling, *Forts Henry and Donelson*, 180.

16. Roland, *Albert Sidney Johnston*, 319.

17. *OR*, 10 (pt. 2): 387. Of course there would not have been room between Owl and Lick Creeks for the three Confederate corps to deploy side by side if each was stretched out in a single line of battle. The obvious and far more desirable formation for Johnston to use would have been corps columns of attack, with most of each corps' units held in reserve behind those that would spearhead the initial assault, much as James Longstreet did in his famous attack at Chickamauga the following year.

18. Roland, *Albert Sidney Johnston*, 323; Larry J. Daniel, *Shiloh: The Battle that Changed the Civil War* (New York: Simon & Schuster, 1997), 118–20, argues that Johnston learned of the faulty deployment in time to have changed it.

19. Daniel, *Shiloh*, 128–29.

Chapter Two. "The Responsibility Is Great"

1. Quoted in Gilbert Govan and James W. Livingood, *A Different Valor, the Story of General Joseph E. Johnston, C.S.A.* (New York: Bobbs-Merrill, 1956), 158.

2. Joseph Eggleston Johnston, *Narrative of Military Operations during the Civil War* (New York: D. Appleton & Company, 1874; reprint, Bloomington: Indiana University Press, 1959), ix.

3. T. Harry Williams, "Military Leadership of the North and the South," in *The Harmon Memorial Lectures in Military History, 1959–1987* (Washington, D.C.: Office of Air Force History, 1988), 58.

4. James M. McPherson, *Battle Cry of Freedom: The Civil War Era* (New York: Oxford University Press, 1988), 857.

5. Clement Eaton, *Jefferson Davis* (New York: Free Press, 1977), 157.

6. Richard M. McMurry, *John Bell Hood and the War for Southern Independence* (Lexington: University Press of Kentucky, 1982), 94.

7. "Longstreet on the War," *New York Times*, July 29, 1879.

8. Henry Kyd Douglas, *I Rode with Stonewall* (Chapel Hill: University of North Carolina Press, 1968), 66.

9. David Hackett Fischer, *Historian's Fallacies* (New York: Harper & Row, 1970), 182–83.

10. Steven E. Woodworth, *Davis and Lee at War* (Lawrence: University Press of Kansas, 1995), 92.

11. Govan and Livingood, *A Different Valor*, 12–13.

12. William Campbell was a leader of the "over-mountain men"—settlers inhabiting the western frontier of Virginia, North Carolina, and South Carolina—who defeated British forces under Maj. Patrick Ferguson at King's Mountain, South Carolina, on October 7, 1780.

13. Peter Johnston bypassed his older sons and gave his sword to Joseph when the boy was only eight years old, probably owing to Joseph's interest in his father's military exploits.

14. Johnston's prewar military history is outlined in George W. Cullum, *Biographical Register of Officers and Graduates of the United States Military Academy at West Point*, vol. 1, *1802–1840* (New York: James Miller, 1879), 343–44.

15. Cecil Eby, *"That Disgraceful Affair": The Black Hawk War* (New York: W. W. Norton, 1973), 222–25. The trip to Fort Dearborn was anything but leisurely. Over half of the men on board contracted cholera, and the crew became mutinous.

16. Craig Symonds, *Joseph E. Johnston: A Civil War Biography* (New York: W. W. Norton, 1992), 28.

17. "Inquiry into Campaigns of Scott and Gaines," United States Senate Document No. 224, 24th Congress, 2d Session, 1837 (National Archives: United States Congressional Set). See also Virginia Bergman Peters, *The Florida Wars* (Hamden, Conn.: Archon Books, 1979), 118.

18. John K. Mahon, *History of the Second Seminole War, 1835–1842* (Gainesville: University Presses of Florida, 1967), 165–67, 219–20.

19. George E. Buker, *Swamp Sailors: Riverine Warfare in the Everglades, 1835–1842* (Gainesville: University Presses of Florida, 1975), 60–63.

20. J. R. Motte, *Journey into Wilderness: An Army Surgeon's Account of Life in Camp and Field during the Creek and Seminole Wars, 1836–1838*, ed. James F. Sunderman (Gainesville: University Presses of Florida, 1953), 182–83.

21. During one of these coastal surveys, a relationship developed between Johnston and Lydia McLane of Baltimore. Lydia was the daughter of former congressman and senator Louis McLane, who had served under President Jackson as secretary of the treasury, secretary of state, and minister to Great Britain. Johnston knew and was good friends with Lydia's brother Robert, a West Pointer himself. Joseph and Lydia were married on July 10, 1845.

22. Douglas Southall Freeman, *R. E. Lee*, 4 vols. (New York: Charles Scribner's Sons, 1934–1935), 1:219.

23. Benjamin Stoddert Ewell, "Notes on the Mexican War," Benjamin Stoddert Ewell Papers, Earl Gregg Swem Library, College of William & Mary.

24. Justin H. Smith, *The War with Mexico* (New York: Macmillan, 1919), 154–57.

25. Robert M. Hughes, *General Johnston* (New York: D. Appleton & Company, 1893), 32.

26. Robert E. Lee to John Mackay, October 2, 1847, Stephen H. Elliott Papers, United States Army War College, Carlisle Barracks, Pennsylvania.

27. J. E. Johnston to Louis T. Wigfall, March 14, 1865, Louis T. Wigfall Papers, Library of Congress.

28. Govan and Livingood, *A Different Valor*, 21. A good description of Johnston's close relationship with McClellan can be found in Symonds, *Joseph E. Johnston*, 77–78.

29. Govan and Livingood, *A Different Valor*, 34.

30. Freeman, *R. E. Lee*, 1:411.

31. Hughes, *General Johnston*, 35. Johnston later wrote, "I believed, like most others, that the division of the country would be permanent; and that, apart from any right of secession, the revolution begun was justified by the maxims so often repeated by Americans, that free government is founded on the consent of the governed, and that every community strong enough to establish and maintain its independence has a right to assert it." See Johnston, *Narrative of Military Operations*, 10. Joseph and Lydia were also opposed to slavery. Mary Chesnut writes, "Mrs. Johnston said she would never own slaves." See C. Vann Woodward, ed., *Mary Chesnut's Civil War* (New Haven, Conn.: Yale University Press, 1981), 729.

32. Woodward, *Mary Chesnut's Civil War*, 187.

33. Govan and Livingood, *A Different Valor*, 28. It is not clear why Mrs. Johnston was so distrustful of Jefferson Davis prior to her husband's Confederate service. Possibly she was angered at Davis's opposition to Johnston's appointment as quartermaster general or was reflecting a long-standing antipathy between the two men going back to their days at West Point. The story that the two men had fought over the affections of a young lady while they were at the academy cannot be substantiated. It is also conceivable that the conversation is inaccurate, having been distorted through time. Mrs. Johnston wrote of the exchange between herself and her husband in a letter to Mrs. Louis T. Wigfall, the wife of one of the most vocal anti-Davis members of the Confederate Congress. The letter was dated August 2, 1863—precisely the same time that General Johnston was defending his handling of the Vicksburg campaign.

34. Ibid.

35. Freeman, *R. E. Lee*, 1:462.

36. Emory Thomas, *The Confederacy as a Revolutionary Experience* (New York: Prentice-Hall, 1971), 1–2.

37. Symonds, *Joseph E. Johnston*, 20–21. Symonds offers a number of possible explanations for this loss of rank.

38. Joseph E. Johnston to Beverly Johnston, June 13, 1837, Joseph E. Johnston Collection, Earl Gregg Swem Library, College of William & Mary.

39. Joseph E. Johnston to Edward Johnston, January 6, 1851, Joseph E. Johnston Collection, Earl Gregg Swem Library, College of William & Mary.

40. Johnston, *Narrative of Military Operations*, 13.

41. George B. McClellan to E. D. Townsend, May 17, 1861, McClellan Papers, Library of Congress.

42. U.S. War Department, *The War of the Rebellion: A Compilation of the Official Records of the Union and Confederate Armies,* 128 vols. (Washington: Government Printing Office, 1881–1901), 2:471 (hereafter cited as *OR*). Johnston wrote, "The force at that point consisted of nine regiments and two battalions of infantry, four companies of artillery, with sixteen pieces without caissons, harness, or horses, and about three hundred cavalry. They were, of course, undisciplined, several regiments without accouterments, and with an entirely inadequate supply of ammunition."

43. Paul E. Steiner, *Disease in the Civil War: Natural Biological Warfare in 1861–1865,* (Springfield, Ill.: Charles C. Thomas, 1968), 27–28.

44. See *OR*, 2:471. Johnston's assessment of the strategic and tactical problems posed by the location of Harpers Ferry was proved correct if one looks at the history of the town throughout the war. Neither Union nor Confederate defenders were ever successful in preventing the town's capture. As a consequence, Harpers Ferry changed hands repeatedly.

45. *OR*, 2:890.

46. James Longstreet, *From Manassas to Appomattox: Memoirs of the Civil War in America,* ed. James I. Robertson, Jr. (Bloomington: Indiana University Press, 1960), 113.

47. *OR*, 2:881.

48. Joseph E. Johnston to R. S. Garnett, May 28, 1861, *OR*, 2:889.

49. Johnston, *Narrative of Military Operations,* 18–19. Col. J. W. Allen wrote to Johnston that "the Federal troops concentrated at Chambersburg number thirteen thousand. The advance guard, of three thousand, left there at 1 p.m. for Hagerstown, where they will encamp to-night, from which force vedettes are to be thrown into Williamsport. . . . The communication in pencil is from a perfectly reliable source. I would wish positive instructions, and, if to make a stand, re-enforcements. My line of defense is too extended for my present force. Owing to disaffection in Captain White's cavalry, they are not as efficient as they should be, and incompetent to guard the river." J. W. Allen to Joseph E. Johnston, May 31, 1861, *OR*, 2:899.

50. Joseph E. Johnston to Robert E. Lee, May 31, 1861, *OR*, 2:896.

51. Robert E. Lee to Joseph E. Johnston, June 1, 1861, *OR*, 2:897.

52. Robert E. Lee to Joseph E. Johnston, June 3, 1861, *OR*, 2:901.

53. Joseph E. Johnston to Robert E. Lee, June 6, 1861, *OR*, 2:907–8. Johnston added, "I offer these opinions for what they are worth, thinking it my duty to present them to you, and being anxious to conform closely to whatever general plan of operations has been determined upon. I beg you, therefore, to let me understand my position."

54. Johnston, *Narrative of Military Operations,* 21–22.

55. Robert E. Lee to Joseph E. Johnston, June 7, 1861, *OR*, 2:910.

56. Johnston, *Narrative of Military Operations,* 20–21.

57. *OR*, 2:66.

58. Jeffrey N. Lash, *Destroyer of the Iron Horse: General Joseph E. Johnston and Confederate Rail Transport, 1861–1865* (Kent, Ohio: Kent State University Press, 1991), 12–13.

59. Lash, *Destroyer of the Iron Horse,* 13; Woodworth, *Davis and Lee at War,* 28.

60. Samuel Cooper to Joseph Johnston, June 19, 1861, *OR*, 2:940.

61. Robert E. Lee to Joseph E. Johnston, June 1, 1861, *OR*, 2:897–98.

62. Lash, *Destroyer of the Iron Horse*, 15.

63. Jefferson Davis, *The Rise and Fall of the Confederate Government*, 2 vols. (New York: Thomas Yoseloff, 1958), 1:345.

64. Johnston, *Narrative of Military Operations*, 33.

65. Jefferson Davis to Joseph E. Johnston, July 20, 1861, OR, 2:985.

66. Special Order No.___, July 21, 1861, Joseph E. Johnston Papers, Henry E. Huntington Library.

67. Johnston, *Narrative of Military Operations*, 48–49. Johnston suggests that Beauregard readily concurred with this arrangement, remarking that command of the troops immediately engaged "belonged to the second in rank, not to the commander of the army." Beauregard claimed, ten years after the publication of Johnston's memoirs, that Johnston had given him command of the Confederate forces and that he, not Johnston, had actually directed the day's operations. P. G. T. Beauregard, "The First Battle of Bull Run," in Robert Underwood Johnson and Clarence Clough Buel, eds., *Battles and Leaders of the Civil War*, 4 vols. (New York: Century Company, 1887–1888), 1:226–27.

68. Gary W. Gallagher, ed., *Fighting for the Confederacy: The Personal Recollections of General Edward Porter Alexander* (Chapel Hill: University of North Carolina Press, 1989), 52–53. Alexander came down from his signal station atop Wilcoxen's Hill to ascertain whether Generals Johnston and Beauregard understood the magnitude of the Federal envelopment.

69. Johnston, *Narrative of Military Operations*, 52–53; Joseph E. Johnston, "Responsibilities of the First Bull Run," in *Battles and Leaders of the Civil War*, 1:249. Johnston's characteristic penchant for precision is reflected in the care that he took to note the exact time the Federal retreat began.

70. In *The Rise and Fall of the Confederate Government*, Davis claims to have arrived on the battlefield in time to see a column of Federal infantry routed by a band of Confederate cavalry—implying that he was on the field before the battle was over. What Davis saw was a column of Confederate troops. See Davis, *Rise and Fall*, 1:349.

71. Jubal Anderson Early, *War Memoirs* (Bloomington: Indiana University Press, 1960), 41.

72. Johnston, *Narrative of Military Operations*, 59–60. Contributing to and supporting the argument that the South made a mistake in not advancing on Washington following the victory at Manassas was R. L. Dabney's popular biography of Stonewall Jackson published in 1866. Dabney states that Jackson had confided to his friends that the Confederate inaction was a "deplorable blunder." See R. L. Dabney, *Life and Campaigns of Lt. General T. J. (Stonewall) Jackson* (Boston: Scrymgeour, Whitcomb & Co., 1866), 234.

73. For example, "The Beauregard Manassas Quick-step" and "Gen'l Beauregard's Grand Polka Militaire." T. Harry Williams, *P. G. T. Beauregard, Napoleon in Gray* (Baton Rouge: Louisiana State University Press, 1955), 91–92; William C. Davis, *Battle at Bull Run* (New York: Doubleday, 1977), 248.

74. Johnston, *Narrative of Military Operations*, 59.

75. Joseph E. Johnston to Jefferson Davis, September 3, 1861, in Linda Crist and Mary Dix, eds., *The Papers of Jefferson Davis* (Baton Rouge: Louisiana States University Press, 1992), 7:321.

76. Davis, *Rise and Fall*, 1:449.

77. OR, 5:884–87.

78. Woodworth does a good job in pointing out this similarity between Davis and Johnston. See *Davis and Lee at War*, 53, 65, 68–69, 97.

79. Joseph E. Johnston to Jefferson Davis, September 12, 1861, *OR*, 4:605–8.

80. Ibid.; italics added.

81. Woodworth, *Davis and Lee at War*, 54–55. See also William C. Davis, *Jefferson Davis, the Man and His Hour* (New York: HarperCollins, 1991), 360–61.

82. Davis to Johnston, September 5, 1861; Davis to Johnston, September 8, 1861; Davis to Johnston, September 13, 1861. All in Joseph E. Johnston Papers, Henry E. Huntington Library. Davis had made this error before, specifically in reference to "Mrs. Johnson," but had since then spelled the general's name correctly in letters to other individuals. Davis to Johnston, August 1, 1861, Joseph E. Johnston Papers, Henry E. Huntington Library. Both *OR* and Dunbar Rowland's *Jefferson Davis Constitutionalist*, 10 vols. (Jackson: Mississippi Department of Archives and History, 1926) correct Davis's misspellings. Crist and Dix's *Papers of Jefferson Davis* preserves the president's misspellings but does not reprint the entirety of these three key letters.

83. Eli N. Evans, *Judah P. Benjamin, the Jewish Confederate* (New York: Free Press, 1988), 116, 121. See also Burton J. Hendrick, *Statesmen of the Lost Cause: Jefferson Davis and His Cabinet* (New York: Literary Guild of America, 1939), 178–81.

84. Stephen R. Mallory Diary, 2:207, Southern Historical Collection, University of North Carolina–Chapel Hill.

85. Quoted in Govan and Livingood, *A Different Valor*, 83.

86. Johnston had earlier suggested that Davis leave Richmond and take the field, in all likelihood knowing that Davis would not (or at least could not) do such a thing. See Joseph E. Johnston to Jefferson Davis, June 26, 1861, in Crist and Dix, *Papers of Jefferson Davis*, 7:213. It was also Johnston's habit to tone down his communiqués with Richmond to reflect a more deferential air. This point is clear if one compares extant original drafts with final versions printed in *OR*.

87. When asked by congressmen at a Richmond dinner party about the future of the Confederate war effort under Benjamin's leadership, Johnston expressed pessimism. Upon learning of the general's reply, a clerk in the War Department wrote in his diary that "Joseph E. Johnston is a doomed fly." See John B. Jones, *A Rebel War Clerk's Diary*, 2 vols. (Philadelphia: Lippincott & Company, 1866), 1:116. Davis remained stubbornly loyal to his friend, eventually responding to the demand for change by shifting Benjamin to secretary of state in March and appointing George Wythe Randolph secretary of war. This change in roles for Benjamin had no detrimental effect on his ability to influence the Confederate president. It is not clear whether Benjamin's opinion that Johnston would not fight persuaded the president to believe the same. What we do know is that for the remainder of the war, Davis found support and encouragement for his views when they conflicted with those of Johnston.

88. Joseph E. Johnston to W. H. C. Whiting, February 28, 1862, *OR*, 5:1085.

89. Jefferson Davis to Joseph E. Johnston, February 28, 1862, *OR*, 5:1084. Davis later denied that this indicated support for a withdrawal.

90. Joseph E. Johnston to Jefferson Davis, March 3, 1862, *OR*, 5:1088.

91. Johnston, *Narrative of Military Operations*, 101–2.

92. John Bakeless, *Spies of the Confederacy* (Philadelphia: J. B. Lippincott, 1970), 96–101.

93. Johnston later estimated that the amount of provisions destroyed at Manassas represented a total of six days' rations for the troops in Virginia. See Joseph E. Johnston, "Responsibilities of the First Bull Run," in *Battles and Leaders of the Civil War*, 1:257.

94. William Willis Blackford, *War Years with J. E. B. Stuart* (New York: Charles Scribner, 1945), 59–60.

95. After the war, Davis wrote that by "first policy" he meant an offensive operation. Davis, *Rise and Fall*, 1:464.

96. Quoted in Govan and Livingood, *A Different Valor*, 102.

97. Ibid.

98. After a poor performance in western Virginia in the fall of 1861, followed by a tour of South Carolina and Georgia supervising the construction of coastal fortifications, Lee was back in his de facto role as military adviser to the president.

99. Joseph E. Johnston to Robert E. Lee, March 27, 1862, *OR*, 11 (pt. 3): 405–6.

100. Beverly Johnston to Joseph E. Johnson, February 23, 1868, Robert Morton Hughes Papers, Old Dominion University.

101. Johnston considered Longstreet to be one of his most capable officers. Since the previous fall, Johnston had been increasing Longstreet's responsibilities and even desired to appoint him second in command—something that he was unable to do because of Smith's seniority. See William Garrett Piston, "Lee's Tarnished Lieutenant: James Longstreet and His Image in American Society," Ph.D. diss., University of South Carolina, 1982, 150.

102. Joseph E. Johnston, "Manassas to Seven Pines," in *Battles and Leaders of the Civil War*, 2:203–7; Johnston, *Narrative of Military Operations*, 114–15.

103. Although he chose not to mention it at the meeting, Longstreet did have a counterproposal. His strategic thinking considered leaving Magruder on the peninsula to delay McClellan while Confederate forces concentrated in the Shenandoah Valley for a strike across the Potomac. The Army of the Potomac would be forced to abandon its operation against Richmond to come to the defense of Washington. Longstreet, *From Manassas to Appomattox*, 66. Gustavus Smith actually suggested a similar (yet more grandiose) idea: leaving enough troops in Richmond to defend the capital while the remainder moved across the Potomac toward Philadelphia or New York.

104. Both Georgia and South Carolina had already sent troops to Tennessee in the wake of defeats suffered by Confederate forces earlier in the year. Freeman, *R. E. Lee*, 2:22.

105. McClellan did order a reconnaissance-in-force on April 16 toward the center of the Confederate line at Dam No. 1. After capturing a few partially occupied rifle pits, the Federals were ordered to return to their original lines.

106. Quoted in Richard Wheeler, *Sword over Richmond: An Eyewitness History of McClellan's Peninsula Campaign* (New York: Harper & Row, 1986), 135.

107. Stephen W. Sears, *To the Gates of Richmond, the Peninsula Campaign* (New York: Ticknor & Fields, 1992), 66.

108. Franklin's division disembarked on May 2 only to embark once again three days later. McClellan's original plans called for McDowell's corps to undertake the turning movement. Once McDowell was withheld from the peninsula, McClellan decided that a division would suffice. He soon developed second thoughts.

109. Robert E. Lee to Joseph E. Johnston, April 23, 1862, *OR*, 11 (pt. 3): 458.

110. Josiah Tatnall to Joseph E. Johnston, April 30, 1862, *OR*, 11 (pt. 3): 477–78.

111. Early, *War Memoirs*, 66.

112. Gallagher, *Fighting for the Confederacy*, 77.

113. Joseph E. Johnston to Robert E. Lee, April 29, 1862, *OR*, 11 (pt. 3): 473.

114. *OR*, 11 (pt. 1): 450, 568–69.

115. Joseph E. Johnston, "Manassas to Seven Pines," in *Battles and Leaders of the Civil War*, 2:208.

116. Steiner, *Disease in the Civil War*, 138–39. Steiner notes that McClellan, as a consequence of the unhealthy terrain, was losing about one regiment a day to sickness and communicable disease.

117. *OR* 11 (pt. 3): 495–96, 501–2, 557.

118. Stephen Sears, *George B. McClellan: The Young Napoleon* (New York: Tickner & Fields, 1988), 188–89; James McPherson, *Battle Cry of Freedom*, 454.

119. Stephen Sears argues in his biography of McClellan that the Federal general had anticipated conducting siege operations ever since the navy had been turned away from Drewry's Bluff and consequently would not relinquish control of the rail line. Sears, *George B. McClellan*, 188–89.

120. Davis, *Rise and Fall*, 2:102.

121. Jefferson Davis to Joseph E. Johnston, May 17, 1862, *OR*, 11 (pt. 3): 523–24.

122. By way of comparison, the Confederate army at Shiloh numbered approximately 42,000.

123. Quoted in Sears, *George B. McClellan*, 193.

124. E. P. Alexander, now serving as Johnston's chief of ordnance, recalled that the general's plan "was an excellent & well devised scheme, & apparently as simple as any plan could be. Properly carried out it is hard to see how it could have failed to overwhelm all the enemy south of the Chickahominy, by a concentrated attack of superior numbers. But note how a single misconception brought chaos over the whole. . . . Gen. Longstreet entirely misconceived his orders." Gallagher, *Fighting for the Confederacy*, 85.

125. Douglas Southall Freeman, *Lee's Lieutenants: A Study in Command*, 3 vols. (New York: Scribner's, 1942–1944), 1:237n.

126. Johnston, *Narrative of Military Operations*, 138–39; Varina Davis, *Jefferson Davis, Ex-President of the Confederate States of America: A Memoir by His Wife*, 2 vols. (New York: Belford, 1890), 2:292.

127. Jeffry Wert, *General James Longstreet* (New York: Simon & Schuster, 1993), 113.

128. "Supplemental Notes," no. 4, Robert M. Hughes Papers, Old Dominion University.

129. Emory Thomas, *Robert E. Lee* (New York: W. W. Norton, 1995), 36–37.

Chapter Three. Fighting for Defeat?

1. Thomas to McClellan, June 22, 1861, in U.S. War Department, *The War of the Rebellion: A Compilation of the Official Records of the Union and Confederate Armies*, 128 vols. (Washington, D.C.: Government Printing Office, 1881–1901), 2: 753 (hereafter cited as *OR*; all references are to series I unless otherwise noted).

2. Stephen W. Sears, *George B. McClellan: The Young Napoleon* (New York: Ticknor & Fields, 1988), xi–xii; James M. McPherson, *Battle Cry of Freedom: The Civil War Era* (New York: Oxford University Press, 1988), 365; Michael C. C. Adams, *Our Masters the Rebels: A Speculation on Union Military Failure in the East*,

1861–1865 (Cambridge, Mass.: Harvard University Press, 1978), 88–103, republished as *Fighting for Defeat: Union Military Failure in the East, 1861–1865* (Lincoln: University of Nebraska Press, 1996).

3. Stephen W. Sears, *To the Gates of Richmond: The Peninsula Campaign* (New York: Ticknor & Fields, 1992), 210–11; McPherson, *Battle Cry of Freedom*, 466–70; Adams, *Our Masters the Rebels*, 90–91.

4. For an excellent critique of the conclusions historians have drawn from psychoanalysis of McClellan that argues that the general has suffered from unfair comparison with Grant and Sherman, who pursued more "realistic" war aims, see Thomas J. Rowland, "In the Shadows of Grant and Sherman: George B. McClellan Revisited," *Civil War History* 40 (September 1994): 202–25. The two most insightful studies of the peninsula campaign provide dramatically different approaches to the campaign and evaluations of McClellan's generalship. Sears's *To the Gates of Richmond* is a comprehensive narrative of the campaign that makes little effort to place it in a broader context and is harshly critical of McClellan. Although less detailed, Rowena Reed's *Combined Operations in the Civil War* (Annapolis, Md.: Naval Institute Press, 1978), 97–189, places the peninsula campaign within the broader context of the evolution of the concept of combined operations during the war and is highly favorable to McClellan. In the most extended defense of McClellan published to date, Warren W. Hassler, Jr., attributes the general's failure in the peninsula campaign to the machinations of his enemies in Washington (Hassler, *General George B. McClellan: Shield of the Union* [Baton Rouge: Louisiana State University Press, 1957]). For an excellent and underappreciated study that places McClellan's endeavors in the context of the emerging culture of military professionalism and the problems of organization, logistics, and strategic and tactical doctrine inherent in the transition from preindustrial to modern warfare that occurred during the Civil War, see Edward Hagerman, *The American Civil War and the Origins of Modern Warfare: Ideas, Organization, and Field Command* (Bloomington: Indiana University Press, 1988), 31–55.

5. This definition of "cultural outlook" is based on intellectual and political historian Daniel Walker Howe's use of the term "culture." Howe, *The Political Culture of the American Whigs* (Chicago: University of Chicago Press, 1979), 2–3.

6. George B. McClellan, "Austria, June 20, 1866—Early Draft of Autobiography," George B. McClellan (Sr.) Papers, Manuscript Division, Library of Congress, Washington, D.C., [container] D9/reel 71 (repository hereafter cited as LC); George McClellan to John M. Clayton, November 2, 1842, February 3, 184[4], John Middleton Clayton Papers, LC, container 1; John W. Forney, *Anecdotes of Public Men* (Washington, D.C.: Harper & Brothers, 1873), 187–88; George B. McClellan, Jr., *The Gentleman and the Tiger: The Autobiography of George B. McClellan, Jr.*, ed. Harold C. Syrett (Philadelphia: J. B. Lippincott, 1956), 60; George McClellan to George B. McClellan, March 17, 1847, McClellan Papers, B1/reel 43; George B. McClellan to John H. B. McClellan, January 21, 1843, ibid., A1/reel 1; George B. McClellan to Frederica M. English, September 25, 1848, ibid. McClellan biographers Sears and William Starr Myers mention the general's early affiliation with the Whigs in passing but make no effort to explain Whig culture nor link it with McClellan's Civil War career. Sears, *George B. McClellan*, 32; William Starr Myers, *A Study in Personality: General George Brinton McClellan* (New York: D. Appleton & Company, 1934), 13.

7. In a speech to his West Point classmates in 1846, McClellan asserted that without educated officers, in wartime "there would be displayed the very worst and meanest of our passions. It is the part of the officer to check by the influence of his character the outbreak of these unruly dispositions . . . to impose . . . order and discipline." Without them, he warned his listeners, "we see the spirit of the ages in which the passions of men had the mastery over his reason." McClellan, "Address to the Dialectic Society," June 1846, McClellan Papers, A1/reel 1. Howe, *Political Culture of the American Whigs*, 19, 29–34; Thomas Brown, *Politics and Statesmanship: Essays on the American Whig Party* (New York: Columbia University Press, 1985), 8–10, 45–53; Irving Bartlett, "Daniel Webster as a Symbolic Hero," *New England Quarterly* 45 (December 1972): 484–507.

8. George B. McClellan to John H. B. McClellan, February 3, 1852, McClellan Papers, A3/reel 2; George B. McClellan to Frederica M. English, July 21, 1851, ibid.; McClellan Diary, Red River Expedition, entries for May 31, June 1, ibid., D3/reel 67; McClellan, "Austria, June 20, 1866—Early Draft of Autobiography," ibid., D9/reel 71. The McClellan, Clay, and Webster households were not the only ones in which terror at the prospect of a victorious Republican party led them to defect to the Democrats. Webster's associates in the Cotton Whig aristocracy gravitated en masse to the Democrats. David M. Potter, *The Impending Crisis, 1848–1861*, completed and ed. Don E. Fehrenbacher (New York: Harper & Row, 1976), 263; Thomas O'Connor, *Lords of the Loom: The Cotton Whigs and the Coming of the Civil War* (New York: Charles Scribner's, 1968), 115, 122, 128.

9. George B. McClellan, *McClellan's Own Story: The War for the Union, the Soldiers Who Fought It, the Civilians Who Directed It, and His Relations to Them*, ed. William C. Prime (New York: Charles L. Webster, 1887), 29–38; Sears, *George B. McClellan*, 65–66; Joseph L. Harsh, "Lincoln's Tarnished Brass: Conservative Strategies and the Attempt to Fight the Civil War as a Limited War," in Lawrence L. Hewitt and Roman J. Heleniak, eds., *The Confederate High Command and Related Topics: The 1988 Deep Delta Civil War Symposium: Themes in Honor of T. Harry Williams* (Shippensburg, Pa.: White Mane Publishing, 1990), 124–41; Mark Grimsley, *The Hard Hand of War: Union Military Policy toward Southern Civilians, 1861–1865* (Cambridge: Cambridge University Press, 1995), 2–3, 23–26, 31–35.

10. Grimsley, *Hard Hand of War*, 8–11; Richard E. Beringer, Herman Hattaway, Archer Jones, and William Still, *Why the South Lost the Civil War* (Athens: University of Georgia Press, 1986), 64–81.

11. The fullest exposition of McClellan's views on how the war should be conducted is contained in a memorandum he submitted to President Lincoln on August 2, 1861. George B. McClellan, "Memorandum for the Consideration of His Excellency the President, submitted at his request," [August 2, 1861], in Stephen W. Sears, ed., *The Civil War Papers of George B. McClellan: Selected Correspondence, 1860–1865* (New York: Ticknor & Fields, 1989), 71–75; Harsh, "Lincoln's Tarnished Brass," 127–28; Sears, *George B. McClellan*, 98–100.

12. McClellan to Stanton, February 3, 1862, in Sears, *Civil War Papers of McClellan*, 167–70. McClellan's appreciation of the power of the tactical defense and his desire to use strategic turning movements to force the enemy to undertake frontal assaults on entrenched positions are discussed in Herman Hattaway and Archer Jones, *How the North Won: A Military History of the Civil War* (Urbana: University of Illinois Press, 1982), 89–94, 145.

13. Discussion of the advantages to the Union of using the Chesapeake as a base are provided in Steven E. Woodworth, *Davis and Lee at War* (Lawrence: University Press of Kansas, 1995), 12–13; and Beringer et al., *Why the South Lost the Civil War*, 158–62.

14. Harsh, "Lincoln's Tarnished Brass," 137. McClellan's unique recognition of the potential effectiveness of combined operations is a central theme of Reed's work. Reed, *Combined Operations in the Civil War*, xxxi–xxxii.

15. McClellan's report, August 4, 1863, *OR*, 5:50–51; McClellan to Stanton, March 19, 1862, in Sears, *Civil War Papers of McClellan*, 215–16.

16. Reed attributes difficulties between McClellan and Goldsborough to the army's liaison to the Navy Department, John G. Barnard, who opposed the peninsula strategy. Reed, *Combined Operations in the Civil War*, 128–29. For Barnard's objections to the idea of taking the army to the lower Chesapeake, see Barnard to McClellan, [c. December 1, 1861], *OR*, 5:671–73; Barnard to McClellan, December 6, 1861, McClellan Papers, A32/reel 14. George B. McClellan, "The Peninsular Campaign," in Robert U. Johnson and Clarence C. Buel, eds., *Battles and Leaders of the Civil War*, 4 vols. (New York: Century Company, 1884–1889), 2:169; Thomas to McClellan, April 4, 1862, *OR*, 11 (pt. 3): 66. For discussion of the role of Lincoln's and Stanton's concern for the capital in compromising the success of operations on the peninsula, see Thomas J. Rowland, "'Heaven Save a Country Governed by Such Counsels!' The Safety of Washington and the Peninsula Campaign," *Civil War History* 42 (March 1996): 5–17.

17. McClellan to Stanton, April 4, 10, 1862, *OR*, 11 (pt. 3): 67, 86; McClellan to Scott, April 11, 1862, in Sears, *Civil War Papers of McClellan*, 236; McClellan to McDowell, April 4, 1862, ibid., 227–28; McClellan to Lincoln, April 5, 6, 1862, ibid., 228, 231; McClellan to Wool, April [7?], 1862, *OR*, 11 (pt. 3): 76–77; McClellan to Goldsborough, April 8, 1862, ibid., 79.

18. McClellan to his wife, April 14, 19, 23, 30, 1862, in Sears, *Civil War Papers of McClellan*, 239, 243–44, 245, 250–51; McClellan to Lincoln, April 7, 1862, ibid., 233; Lincoln to McClellan, April 6, 9, 1862, in Roy P. Basler, ed., *The Collected Works of Abraham Lincoln*, 9 vols. (New Brunswick, N.J.: Rutgers University Press, 1953–1955), 5: 182, 184–85; Grimsley, *Hard Hand of War*, 71–72; Eric T. Dean, Jr., "'We Live under a Government of Men and Morning Newspapers': Image, Expectation, and the Peninsula Campaign of 1862," *Virginia Magazine of History and Biography* 103 (January 1995): 9–15, 22–24. Although he does not challenge Dean's assertion that public expectations were unrealistically high in 1862, Brooks D. Simpson disagrees with his argument that the press developed a better appreciation of military realities by 1864 that helped Grant succeed where McClellan had failed. Simpson, "Great Expectations: Ulysses S. Grant, the Northern Press, and the Opening of the Wilderness Campaign," in Gary W. Gallagher, ed., *The Wilderness Campaign* (Chapel Hill: University of North Carolina Press, 1997), 1–35. Concerns that McClellan and military professionals in general lacked a "proper" spirit, which were particularly prevalent among the members of the Joint Committee on the Conduct of the War, are discussed in T. Harry Williams, "The Attack upon West Point during the Civil War," *Mississippi Valley Historical Review* 25 (March 1939): 491–504; Phillip Shaw Paludan, *"A People's Contest": The Union and the Civil War, 1861–1865* (New York: Harper & Row, 1988), 63–65, 72, 83–84; and, especially, Bruce Tap, *Over Lincoln's Shoulder: The Joint Committee on the Conduct of the War* (Lawrence: University Press of Kansas, 1998).

19. Johnston to Lee, April 29, 30, 1862, *OR*, 11 (pt. 3): 473, 477; Craig L. Symonds, *Joseph E. Johnston: A Civil War Biography* (New York: W. W. Norton, 1992), 148–50; Magruder to Rhett, April 24, 1862, *OR*, 11 (pt. 3): 463; Huger to Lee, April 29, 1862, ibid., 474; Woodworth, *Davis and Lee at War*, 111–19.

20. McClellan to Goldsborough, April 10, 1862, *OR*, 11 (pt. 3): 87; McClellan to Franklin, April 10, 1862, ibid., 87–88; McClellan to Stanton, April 12, 1862, in Sears, *Civil War Papers of McClellan*, 237; McClellan to his wife, April 18, 19, 27, 1862, ibid., 240–41, 243, 249–50; Special Orders No. 126, April 27, 1862, *OR*, 11 (pt. 3): 125.

21. McClellan to Franklin, May 5, 1862, *OR*, 11 (pt. 3): 143; McClellan to Stanton, May 5, 7, 8, 10, 14, 15, 1862, ibid., 142, 148–49, 150, 151, 160, 170–71, 174; McClellan to Rodgers, May 9, 1862, ibid., 156–57; Special Orders No. 147, May 14, 1862, ibid., 172–73; Entries for May 2, 4, 1862, Excerpts from the Journal of Brigadier-General Samuel Peter Heintzelman, U.S. Army, March 17–August 22, 1862, in Janet B. Hewitt et al., eds., *Supplement to the Official Records of the Union and Confederate Armies, Part 1: Reports*, 10 vols. (Wilmington, N.C.: Broadfoot Publishing, 1995), 2: 42, 44 (hereafter cited as Heintzelman journal, *OR Supplement*). For full accounts of the fight at Williamsburg, see Earl C. Hastings and David S. Hastings, *"A Pitiless Rain": The Battle of Williamsburg, 1862* (Shippensburg, Pa.: White Mane Publishing, 1997), and Sears, *To the Gates of Richmond*, 68–82.

22. Stanton to McClellan, May 11, 1862, McClellan Papers, A57/reel 22; Kurt Hackemer, "The Other Union Ironclad: The USS *Galena* and the Critical Summer of 1862," *Civil War History* 40 (September 1994): 233–37; Sears, *To the Gates of Richmond*, 92–94.

23. Albert Castel, "Mars and the Reverend Longstreet, or, Attacking and Dying in the Civil War," *Civil War History* 33 (June 1987): 112.

24. President's General War Order No. 2, March 8, 1862, in Basler, *Collected Works of Lincoln*, 5: 149–50; Erasmus D. Keyes, *Fifty Years Observations of Men and Events Civil and Military* (New York: Charles Scribner's Sons, 1884), 437–38; Robert M. Epstein, "The Creation and Evolution of the Army Corps in the American Civil War," *Journal of Military History* 55 (January 1991): 30–34; Entry for March 8, 1862, Heintzelman Diary, Samuel P. Heintzelman Papers, LC, container 5/reel 7; Sears, *George B. McClellan*, 159–60.

25. Porter to Butterfield, May 5, 1862, Fitz-John Porter Papers, LC, container 53; McClellan to his wife, May 6, 8, 1862, in Sears, *Civil War Papers of McClellan*, 257–58, 260; McClellan to Stanton, May 9, 1862, ibid., 258.

26. Stanton to McClellan, May 9, 1862, *OR*, 11 (pt. 3): 154; Lincoln to McClellan, May 9, 1862, ibid., 154–55. A perception that McClellan was unfairly favoring certain officers over others was prevalent not only in Washington. During the siege of Yorktown, Heintzelman noted in his journal that McClellan's closeness to Porter was creating "great dissatisfaction. . . . No less than three generals report to me about it, and one of them this morning was afraid his name would have to be changed to Porter before he would be able to do anything." Entry for April 29, 1862, Heintzelman journal, *OR Supplement* 2: 40. McClellan's initial report on the battle of Williamsburg, in which he singled out Winfield Scott Hancock for praise without mentioning other officers whose forces had participated in the fighting, stimulated further grumbling. Entries for May 10, 13, 1862, ibid., 52, 54; Orlando M. Poe to his wife, May 12, 1862, Orlando Metcalfe Poe Papers, LC, box 2; Philip Kearny to O. S. Halstad, May 15, 1862, James William Eldridge Papers, Henry E. Huntington Library, San Marino, Calif., box 33.

27. Special Orders Nos. 146 and 147, May 12, 14, 1862, ibid., 168, 172–73; General Orders, No. 125, ibid., 181; Frank J. Welcher, *The Union Army: Organization and Operations*, Vol. 1, *The Eastern Theater* (Bloomington: Indiana University Press, 1989), 804–6.

28. McClellan, "The Peninsular Campaign," 173; McClellan to Stanton, May 10, 1862, in Sears, *Civil War Papers of McClellan*, 251.

29. Johnston to Lee, April 29, 1862, *OR*, 11 (pt. 3): 473; Johnston to Cooper, May 19, 1862, ibid., 11 (pt. 1): 276; Symonds, *Joseph E. Johnston*, 150–52, 156–57; Sears, *To the Gates of Richmond*, 95.

30. Lee to Johnston, May 17, 1862, in Clifford Dowdey and Louis H. Manarin, eds., *The Wartime Papers of R. E. Lee* (Boston: Little, Brown, 1961), 175; Davis to Johnston, May 17, 1862, *OR*, 11 (pt. 3): 523–24; Woodworth, *Davis and Lee at War*, 132.

31. McClellan to Lincoln, May 14, 1862, in Sears, *Civil War Papers of McClellan*, 264–65; Stanton to McClellan, May 18, 1862, *OR*, 11 (pt. 1): 27.

32. McClellan's report, August 4, 1863, *OR*, 5:28; McClellan, "The Peninsular Campaign," 173.

33. Reed, *Combined Operations in the Civil War*, 161, 169–77; McClellan to Rodgers, June 24, 1862, in Sears, *Civil War Papers of McClellan*, 307; Sears, *To the Gates of Richmond*, 104–6.

34. Lincoln to McClellan, May 24, 1862, *OR*, 11 (pt. 1): 30; Lincoln to McDowell, May 24, 1862, in Basler, *Collected Works of Lincoln*, 5:232; McDowell to Lincoln, May 24, 1862 [two telegrams], *OR*, 12 (pt. 3): 219–20, 220–21; McDowell to McClellan, June 8, 1862, *OR*, 11 (pt. 3): 220–21; Rowland, "Heaven Save a Country Governed by Such Counsels," 12–13.

35. McClellan's report, August 4, 1863, *OR*, 11 (pt. 1): 25; McClellan's complaints about the weather and the state of the Chickahominy can be found in McClellan to Lincoln, June 4, 1862, in Sears, *Civil War Papers of McClellan*, 288–89 *OR*, 11 (pt. 1): 45; McClellan to his wife, May 26, June 10, 1862, in Sears, ibid., 277, 294; McClellan to Stanton, June 5, 7, 10, 1862, *OR*, 11 (pt. 1): 45–47. The heavy rains also complicated efforts to keep the army supplied. Although I do not agree with all of its conclusions, for an extensively researched and informative study of the difficulties encountered by Union quartermasters, see William J. Miller, "'Scarcely any Parallel in History': Logistics, Friction, and McClellan's Strategy for the Peninsula Campaign," in William J. Miller, ed., *The Peninsula Campaign of 1862: Yorktown to the Seven Days*, vol. 2 (Campbell, Calif.: Savas Woodbury Publishers, 1995), 125–83. The three volumes so far published in this series offer a number of valuable essays that supplement more general works on the campaign. A full account of the battle of Fair Oaks is provided in Sears, *To the Gates of Richmond*, 117–51.

36. When the Seven Days battles commenced on June 25, Lee's army enjoyed numerical superiority, although not to the extent that McClellan believed at the time. With the addition of Jackson's forces, Lee's army numbered 112,220 on June 20, 1862, a number that swelled to 113,282 with the arrival of two regiments, the 44th Alabama and the 52nd Georgia, during the Seven Days. The Army of the Potomac numbered 101,434 on June 20 and received no reinforcements until it reached Harrison's Landing. Leon Walter Tenney, "Seven Days in 1862: Numbers in Union and Confederate Armies before Richmond," master's thesis, George Mason University, 1992, pp. 93–122, 133, 208.

37. McClellan to Stanton, June 12, 1862, in Sears, *Civil War Papers of McClellan*, 297–98. McClellan's opinion that McDowell should be sent by water

was seconded by Winfield Scott, who stated in a memorandum he handed to Lincoln when the president made an impromptu visit to West Point to consult with him on June 24 (which was of course too late to alter the course of events near Richmond): "The force at Fredericksburg seems entirely out of position, & it cannot be called up, directly & in time, by McClellan, from the want of rail-road transportation, or an adequate supply train. . . . If, however, there be a sufficient number of vessels, at hand, that force might reach the head of the York river, by water, in time to aid the operation against Richmond." Scott to Lincoln, June 24, 1862, in Basler, *Collected Works of Lincoln*, 5:284n1.

38. Fitz-John Porter, "Hanover Court-House and Gaines Mill," in Johnson and Buel, *Battles and Leaders of the Civil War*, 2:324; Myer to Marcy, undated, *OR*, 11 (pt. 1): 998–99; Peck to Williams, June 25, 1862, *OR*, 11 (pt. 3): 255–56; Van Vliet's report, August 2, 1862, *OR*, 11 (pt. 1): 159; McClellan's report, August 4, 1863, ibid., 52; Clifford Dowdey, *The Seven Days: The Emergence of Robert E. Lee* (New York: Little, Brown, 1964), 136.

39. Lee to Davis, June 5, 1862, in Dowdey and Manarin, *Wartime Papers of R. E. Lee*, 184.

40. Lee to Davis, June 10, 1862, in ibid., 188; Lee to Jackson, June 11, 16, 1862, *OR*, 11 (pt. 3): 589–90, 602. For analysis of Lee's plans to relieve the siege of Richmond and his overall strategic views, see Woodworth, *Davis and Lee at War*, 156–59, 197, and passim; Emory M. Thomas, *Robert E. Lee: A Biography* (New York: W. W. Norton, 1995), 227–29; Russell F. Weigley, "American Strategy from Its Beginnings through the First World War," in Peter Paret and Gordon A. Craig, eds., *Makers of Modern Strategy: From Machiavelli to the Nuclear Age* (Princeton, N.J.: Princeton University Press, 1986), 421–29; and Hattaway and Jones, *How the North Won*, 188, 192–94, 351–54. Woodworth, Thomas, and Weigley contend that Lee's strategic objective throughout the war was a quick victory through the destruction of the Union army in battle. Hattaway and Jones argue that after failing to achieve this unrealistic goal in the summer of 1862, Lee looked to avoid battle and instead relied on strategic turning movements to protect his supply base in central Virginia and the Shenandoah Valley and foster war weariness in the North.

41. McClellan to Stanton, June 24, 25, 1862, in Sears, *Civil War Papers of McClellan*, 308–10; McClellan to his wife, June 26, 1862, in ibid., 313.

42. McClellan to his wife, July 2, 1862, in ibid., 330; McClellan to Porter, June 26, 1862, in ibid, 314–15; McClellan's report, August 4, 1863, *OR*, 11 (pt. 2): 20–21; Van Vliet to Ingalls, June 26, 1862, McClellan Papers, A69/reel 28.

43. McClellan's report, August 4, 1863, *OR*, 11 (pt. 1): 53; McClellan to Franklin, June 27, 1862, in Sears, *Civil War Papers of McClellan*, 319; McClellan to Porter, June 27, 1862, in ibid., 320, 321; McClellan to Goldsborough, June 27, 1862, in ibid., 322; Council of War, June 27, 1862, from "The Soldier of Indiana," Porter Papers, container 3; McClellan to Stanton, June 28, 1862, in Sears, *Civil War Papers of McClellan*, 322–23.

44. McClellan, "The Peninsular Campaign," 180; McClellan to Heintzelman, June 24, 1862, in Sears, *Civil War Papers of McClellan*, 308; Entries for June 24, 25, 1862, Heintzelman journal, *OR Supplement*, 2:80–82; McClellan to Stanton, June 25, 1862, *OR*, 11 (pt. 3): 250–51; Sears, *To the Gates of Richmond*, 183.

45. Lincoln to McClellan, June 26, 1862, *OR*, 11 (pt. 3): 259; Lee's report, March 6, 1863, *OR*, 11 (pt. 2): 490.

46. Lincoln to Halleck and Buell, January 13, 1862, in Basler, *Collected Works*

of Lincoln, 5:98–99; Lincoln to de Gasparin, August 4, 1862, ibid., 355. The agreement between Halleck and Lincoln on strategy is not surprising when one considers that one of the main books Lincoln turned to in his efforts to educate himself on military matters was Halleck's *Elements of Military Art and Science.* C. Percy Powell, *Lincoln Day by Day: A Chronology, 1809–1865,* 3 vols. (Washington, D.C.: Lincoln Sesquicentennial, 1960), 3:88; Hattaway and Jones, *How the North Won,* 210–11.

47. McClellan did in fact mention such a move at the council of war on the evening of June 27 but rejected it as logistically unfeasible. Council of War, June 27, 1862, from "The Soldier of Indiana," Porter Papers, container 3.

48. It is ironic to note that many have criticized McClellan's generalship for being "place oriented" (i.e., focused on the capture of Richmond), yet this place-oriented option has frequently been advanced as a solution to the problem McClellan faced at this time. For this criticism of McClellan, see T. Harry Williams, *Lincoln and His Generals* (New York: Alfred A. Knopf, 1952), 31. Arguments for the "attack Richmond" strategy can be found in McPherson, *Battle Cry of Freedom,* 467–68; Sears, *George B. McClellan,* 207–8; and Kenneth P. Williams, *Lincoln Finds a General: A Military Study of the Civil War,* 5 vols. (New York: Macmillan, 1949–1959), 2:228–31.

49. Daniel H. Hill, "McClellan's Change of Base and Malvern Hill," in Johnson and Buel, *Battles and Leaders of the Civil War,* 2:395; Lee's report, March 6, 1863, *OR,* 11 (pt. 2): 494. In his report on the Seven Days battles, Lee commented that "under ordinary circumstances, the Federal Army should have been destroyed" (ibid., 497), suggesting McClellan's move to the James would have failed but for Confederate mistakes. Given the resiliency of nineteenth-century armies, which was to be demonstrated time and again during the Civil War, it is unlikely that Lee, even "under ordinary circumstances," could have achieved so decisive a victory as to cancel out the operational advantages the Army of the Potomac gained by the move to the James. Hattaway and Jones, *How the North Won,* 199–201.

50. Thomas L. Livermore, *Numbers and Losses in the Civil War in America, 1861–1865,* (Boston: Houghton, Mifflin, 1901), 86; Hattaway and Jones, *How the North Won,* 199–200. For detailed descriptions of the battles of Savage's Station, Frayser's Farm (Glendale), and Malvern Hill, see Sears, *To the Gates of Richmond,* 249–336.

51. Lee to Davis, July 4, 1862, in Dowdey and Manarin, *Wartime Papers of R. E. Lee,* 208; Lee to Jackson, August 7, 1862, in ibid., 247–48; Lee to D. H. Hill, August 13, 1862, in ibid., 251–52; Lee to Smith, August 14, 1862, in ibid., 254–55; Lee to Davis, August 24, 1862, in ibid., 263–64; John J. Hennessy, *Return to Bull Run: The Campaign and Battle of Second Manassas* (New York: Simon & Schuster, 1993), 24–26, 30.

52. Halleck to Stanton, July 27, 1862, *OR,* 11 (pt. 3): 337; George B. McClellan, "From the Peninsula to Antietam," in Johnson and Buel, *Battles and Leaders of the Civil War,* 2:548.

53. Carl von Clausewitz, *On War,* rev. ed., trans. and ed. Michael Howard and Peter Paret (Princeton, N.J.: Princeton University Press, 1984), 85–86, 89, 100–102, 119–21.

54. Grimsley, *Hard Hand of War,* 73–78; Dean, "We Live under a Government of Men and Morning Newspapers," 17–19, 26.

55. Hattaway and Jones, *How the North Won,* 211; McClellan to Lincoln, July 7, 1862, in Sears, *Civil War Papers of McClellan,* 344–45; Grimsley, *Hard Hand*

of War, 68–70, 74–78, 85–89, 130–37; Abraham Lincoln, "Emancipation Proclamation—First Draft," July 22, 1862, in Basler, *Collected Works of Lincoln,* 5:336. On Lincoln's move to adopt emancipation as a war aim, see McPherson, *Battle Cry of Freedom,* 490–510; David Herbert Donald, *Lincoln* (New York: Simon & Schuster, 1995), 359–76; and John Hope Franklin, *The Emancipation Proclamation* (Garden City, N.Y.: Doubleday, 1963), 28–46.

Chapter Four. Generalship on Trial

1. Scholars who have examined Don Carlos Buell's role in the Civil War and who have characterized him as slow include T. Harry Williams, *Lincoln and His Generals* (New York: Alfred A. Knopf, 1952); see also Williams's essay "The Military Leadership of North and South," in David Donald, ed., *Why the North Won the Civil War* (Baton Rouge: Louisiana State University Press, 1960), 33–54; Kenneth P. Williams, *Lincoln Finds a General,* 5 vols. (New York: Macmillan, 1949–1959); Bruce Catton, *Terrible Swift Sword* (New York: Doubleday, 1963); Herman Hattaway and Archer Jones, *How the North Won: A Military History of the Civil War* (Urbana: University of Illinois Press, 1983); James M. McPherson, *Battle Cry of Freedom: The Civil War Era* (New York: Oxford University Press, 1988); and James Lee McDonough, *War in Kentucky: From Shiloh to Perryville* (Knoxville: University of Tennessee Press, 1994). Contemporaries include, for example, George A. Bruce, "General Buell's Campaign against Chattanooga," in *Papers of the Military Historical Society of Massachusetts* (Boston: Military Historical Society of Massachusetts, 1910), 8:99–148, and in the same collection, Henry Stone, "The Operations of General Buell in Kentucky and Tennessee in 1862," 7:257–91; Benjamin F Scribner, *How Soldiers Were Made: Or the War as I Saw It under Buell, Rosecrans, Thomas, Grant and Sherman* (New Albany, Ind.: Donahue & Hanneberry, 1887); Ephraim Allen Otis, "Recollections of the Kentucky Campaign of 1862," in *Military Essays and Recollections: Papers Read before the Commandery of the State of Illinois, Military Order of the Loyal Legion of the United States* (Chicago: Dial Press, 1899), 4:122–47. For a favorable treatment of Buell, see James R. Chumney, "Don Carlos Buell: Gentleman General," Ph.D. diss., Rice University, 1964. For a recent assessment of Buell's conciliatory policy, see Mark Grimsley, *The Hard Hand of War* (New York: Cambridge University Press, 1996); see also *New York Daily Tribune,* October 23, 25, 1862.

2. U.S. War Department, *The War of the Rebellion: A Compilation of the Official Records of the Union and Confederate Armies,* 128 vols. (Washington, D.C.: Government Printing Office, 1881–1901), series I, 16:6–7 (hereafter cited as *OR*; all references are to series I unless otherwise noted). Buell incurred the wrath of Governor Morton almost from the beginning of his tenure as commander of the Army of the Ohio, because Buell centralized the command of the army in himself in an attempt to reduce the interference of politicians. Johnson had been frustrated by Buell's refusal to move into east Tennessee in the winter of 1861–1862. When he was appointed military governor of Tennessee in March 1862, Johnson and Buell clashed over the defense of Nashville and over Buell's policy of conciliation. During the summer, both governors stepped up their criticism of Buell for his conciliatory policy and for not getting to Chattanooga. The failure to defeat Braxton Bragg at Perryville or to pursue him after the battle further intensified the animosity toward Buell. See also Donn Piatt, *General George H. Thomas: A Critical Biography* (Cincinnati, Ohio: Robert Clarke, 1983),

178; James B. Fry, *Operations of the Army under Buell* (New York: D. Van Nostrand, 1884), 116.

3. Lew Wallace, *Lew Wallace: An Autobiography*, 2 vols. (New York: Harper & Brothers, 1906), 2:644. For the entire contents of the commission, see *OR*, 16:7–726; Lee Scott Theisen, "The Public Career of General Lew Wallace, 1845–1905," Ph.D. diss., Arizona State University, 1973; Francis F. McKinney, "The Trial of General Buell," *Michigan Alumnus Quarterly Review* 64 (March 1956): 163–78. Secretary of War Edwin M. Stanton designated the Buell investigation a "military commission," which was not recognized by the *Articles of War* published in 1861. See U.S. Department of War, *Revised Regulations for the Army of the United States, 1861* (Philadelphia, 1862), 499–516; Mark A. Peine, "The Buell Military Commission," master's thesis, University of North Dakota, 1977, 77–123.

4. Wallace, *Autobiography*, 645; *OR*, 16:13, 571–72; Peine, "Buell Commission," 77–123; Williams, "Military Leadership of North and South," 36–46; see also Stephen E. Ambrose, *Halleck: Lincoln's Chief of Staff* (Baton Rouge: Louisiana State University Press, 1962) Stephen W. Sears, *George B. McClellan: The Young Napoleon* (New York: Ticknor & Fields, 1988); and Edward Hagerman, *The American Civil War and the Origins of Modern Warfare* (Bloomington: University of Indiana Press, 1988); Piatt, *George H. Thomas*, 179.

5. See Inclosure No. 2, *OR*, 16:12–14. Before the investigation began, the prosecution added this enclosure regarding Buell's march to Chattanooga.

6. *OR*, 16:32.

7. *OR*, 16:65. Because Buell and McClellan have often been compared in their prosecution of the war, it is important to understand that their conduct and brand of war has generally been viewed in the context of what Joseph Harsh calls the Union interpretation of the Civil War. Anything that can be attributed to the Union's success, he argues, has generally been applauded by historians, and anything that thwarted that success has generally been condemned. Thus, because McClellan and Buell did not prosecute the war more vigorously, they are ultimately viewed as failures, and their brand of war is considered simply wrong. Thus, Buell falls into the category of preventing success by being too slow, too lenient, too traditional, and simply unsuited temperamentally to bring about success. See Joseph L. Harsh, "On the McClellan-Go-Round," *Civil War History* 19 (June 1973): 101–18.

8. *OR*, 16:8–20; Peine, "Buell Commission," 77–117; Hagerman, *Origins of Modern Warfare*, xvii; Joseph T. Glatthaar, *Partners in Command: The Relationship between Leaders in the Civil War* (New York: Free Press, 1994), 236; Williams, "Military Leadership of North and South," 33–54.

9. Bruce, "Buell's Campaign against Chattanooga," 147; Hagerman, *Origins of Modern Warfare*, xi, 32; Williams, "Military Leadership of North and South," 33–54; Ambrose, *Halleck*, 10; T. Harry Williams, *McClellan, Sherman and Grant* (New Brunswick, N.J.: Rutgers University Press, 1962), 22–23; Sears, *McClellan*, 95–117.

10. Roy P. Basler, ed., *The Collected Works of Abraham Lincoln*, 8 vols. (New Brunswick, N.J.: Rutgers University Press, 1953), 5:591; Williams, *Lincoln and His Generals*, 47–48; R. W. Johnson, *A Soldier's Reminiscences in Peace and War* (Philadelphia: J. B. Lippincott, 1886), 322; Sears, *George B. McClellan*, 129.

11. Buell to McClellan, December 10, 1861, from Louisville, Ky., Don Carlos Buell Papers, Huntington Library, San Marino, California (hereafter cited as Buell Papers); *OR*, 7:468, 487–89, 4:355–56.

12. Buell to McClellan, November 16, 30, 1861, George B. McClellan Papers, Library of Congress Manuscript Division, Washington, D.C., microfilm reel 47 (hereafter cited as McClellan Papers); *OR*, series I, 7:450–51; Williams, *Lincoln and His Generals*, 49; Bruce, "Buell's Campaign against Chattanooga," 112; see also Walter T. Durham, *Nashville: The Occupied City* (Nashville: Tennessee Historical Society, 1985).

13. Buell to McClellan, December 10, 1861, from Louisville, Ky., Buell Papers.

14. *OR*, 16:51–59.

15. *OR*, 7:587–88; Ambrose, *Halleck*, 26. On the capture of Forts Henry and Donelson, see Benjamin Franklin Cooling, *Forts Henry and Donelson: The Key to the Confederate Heartland* (Knoxville: University of Tennessee Press, 1987); on the battle of Shiloh, see James Lee McDonough, *Shiloh: In Hell before Night* (Knoxville: University of Tennessee Press, 1977). According to Eric Foner, "By an accident of war, Tennessee's Reconstruction began not in the staunchly Unionist eastern mountains, but in the middle and western parts of the state, where slavery was deeply entrenched and Confederate sentiment dominant." See Foner, *Reconstruction: America's Unfinished Revolution: 1863–1877* (New York: Harper, 1988), 43.

16. Ambrose, *Halleck*, 41–57; Hans L. Trefousse, *Andrew Johnson: A Biography* (New York: Alfred A. Knopf, 1989), 152–63; see also Stephen V. Ash, *Middle Tennessee Society Transformed: 1860–1870* (Baton Rouge: Louisiana State University Press, 1988); *OR*, 10:671, 16 (pt. 2): 3; Ambrose, *Halleck*, 56; Hagerman, *Origins of Modern Warfare*, 176. The orders outlining Halleck's strategy reinstated Grant to his old command, and he remained in west Tennessee.

17. *Cincinnati Daily Commercial*, November 15, 1861; *New York Weekly Tribune*, January 18, 1862; Governors Andrew Johnson and Oliver P. Morton continued to clamor to the president regarding Buell's refusal to redeem east Tennessee. See Trefousse, *Andrew Johnson*, 157–58; Leroy P. Graf and Randolph W. Haskins, eds., *The Papers of Andrew Johnson*, 8 vols. (Knoxville: University of Tennessee Press, 1967–1989), 5:485–86; *Frank Leslie's Illustrated Newspaper*, March 8, May 10, 1862.

18. Catton, *Terrible Swift Sword*, 354; *OR*, 10 (pt. 2): 244, 281; Don Carlos Buell, *Statement of Major General Buell in Review of the Evidence before the Military Commission Appointed by the War Department in November 1862. Campaign in Kentucky, Tennessee Northern Mississippi and North Alabama in 1861 and 1862* (Cincinnati, n.p., 1863), 11–12; James B. Fry, *Operations of the Army under Buell from June 10th to October 30th, 1862, and the Buell Commission* (New York: D. Van Nostrand, 1884), 81.

19. Basler, *Collected Works of Lincoln*, 5:295; Robert C. Black III, *The Railroads of the Confederacy* (Chapel Hill: University of North Carolina Press, 1952; reprint, Wilmington, 1987), 180–82; Bruce, "Buell's March against Chattanooga," 106.

20. *OR*, 16 (pt. 2): 8; see also *OR*, 10 (pt. 2): 20.

21. *OR*, 10 (pt. 2): 20; on Buell's prewar military background, see George W. Cullum, *Biographical Register of the Officers and Cadets of the United States Military Academy at West Point*, 3 vols. (New York: Association of Graduates, 1868), 2:26; *New York Daily Tribune*, August 7, November 12, 1862.

22. *OR*, 16 (pt. 2): 5–8, 62–63; Williams, *Lincoln Finds a General*, 4:27; Ambrose, *Halleck*, 56–57; McDonough, *War in Kentucky*, 40.

23. Ambrose, *Halleck*, 56–57; Black, *Railroads of the Confederacy*, 181–82; Williams, *Lincoln Find a General*, 4:26–27; McDonough, *War in Kentucky*, 40–41.

24. Basler, *Collected Works of Lincoln*, 5:295; *OR*, 10 (pt. 2): 232–33, 244, 254, 267–68, 280–81, 16 (pt. 1): 30–31, 16 (pt. 2): 62–63; Bruce, "Buell's March against Chattanooga," 110–15; Ambrose, *Halleck*, 57–59; Gerald Prokopowicz, "All for the Regiment: Unit Cohesion and Tactical Stalemate in the Army of the Ohio, 1861–1862," Ph.D. diss., Harvard University, 1994, 226–27; Hattaway and Jones, *How the North Won*, 214–17.

25. McDonough, *War in Kentucky*, 42; Bruce, "Buell's March against Chattanooga," 110–15.

26. *OR*, 16 (pt. 2): 33, 44, 16: 32–34, also 10 (pt. 2): 118, 236–37, 250–51; Don Carlos Buell, "East Tennessee and the Campaign of Perryville," in Robert U. Johnson and Clarence C. Buel, eds., *Battles and Leaders of the Civil War*, 4 vols. (New York: Castle, 1956; reprint), 3: 31–51.

27. *OR*, 16: 30–34, 472–81; Bruce, "Buell's Campaign against Chattanooga," 106.

28. Grimsley, *Hard Hand of War*, 81–85.

29. Hattaway and Jones, *How the North Won*, 250; McDonough, *War in Kentucky*, 43; Williams, *Lincoln Finds a General*, 4: 27–28. In his autobiography, Lew Wallace claimed that Halleck's *Indorsement* to the commission was "wholly without proof." He further implied that it was Halleck who was partially to blame for the failed Chattanooga campaign and that he was responsible for losing the commission's opinion after the war, perhaps to exonerate himself from any blame about the failed Chattanooga campaign. See Wallace, *Autobiography*, 2:653; *OR*, 16:12, 31; Bruce, "Buell's Campaign against Chattanooga," 104. Bruce argues that the controversy over whether repairing the Memphis and Charleston Railroad delayed Buell's march to Chattanooga was irrelevant, since the railroad was completed and put in use by June 29. He argued that it was the use, not the repair, of the railroad that slowed Buell, since Halleck had diverted his engineer forces to the track extending from Memphis to Columbus instead of east as he had promised Buell. He further blamed Halleck for not making sufficient preparations for the movement east. The commission also revealed that in June the divisions of McCook and Crittenden crossed the Tennessee River at Florence and marched through Athens without repairing the railroad. Furthermore, Nelson's division, after making some repairs on the line near Iuka, followed those of McCook and Crittenden without any interval of time. Wood's division alone advanced along the railroad, and it arrived at Decatur only two days after the head of the other column had passed through Athens.

30. *OR*, 10 (pt. 2): 628, 16:32–34, 247–50, 325–27, 516–602, 603–11, 709, 16 (pt. 2): 22–23, 41–44, 68–69, 77, 85; Buell, *Statement*, 12; Williams, *Lincoln Finds a General*, 4:27; Chumney, "Gentleman General," 102–3; McDonough, *War in Kentucky*, 45. Buell was in such desperate need of cavalry that he ordered the purchase of 5,000 cavalry horses.

31. *OR*, 16 (pt. 2): 15, 31, 127; Hagerman, *Origins of Modern Warfare*, 176–85.

32. John W. Switzer Diary, July 20, 1862, Switzer Papers, Indiana Historical Society, Indianapolis, Indiana; Hagerman, *Origins of Modern Warfare*, 175–76; Prokopowicz, "All for the Regiment," 245–47; Bruce, "Buell's Campaign against Chattanooga," 117; General Orders No. 26, June 24, 1862, Department of the Ohio, RG 393, National Archives and Records Administration, Washington,

D.C., *OR*, 16 (pt. 2): 23, 32–35, 39, 54, 60–61, 73; see also *New York Daily Tribune*, June 30, 1862.

33. Joseph Warren Keifer to Eliza, July 12, 1862, Keifer Papers, Library of Congress Manuscript Division, Washington, D.C.

34. *OR*, 16 (pt. 2): 74–75. Lincoln apparently considered the Chattanooga campaign so important that he followed up Stanton's telegram to Halleck the same day with a message of his own saying that the campaign was "as important as the taking and holding of Richmond." See also Prokopowicz, "All for the Regiment," 241–45; Ulysses S. Grant, "Battle of Shiloh," in *Battles and Leaders of the Civil War*, 1:482; *New York Daily Tribune*, June 30, July 12, November 12, 1862.

35. "Buell's March to Chattanooga," pp. 7–10, Kenneth P. Williams Papers, University of Indiana, Lilly Library Manuscript Division, Bloomington, Indiana (hereafter cited as Williams Papers). Stone, "Operations of Buell in Kentucky and Tennessee," 261–63.

36. Buell's conception of war had not changed since McClellan's initial instructions in November outlining the kind of war the Union government was waging. McClellan had urged Buell to respect the constitutional rights of Southern citizens while he was in command in Kentucky and told him that he should "carefully regard the local institutions of the region" and "religiously respect the constitutional rights of all." But even McClellan recognized—and Buell must have as well—that only "the dictates of military necessity" should cause Buell to "depart from the spirit of these instructions." By the summer of 1862, certainly the condition of the army and the countryside and the transportation situation should have caused Buell to depart from the policy McClellan had outlined. But apparently Buell was more religious than sensible in carrying out the government's initial policy. See *OR*, 4:342, 355–56, 16:23, 474; Buell to McClellan, November 2, 16, 1861, McClellan Papers, reel 47; "Buell's March to Chattanooga," pp. 9–10, Williams Papers; Williams, *Lincoln Finds a General*, 4:33. Buell also reiterated McClellan's points when on February 26 he issued General Orders 13a: "We are not in arms for the purpose of invading the rights of our fellow-countrymen anywhere, but to maintain the integrity of the Union and protect the Constitution, under which its people have been prosperous and happy." See General Orders No. 13a, February 26, Department of the Ohio, RG 393.

37. *OR*, 16 (pt. 2): 474, 485–96, 324–63, 603. Robert MacFeely, captain of commissary of subsistence of the U.S. Army in Nashville, testified that he purchased supplies from Nashvillians to support the army. He further stated that different commissaries along the route to Chattanooga seized and even purchased cattle for the army. Interestingly, at a time when several commanders complained of not being able to find forage, several soldiers wrote that the countryside abounded with food. See, for example, Keifer to My Dear Wife, July 22, 1862, Keifer Papers, Library of Congress; *OR*, 16 (pt. 2): 85. Williams uses, or rather misuses, a dispatch from Thomas J. Wood to Colonel Fry on July 10, saying, "I telegraphed you to-day to have a train sent down to move some of the corn which my command has collected here." Williams cites this portion of the dispatch to make the case that Wood's division was having little trouble finding food at a time when others could find none. He does this to undermine further what Buell reasoned was one of the causes for his slow march to Chattanooga.

38. *OR*, 16 (pt. 2): 75, 104. It should be noted that Stanton characterized Lincoln's position by saying that the president was "not pleased with the tar-

diness of the movement toward Chattanooga." In Halleck's dispatch to Buell, he translated this into: "The President telegraphs that your progress is not satisfactory and that you should move more rapidly." Halleck no doubt sensed that a message from the president himself might alarm Buell into moving more rapidly, since Halleck was apparently having little success in getting him to do so.

39. *OR*, 16 (pt. 2): 104; Bruce, "Buell's March against Chattanooga," 118.

40. *OR*, 16 (pt. 2): 122–23, 16:33; Black, *Railroads of the Confederacy*, 180; Bruce, "Buell's March against Chattanooga," 106.

41. *OR*, 16 (pt. 2): 122–23.

42. *OR*, 16 (pt. 2): 118–19, 135; Trefousse, *Andrew Johnson*, 144–48; It should also be noted that Andrew Johnson, military governor of Tennessee, was constantly badgering Lincoln and Halleck regarding the defense of Nashville. This further compounded Buell's dilemma in marching to Chattanooga, since Johnson had trouble viewing the Chattanooga campaign as any aid to his political efforts to Reconstruct the area under his command. Moreover, Johnson was close to Lincoln and could use his political influence to discredit Buell. Thus, an already frustrating situation for the president—Buell's tardiness—was compounded by Johnson's frustration at Buell for not supporting his Reconstruction efforts.

43. *OR*, 16 (pt. 2): 128, 167–68.

44. *Indianapolis Daily Journal*, July 16, 1862; *New York Daily Tribune*, July 12, 22, 1862.

45. *Daily Nashville Union*, July 23, 1862; *New York Daily Tribune*, July 10, 12, August 7, 1862.

46. Keifer to My Dear Eliza, July 5, and to My Dear Wife, July 8, 1862, Keifer Papers, Library of Congress.

47. A good estimation of the mood of the army can be found in the Keifer Papers, Library of Congress. Keifer was a major in the 3rd Ohio, Mitchell's Division. The daily letters to his wife are highly illuminating in this regard. On July 9, he wrote, "I am not alone in my views on Buell. Large numbers have resigned in consequence of some of his orders. Others will." Perhaps the only subordinate totally supportive of Buell's efforts all along was William "Bull" Nelson, who wrote to Treasury Secretary Salmon P. Chase in late July that Buell's policy was the best to "put this rebellion down soonest." See Nelson to Chase, July 30, 1862, Salmon P. Chase Papers, Claremont Graduate School, Microfilm Edition, Claremont, California. See also *New York Daily Tribune*, July 10, 12, August 7, 1862.

48. *OR*, 16 (pt. 2): 75, 146, 155; Williams, *Lincoln Finds a General*, 4:41–42; McDonough, *War in Kentucky*, 46–47.

49. *OR*, 16 (pt. 2): 127, 162–64, 16 (pt. 1): 247–51; Stone, "Operations of Buell in Kentucky and Tennessee," 261–64; John Allan Wyeth, *That Devil Forrest: Life of General Nathan Bedford Forrest* (New York: Harper & Brothers, 1959; reprint), 28–68; Williams, *Lincoln Finds a General*, 4:38–41.

50. *OR*, 16 (pt. 2): 188, 221, 237.

51. *OR*, 16 (pt. 2): 236, 266.

52. James A. Ramage, *Rebel Raider: The Life of John Hunt Morgan* (Lexington: University Press of Kentucky, 1986), 111; McDonough, *War in Kentucky*, 56–58; Hagerman, *Origins of Modern Warfare*, 117; Bruce, "Buell's Campaign against Chattanooga," 119; *OR*, 16 (pt. 2): 322, 328–30; *New York Daily Tribune*, August 7, 1862.

53. *OR,* 16 (pt. 2): 278–79.

54. Buell and Bragg would battle at Perryville, Kentucky, on October 8, 1862. On the battle of Perryville, see McDonough, *War in Kentucky,* 159–325, and Kenneth A. Hafendorfer, *Perryville: Battle for Kentucky* (Louisville: Kenneth Hafendorfer, 1991).

55. Keifer to Dear Eliza, July 3, 1862, Keifer Papers, Library of Congress; Ephraim A. Otis, "Recollections of the Kentucky Campaign of 1862," in *Papers of the Military Historical Society of Massachusetts,* 7:232–36; Catton, *Terrible Swift Sword,* 356.

56. Catton, *Terrible Swift Sword,* 356. Buell has received considerable criticism for his failure to get to Chattanooga. Kenneth P. Williams and Bruce Catton are among the more critical, whereas James McDonough is more sympathetic to the logistical problems Buell faced; *OR,* 16 (pt. 2): 360; John Niven, *Salmon P. Chase: A Biography* (New York: Oxford University Press, 1995), 292–94.

57. *OR,* 16 (pt. 2): 387–88; Grady McWhiney, "Controversy in Kentucky: Braxton Bragg's Campaign of 1862," *Civil War History* 6 (1969): 5–14.

58. Hagerman, *Origins of Modern Warfare,* 178; *OR,* 16 (pt. 2). 2, 3, 5, 10 (pt. 2): 235; Williams, *Lincoln and His Generals,* 151.

59. *OR,* 16:354–55.

60. *OR,* 16:59–60.

61. Johnson, *A Soldier's Reminiscences,* 196–98.

62. *OR,* 16 (pt. 2): 421; Williams, *Lincoln and His Generals,* 151–52.

Chapter Five. In Defense of Fighting Joe Hooker

1. T. Harry Williams, *Lincoln and His Generals* (New York: Alfred A. Knopf, 1952), 239. The most recent charge that Hooker was drunk at Chancellorsville is in Ernest B. Furgurson, *Chancellorsville 1863: The Souls of the Brave* (New York: Alfred A. Knopf, 1992), 285–87. The Army of the Potomac was manifestly (if unofficially) under Pope's command at Second Bull Run.

2. James M. McPherson, *Battle Cry of Freedom: The Civil War Era* (New York: Oxford University Press, 1988), 645; Shelby Foote, *The Civil War: A Narrative,* 3 vols. (New York: Random House, 1963), 2:315; Bruce Catton, *Glory Road: The Bloody Route from Fredericksburg to Gettysburg* (New York: Doubleday, 1954), 230; Kenneth P. Williams, *Lincoln Finds a General: A Military Study of the Civil War,* 5 vols. (New York: Macmillan, 1949), 2:604; Walter H. Hebert, *Fighting Joe Hooker* (Indianapolis: Bobbs-Merrill, 1944), chap. 14; Gene Smith, "The Destruction of Fighting Joe Hooker," *American Heritage* (October 1993): 95–103; Ken Burns, *The Civil War* (PBS, 1990), episode four.

3. Albert Castel, *Decision in the West: The Atlanta Campaign of 1864* (Lawrence: University Press of Kansas, 1992), 291.

4. Theodore A. Dodge, Lowell Lecture: "The Battle of Chancellorsville," *Southern Historical Society Papers,* 14:276–92; Theodore A. Dodge, *The Campaign of Chancellorsville,* (Boston: Ticknor & Co., 2d ed., 1886), 266–67.

5. *Report of the Joint Committee on the Conduct of the War,* Vol. 1 (1865), 111–49.

6. Hooker's 1876–1879 letters, Samuel P. Bates Collection, Pennsylvania Historical and Museum Commission, Pennsylvania State Archives; Jedediah Hotchkiss and William Allan, *The Battle-Fields of Virginia: Chancellorsville* (New York: Van Nostrand, 1867).

7. Samuel P. Bates, "Hooker's Comments on Chancellorsville," in Robert U. Johnson and Clarence C. Buel, eds., *Battles and Leaders of the Civil War*, 3 vols. (New York: Century, 1887–1888), 3:215–23; Samuel P. Bates, *The Battle of Chancellorsville* (1882); Allan Nevins, James I. Robertson, Jr., and Bell I. Wiley, *Civil War Books: A Critical Bibliography*, 2 vols. (Baton Rouge: Louisiana State University Press, 1967), 1:23.

8. John Bigelow, Jr., *The Campaign of Chancellorsville: A Strategic and Tactical Study* (New Haven, Conn.: Yale University Press, 1910), 477–78n.

9. E. P. Halstead, April 19, 1903, Bigelow Papers, Library of Congress.

10. Hebert, *Fighting Joe Hooker*, 38; George B. McClellan, memoirs draft, McClellan Papers, Library of Congress.

11. John Hay, *Lincoln and the Civil War in the Diaries and Letters of John Hay*, ed. Tyler Dennett (New York: Dodd, Meade, 1939), 86; Darius Couch, in *Battles and Leaders of the Civil War*, 3:170; George G. Meade, *Life and Letters of George Gordon Meade* (New York: Scribner's, 1913), 1:365; Charles S. Wainwright, *A Diary of Battle: The Personal Journals of Colonel Charles S. Wainwright*, ed. Allan Nevins (New York: Harcourt, Brace & World, 1963), 202, 214; George H. Sharpe memorandum, Joseph Hooker Papers, Huntington Library.

12. Custer to McClellan, May 6, 1863, McClellan Papers, Library of Congress; George W. Smalley, *Anglo-American Memories* (New York: Putnam's, 1911), 158.

13. Wainwright, *Diary of Battle*, 162; Charles Francis Adams, Jr., *Charles Francis Adams, 1835–1916, An Autobiography* (Boston: Houghton Mifflin, 1916), 161; E. N. Gilpin, April 7, 1911, Bigelow Papers, Library of Congress; Margaret Leech, *Reveille in Washington, 1860–1865* (New York: Harper & Brothers, 1941), 264.

14. *The American Heritage Dictionary*, 3d ed., 869.

15. Halleck to Sherman, September 16, 1864, in Sherman, *Memoirs* (New York: Appleton, 1875), 590; Hooker to Bates, June 28,1878, Bates Collection.

16. Hooker testimony, *Report of Joint Committee*, Vol. 1 (1865), 175, 112; Halleck to Stanton, May 18, 1863, in U.S. War Department, *The War of the Rebellion: A Compilation of the Official Records of the Union and Confederate Armies*, 128 vols. (Washington, D.C.: Government Printing Office, 1881–1901), 25:2, 506 (hereafter cited as *OR*).

17. Hooker testimony, *Report of Joint Committee*, Vol. 1 (1865), 175; Lincoln to Hooker, June 16, 1863, in Roy P. Basler, ed., *The Collected Works of Abraham Lincoln*, 9 vols. (New Brunswick, N.J.: Rutgers University Press, 1953), 6:281.

18. Hooker testimony, *Report of Joint Committee*, vol.1 (1865), 175.

19. Williams, *Lincoln and His Generals*, 259; *OR*, 27:3, 349; Lincoln to Hooker, May 14, 1863, *OR* 25:2, 479; Hooker to Bates, October 5, 1878, Bates Collection.

20. Alexander K. McClure, *Abraham Lincoln and Men of War-Times* (Philadelphia: Times Publishing, 1892), 180.

21. Meade, *Life and Letters*, 2:142; Lincoln to Hooker, May 14,1863, *OR*, 25:2, 479.

22. Hebert, *Fighting Joe Hooker*, 25–33; *San Francisco Chronicle*, November 1, 1879.

23. Alpheus S. Williams, *From the Cannon's Mouth: The Civil War Letters of General Alpheus S.Williams*, ed. Milo M. Quaife (Detroit: Wayne State University Press, 1959), 265; Hooker to Bates, January 3, 1878, Bates Collection; Alexander K. McClure, *Recollections of Half a Century* (Salem, Mass.: Salem Press, 1902), 347; *OR*, 25:1, 171.

24. Lincoln to Hooker, January 26, 1863, in *Collected Works of Lincoln*, 6:78–79; Noah Brooks, *Washington in Lincoln's Time* (New York: Rinehart, 1958), 57–58; Anson G. Henry, April 12, 1863, Illinois State Historical Library.

25. Henry L. Abbott, *Fallen Leaves: The Civil War Letters of Major Henry Livermore Abbott*, ed. Robert Garth Scott (Kent, Ohio: Kent State University Press, 1991), 165, 170; *New York Times*, March 1, 1863; Andrew E. Ford, *The Story of the Fifteenth Massachusetts Volunteer Infantry* (1898), 253.

26. Hooker testimony, *Report of Joint Committee*, Vol. 1 (1863), 668.

27. Warren to Butterfield, May 3, 1863, Hooker Papers, Huntington Library.

28. Hooker memorandum, March 21, 1877, courtesy Abraham Lincoln Book Shop; Jonathan Letterman, *Medical Recollections of the Army of the Potomac* (New York: Appleton, 1866), 137; William Candler, May 7, 1863, in Bigelow, *The Campaign of Chancellorsville: A Strategic and Tactical Study* (New Haven, Conn.: Yale University Press, 1910), 363n; Doubleday memorandum, Doubleday Papers, New York Historical Society.

29. Couch, in *Battles and Leaders*, 3:167.

30. Lincoln to Meade, July 27, 1863, in *Collected Works of Lincoln*, 6:350; Meade, *Life and Letters*, 2:142.

31. Dana to Stanton, October 29, 1863, *OR*, 31:1, 73; John Russell Young, *Around the World with General Grant* (New York: American News Company, 1879), 2: 306; Hooker to Stanton, February 25, 1864, *OR*, 32:2, 469; Castel, *Decision in the West*, 97.

32. M. A. De Wolfe Howe, ed., *Home Letters of General Sherman* (New York: Scribner's, 1909), 250.

33. *OR*, 38:5, 273.

34. Hooker to Bates, April 2, 1877, Bates Collection; Lincoln to Meade, July 27, 1863, in *Collected Works of Lincoln*, 6:350.

Chapter Six. Misused Merit

1. The story of Pemberton's roots and pre–West Point years is in Michael B. Ballard, *Pemberton: A Biography* (Jackson: University Press of Mississippi, 1991) , 3–11.

2. Ibid., 6, 10–11.

3. For details of Pemberton's West Point years, see ibid., 12–25.

4. Pemberton Cadet Record, John C. Pemberton Papers (JCPP), Pemberton Family Papers (PFP), Historical Society of Pennsylvania (HSP), Philadelphia.

5. Adjutant General's Office to John C. Pemberton (JCP), June 29, 1837; General Orders No. 46, Head Quarters of the Army Adjutant General's Office, Washington, D.C., July 12, 1837, all in ibid.; Ballard, *Pemberton*, 22, 26–27, 30–31, 32–33.

6. JCP to Parents, January 27, 1838, to John Pemberton, April 22, 1838, to Anna Pemberton, January 23, 1839, to Rebecca Pemberton, April 16, 1839, and to Israel Pemberton, February 13, 1839, JCPP, PFP, HSP; Rebecca to Israel, November 16, 1838, Israel Pemberton Papers, PFP, HSP.

7. See Ballard, *Pemberton*, 35–40.

8. Ibid., 40–41; Marriage Record of John Clifford Pemberton and Martha Thompson, JCPP, Southern Historical Collection (SHC), University of North Carolina at Chapel Hill.

9. The changes in Pemberton's personality are discussed in Ballard, *Pemberton*, 37, 58, 77–78, 79.

10. JCP to Israel, May 28, 1846, to John Pemberton, May 10, June 9, 1846, JCPP, PFP, HSP; George Meade to Israel, June 10, 1846, Israel Pemberton Papers, PFP, HSP. For Pemberton's experiences in the Mexican War, see Ballard, *Pemberton*, 43–63.

11. JCP to Rebecca, August 5, 1846, JCPP, PFP, HSP; Ballard, *Pemberton*, 52.

12. *Niles' National Register* 71 (November 21, 1846), 180–81; G. W. Cullum, *Biographical Register of Officers and Graduates, U. S. Military Academy* (West Point, N.Y.: U.S. Military Academy, 1891), excerpt in Pemberton Papers, SHC.

13. Pemberton's years between the Mexican and Civil Wars are covered in Ballard, *Pemberton*, 64–82.

14. Israel Pemberton to JCP, April 15, 1861, JCPP, PFP, HSP.

15. Ibid.; Rebecca Pemberton to Caroline Hollingsworth Pemberton, April 23, 1861, Pemberton Papers, SHC; U.S. War Department, *The War of the Rebellion: A Compilation of the Official Records of the Union and Confederate Armies*, 128 vols. (Washington, D.C.: Government Printing Office, 1881–1901), 2:580 (hereafter cited as *OR*; all references are to series I unless otherwise noted).

16. Pemberton's decision is analyzed in Ballard, *Pemberton*, 85–86.

17. *OR*, 2:856, 963; Certificates of Rank, Pemberton Papers, SHC; Joseph E. Johnston, *Narrative of Military Operations, Directed, during the Late War between the States* (New York: D. Appleton & Company, 1874), 12.

18. *OR*, 2:982–83, 4:666.

19. *OR*, 6:334.

20. Douglas Southall Freeman, *R. E. Lee: A Biography*, 4 vols. (New York: Charles Scribner's Sons, 1934–1935), 1: 613, 630–31; *OR*, 6:366.

21. Certificates of Rank, Pemberton Papers, SHC; *OR*, 6:402, 407.

22. *OR*, 6:414, 523.

23. Pemberton's administrative challenges in South Carolina are discussed at length in Ballard, *Pemberton*, 91–106.

24. Charles E. Cauthen, *South Carolina Goes to War, 1860–1865* (Chapel Hill: University of North Carolina Press, 1950), 142, 144, 161. The council was generally unpopular among the South Carolina public and was eventually abolished, but not until Pemberton had left the state.

25. JCP to Samuel Cooper, March 27, 1862, Record Group (RG) chap. II, vol. 21, National Archives (NA); *OR*, 14:423–24.

26. *OR*, 14:424–25.

27. Freeman, *R. E. Lee*, 1:627; JCP to R. E. Lee, April 10, 1862, RG 109, chap. II, vol. 21, NA; *OR*, 6:366.

28. *OR*, 14:13–15, 483; JCP to W. H. Taylor, May 14, 1862, and to A. L. Long, May 21, 1862, RG 109, chap. II, vol. 21, NA.

29. JCP to A. L. Long, May 21, 1862, RG 109, chap. II, vol. 21, NA.

30. *OR*, 14:490–91, 513–14.

31. Francis Pickens to JCP, May 23, 1862, RG 109, chap. II, vol. 21, NA.

32. *OR*, 14: 523–24. See also F. W. Pickens to Jefferson Davis, August 20, 1862 in Dunbar Rowland, ed., *Jefferson Davis, Constitutionalist: His Letters. Papers, and Speeches*, 10 vols. (Jackson: Mississippi Department of Archives and History, 1923), 5:326–27.

33. JCP to Jefferson Davis, June 2, 5, 1862, to George Randolph, June 3, 1862 (three messages that date), to James Chesnut, June 6, 1862, all in RG 109,

chap. II, vol. 21, NA; *OR*, 14:89, 90, 567; Milby Burton, *The Siege of Charleston, 1861–1865* (Columbia: University of South Carolina Press, 1970), 99, 105–9.

34. For examples, see Ballard, *Pemberton*, 107–10.

35. *OR*, 14:560.

36. C. Vann Woodward, ed., *Mary Chesnut's Civil War* (New Haven, Conn.: Yale University Press, 1981), 332; John F. Marszalek, ed., *The Diary of Miss Emma Holmes 1861–1866* (Baton Rouge: Louisiana State University Press, 1979), 174, 177.

37. JCP to A. L. Long, May 21, 1862, RG 109, chap. II, vol. 21, NA; *OR*, 14:503–4, 524; Ballard, *Pemberton*, 107–8.

38. *OR*, 14:560, 569–70, 601.

39. Ibid., 601. For examples of support, see *Charleston Daily Courier*, September 26, 1862, and *Charleston Mercury*, September 29, 1862.

40. *OR*, 15:820, 17 (pt. 2): 718; Ballard, *Pemberton*, 120.

41. See Michael B. Ballard, *The Campaign for Vicksburg* (Conshohocken, Penn.: Eastern National Park and Monument Association, 1996), 1–6, for background prior to Pemberton's arrival; David D. Porter, *Incidents and Anecdotes of the Civil War* (New York: D. Appleton & Company, 1885), 95–96.

42. *New York Herald*, August 17, 1881, clipping in John Clifford Pemberton Papers, Library of Congress.

43. Richard M. McMurry, *Two Great Rebel Armies: An Essay in Confederate Military History* (Chapel Hill: University of North Carolina Press, 1989), 133–34.

44. Ballard, *Campaign*, 5, 6, 13, 22, and *Pemberton*, 123, 125.

45. For comparisons of troop strength, see *OR*, 17 (pt. 2): 576–78, 661–62, 699.

46. Ibid., 757–58; Ballard, *Pemberton*, 118–19.

47. Ballard, *Pemberton*, 119–20, 144.

48. *OR*, 17 (pt. 2): 758.

49. *Jackson Daily Mississippian* quoted in *Memphis Daily Appeal*, November 28 [29], 1862; R. W. Memminger, "The Surrender of Vicksburg—A Defence of General Pemberton," *Southern Historical Society Papers* 12 (July, August, September 1984): 353; Ballard, *Pemberton*, 121–23.

50. Robert G. Hartje, *Van Dorn: The Life and Times of a Confederate General* (Nashville: Vanderbilt University Press, 1967), 254–69; *OR*, 17 (pt. 2): 451; Ballard, *Pemberton*, 127.

51. Edwin Cole Bearss, *The Vicksburg Campaign*, 3 vols. (Dayton, Ohio: Morningside, 1985–1986), 1:143–46, 154, 172, 190, 200, 208–9; R. S. Bevier, *History of the First and Second Missouri Brigades* (St. Louis: Inland Printer, 1985; reprint), 166–67; *OR*, 17 (pt. 2): 669; Ballard, *Pemberton*, 128–29.

52. For a brief survey of Grant's diversionary activities, see Ballard, *Campaign*, 18–24.

53. Bearss, *Vicksburg Campaign*, 1: 475–507, 539; Ezra J. Warner, *Generals in Gray: Lives of the Confederate Commanders* (Baton Rouge: Louisiana State University Press, 1970), 194; William A. Drennon Diary, May 30–July 4, 1862, p. 6, Mississippi Department of Archives and History, Jackson; F. W. M., "Career and Fate of Gen. Lloyd Tilghman," *Confederate Veteran* 9 (September 1893): 274–75; JCP, General Orders No. 33, February 1, 1863, Orders and Circulars, 1862–1865, Records of the Department of Mississippi and East Louisiana and of the Department of Alabama, Mississippi, and East Louisiana, entry 94, Lloyd Tilghman to John Waddy, January 27, 1863, General John C. Pemberton Papers, 1862–1864, entry 131, all in RG 109, NA.

54. The expedition is discussed in detail in Bearss, *Vicksburg Campaign*, 1:549–91. The failure of Confederate command during this episode is dis-

cussed in Samuel W. Ferguson Memoir, pp. 38–41, Vicksburg National Military Park.

55. The standard account of Grierson's raid is D. Alexander Brown, *Grierson's Raid* (Urbana: University of Illinois Press, 1962). See also *OR*, 24 (pt. 1): 532, 24 (pt. 3): 776, 783–87, 791, 792, 794, 802–3; JCP to Daniel Ruggles, April 20, 1863, JCPP, U. S. Naval Academy Archives.

56. Ballard, *Campaign*, 21–32.

57. *OR*, 24 (pt. 3): 810–13. Details of the struggle at Port Gibson are in Bearss, *Vicksburg Campaign*, 2:317–407.

58. *OR*, 24 (pt. 3): 821.

59. Ibid., 808, 815, 839, 842.

60. Bearss, *Vicksburg Campaign*, 2:480, 512–14; Johnston, *Narrative of Military Operations*, 506; *OR*, 24 (pt. 1): 239–41, 262–63, 24 (pt. 2): 74, 75, 24 (pt. 3): 876, 882, 883. Ballard, *Pemberton*, 156–59.

61. *OR*, 24 (pt. 1): 263.

62. Ballard, *Pemberton*, 160–64.

63. Ibid., 164–65.

64. *OR*, 24 (pt. 1): 241, 272. On Pemberton and the siege, see Ballard, *Pemberton*, 167–80.

65. *OR*, 24 (pt. 1): 285; Ballard, *Pemberton*, 153–54, 182–86, 200–201. A lengthy account of the Vicksburg campaign by Pemberton has recently been discovered and is in private hands. The owner has assured the author that the contents do not differ markedly from those of Pemberton's published writings in the *OR*; John C. Pemberton [III], *Pemberton: Defender of Vicksburg* (Chapel Hill: University of North Carolina Press, 1942), 281–319; Robert Underwood Johnson and Clarence Clough Buel, eds., *Battles and Leaders of the Civil War*, 4 vols. (New York: Thomas Yoseloff, 1956, reprint), 3:543–45.

Chapter Seven. "If Properly Led"

1. Lee to Hood, May 21, 1863, in Clifford Dowdey and Louis A. Manarin, eds., *The Wartime Papers of Robert E. Lee* (New York: DaCapo Press, 1987 [1961]), 490.

2. Meade to Mrs. Meade, May 8, 1863, in George Meade, ed., *The Life and Letters of General George Gordon Meade* (New York: Charles Scribner's Sons, 1913), 1: 372.

3. Joseph T. Glatthaar, *Partners in Command: The Relationship between Leaders in the Civil War* (New York: Free Press, 1994), does not discuss Gettysburg (the battle is not even mentioned in the index).

4. Although the historiography of the debate over Confederate leadership at Gettysburg is implicitly present (and sometimes explicitly recounted) in a number of sources, three of the most important assessments that set the controversy in the larger context of the effort to create a Confederate history are Thomas L. Connelly, *The Marble Man: Robert E. Lee and His Image in American Society* (New York: Alfred A. Knopf, 1977); Thomas L. Connelly and Barbara L. Bellows, *God and General Longstreet: The Lost Cause and the Southern Mind* (Baton Rouge: Louisiana State University Press, 1982); and William Garrett Piston, *Lee's Tarnished Lieutenant: James Longstreet and His Place in Southern History* (Athens: University of Georgia Press, 1987).

5. Lee to Davis, August 8, 1863, in *Wartime Papers of Lee*, 589–90.

6. William Allan, "Memoranda of Conversations with General Robert E. Lee," in Gary W. Gallagher, ed., *Lee the Soldier* (Lincoln: University of Nebraska Press, 1996), 13–14, 18.

7. Emory M. Thomas, *Robert E. Lee: A Biography* (New York: W. W. Norton, 1995), 292–93.

8. Ibid.

9. Allan, "Memoranda," 11. Douglas Southall Freeman claims that "Lee could not be expected to change his system for Ewell, nor could Ewell be expected to change his nature after only two months under Lee." Freeman, *R. E. Lee* (New York: Charles Scribner's Sons, 1935), 3:148. In fact, the sign of a superior commander is the ability to tailor instructions according to an estimate of a subordinate's capacity.

10. Gary W. Gallagher, "Confederate Corps Leadership on the First Day of Gettysburg: A. P. Hill and Richard S. Ewell in a Difficult Debut," in Gary W. Gallagher, ed., *The First Day at Gettysburg: Essays on Confederate and Union Leadership* (Kent, Ohio: Kent State University Press, 1992), 30–56, is a superior analysis of Confederate command problems on July 1.

11. E. Porter Alexander, *Fighting for the Confederacy*, ed. Gary Gallagher (Chapel Hill: University of North Carolina Press, 1989), 278.

12. Glenn Tucker, *Lee and Longstreet at Gettysburg* (Dayton, Ohio: Morningside Books, 1982 [1968]), offers an extensive examination of the Lee-Longstreet controversy. Also essential are Gary W. Gallagher, "'If the Enemy Is There, We Must Attack Him': R. E. Lee and the Second Day at Gettysburg," and Robert K. Krick, "'If Longstreet . . . Says So, It Is Most Likely Not True': James Longstreet and the Second Day at Gettysburg," in Gary W. Gallagher, ed., *The Second Day at Gettysburg: Essays on Confederate and Union Leadership* (Kent, Ohio: Kent State University Press, 1993), 1–32, 57–86. I find the Gallagher essay far more balanced and persuasive than Krick's analysis, the thrust of which is clearly indicated by its title.

13. Krick, "'If Longstreet Says So,'" 80.

14. G. Moxley Sorrel, *Recollections of a Confederate Staff Officer* (Jackson, Tenn.: McCowat-Mercer, 1958), 157.

15. Freeman, *R. E. Lee*, 3:150, offers two pertinent observations: "It is scarcely too much to say that on July 2 the Army of Northern Virginia was without a commander. . . . This psychological factor of the overconfidence of the commanding general is almost of sufficient importance to be regarded as a separate reason for the Confederate defeat."

16. Alexander, *Fighting for the Confederacy*, 278; Jeffry D. Wert, *General James Longstreet: The Confederacy's Most Controversial Soldier* (New York: Simon & Schuster, 1993), 268.

17. Arthur J. L. Fremantle, *The Fremantle Diary*, ed. Walter Lord (Boston: Little, Brown, 1954), 208, which also establishes Lee's location at the time of Longstreet's attack; William G. Piston, "Cross Purposes: Longstreet, Lee, and Confederate Attack Plans for July 3 at Gettysburg," in Gary W. Gallagher, ed., *The Third Day at Gettysburg and Beyond* (Chapel Hill: University of North Carolina Press, 1994), 43.

18. See Gallagher, "Confederate Corps Leadership," 31–36, for examples of attempts to invoke Jackson's spirit as a remedy to the actions of Hill and Ewell on July 1; Krick, "'If Longstreet Says So,'" 78–79, indulges in a somewhat more restrained Longstreet-Jackson comparison.

19. Piston, "Cross Purposes," contains a careful analysis of this matter.

20. Piston, "Cross Purposes," 31–55.

21. Douglas Southall Freeman, *Lee's Lieutenants* (New York: Charles Scribner's Sons, 1942–1944), 3:180–87, offers a detailed analysis of the problems in these two divisions on July 3.

22. Lee's comment about support was reported by John Imboden, whose account made it clear that Lee was discussing Pettigrew and Trimble; Walter Taylor also made it clear that he believed that the reason Pickett's division suffered seriously was because "it was not supported by the division on the left." R. Lockwood Tower with John S. Belmont, eds., *Lee's Adjutant: The Wartime Letters of Colonel Walter Herron Taylor, 1862–1865* (Columbia: University of South Carolina, 1995), 61.

23. Alexander, *Fighting for the Confederacy*, 280–83; Thomas, *Lee*, 301–2.

24. Alexander, *Fighting for the Confederacy*, 280.

25. Allan, "Memoranda," 14; Alexander, *Fighting for the Confederacy*, 242.

26. Allan, "Memoranda," 14, 18; Lee to Davis, August 8, 1863, in *Wartime Papers of Lee*, 589; Freeman, *Lee's Lieutenants*, 3:187. In remarking on the criticism directed at Ewell for his decision on July 1, Longstreet, who did not think highly of his fellow corps commander, said that "the censure of his failure is unjust and *very ungenerous.*" James Longstreet, *From Manassas to Appomattox* (Bloomington: Indiana University Press, 1960), 381.

27. Charles F. Adams, Jr., to Charles F. Adams, Sr., August 27, November 19, 1862, in Worthington C. Ford, ed., *A Cycle of Adams Letters*, 2 vols. (Boston: Houghton Mifflin, 1920), 1:180, 194.

28. Freeman, *R. E. Lee*, 2:428.

29. Meade to Mrs. Meade, June 25, 1863, in Meade, *Life and Letters*, 1:389; Halleck to Grant, July 11, 1863, in John Y. Simon et al., eds., *The Papers of Ulysses S. Grant* (Carbondale: Southern Illinois University Press, 1967–), 9:99.

30. Noah Andre Trudeau, *Bloody Roads South: The Wilderness to Cold Harbor, May–June 1864* (Boston: Little, Brown, 1989), 140.

31. Freeman, *Lee's Lieutenants*, 3:170.

32. Thomas, *Lee*, 293.

33. In contrast, one could observe that students of Union operations do not entangle their explanations of battles by indulging in these sorts of counterfactual speculations, although it might be perfectly reasonable to ask what would have happened if Charles F. Smith had commanded his division at Shiloh, Phil Kearney had led his men at Antietam, or John F. Reynolds had been one of Grant's corps commanders in 1864.

Conclusion

1. On this theme, see Edward N. Luttwak, *Strategy: The Logic of War*.

2. Of course, by the end of the Seven Days battles, McClellan had his army safely ensconced at Harrison's Landing on the James River, a position that still gave him considerable strategic leverage against Lee and Richmond. However. the *political* effect of the Seven Days exacerbated McClellan's already tenuous political situation and caused Lincoln to recall the Army of the Potomac from the peninsula. Thus it was as a *political* victory that the Seven Days completed the cancellation of McClellan's strategic advantages.

Index